Shakespeare's Dramatic Heritage

D1520843

Shakespeare's Dramatic Heritage

*Collected Studies in Mediaeval, Tudor
and Shakespearean Drama*

Glynne Wickham
Professor of Drama in the University of Bristol

NEW YORK
BARNES & NOBLE, INC.

First published in Great Britain 1969

Published in the United States of America 1969
by Barnes & Noble, Inc., New York, N.Y. 10003

Printed in Great Britain

To N. C.
whose teaching, writings and productions
have informed so much of this book

Contents

CONTENTS

4
Studies in Shakespeare

List of Illustrations

ix

LIST OF ILLUSTRATIONS

two rectangular paintings flanking the Apotheosis of James I and depicts the Union as an infant identifiable by means of the armorial shield in the top left-hand corner in which the Arms of the King of Scotland are crossed with those of the King of England. Britannia is depicted in the act of crowning the child (the United Kingdom in the person of Charles I) in the presence of King James. (*Facing p. 175*)

Reproduced by permission of the British Museum

FIGURES IN THE TEXT

xiii

Preface and Acknowledgements

THE form and context of this book of Essays stems from a paper which Professor T. J. B. Spencer asked me to deliver to the 12th International Shakespeare Conference at Stratford-upon-Avon in 1966 which was devoted to discussion of 'Shakespearean and Other Tragedy'. This paper, '*Genesis* and the Tragic Hero: Marlowe to Webster', is now printed as Essay 3 in this book.

Essays 1 and 2 are preparatory studies which attempt to show how the subjects of the Fall of Man, the Redemption and the concept of a day of Judgement were developed dramatically by the mediaeval Church, first by way of ornament to the latin liturgy and then in the vernacular as one aspect of an evangelistic crusade based in part on preaching and in part on a newly formulated Calendar Festival, the Feast of Corpus Christi. Essay 1, 'Drama and Religion in the Middle Ages' was prepared initially as a public lecture which I had the honour to deliver in the University of St. Andrews: Essay 2, 'Dramatic Qualities of the English Morality Play and Moral Interlude', was similarly prepared as a lecture in the first instance which I was invited by Professor William Melnitz to deliver to open a Colloquium organized by the Centre for Renaissance Studies in the University of California at Los Angeles in November 1966.

Essays 4, 5 and 6 examine from various aspects the impact of the revival of interest in the drama and theatre of classical antiquity upon the native English tradition and the retarding effects of the Reformation upon the development of these new ideas in Britain. Essay 4, 'Neo-classical Drama in England', is a reprint of a study which I contributed to a volume of Essays presented to Professor H. D. F. Kitto on his retirement from the Chair of Greek in the University of Bristol, edited by M. J. Anderson under the title *Classical Drama and its Influence* and published by Methuens in 1965. Essay 5, 'Shakespeare's "Small Latine and Less Greeke",' is also reprinted, but in expanded and revised form, from an essay in *Talking of Shakespeare* edited by the late John Garrett and published in 1954 by Hodder and Stoughton with Max Reinhardt. Essay 6, 'The Stuart Mask', is published here for the first time.

In the third section of the book, Stages and Stage-Directions, I have switched attention from thoughts about early English drama to consideration of strictly practical, theatrical matters —auditoriums, stages and stage conventions. Essay 8, 'Shakespeare's Stage', offers the reader a synthesis of recent scholarly views on the origins and nature of the stage-craft of Elizabethan and Jacobean dramatists and is flanked by notes on two specific topics at either end of Shakespeare's working life—Marlowe's theatre and a neglected theatre built for Shakespeare's Company in 1630 by Inigo Jones, the Cockpit-in-Court: these two groups of notes are reprinted respectively from the *Tulane Drama Review*, vol. 8 (1964), Marlowe Issue, and from *New Theatre Magazine*, vol. VII (1966/7), No. 2.

All nine essays therefore in the first three sections, while supplementing Essay 3—'*Genesis* and the Tragic Hero: Marlowe to Webster'—with detailed comment on particular aspects of that subject, look forward to the six studies of particular Shakespeare plays contained in Section Four. Both individually and collectively these six studies are designed to provoke the asking of two questions: how much of his dramatic skill did Shakespeare derive from earlier, English, dramaturgical traditions, and how far is a knowledge of these earlier traditions of service to the interpretative artist today? Professor Jan Kott in claiming that Shakespeare was 'our contemporary' has wilfully ignored, as it appears to me, the fact that he was undeniably a product of his own society and that that society, at least where the theatre is concerned, was the direct heir to the values of the mediaeval past: it therefore reflected these values in a much more accurate sense than it could hope to forecast or anticipate twentieth-century thought. That Elizabethan drama, like ancient Greek drama, possesses lasting qualities as relevant to us today as to its first begetters no one would wish to deny; but it is an inevitable and dangerous consequence of plucking a random harvest of correspondences with our own ideological viewpoints out of Shakespeare's plays while ignoring the artistic and historical contexts out of which they came, that the director, actor, or both together, will be obliged to cut and deface or otherwise distort the original text in order to eliminate those features of it which do not correspond so conveniently. It thus becomes an open question, for example, whether posterity will regard such alterations as were made to the text of *King Lear* by the Royal Shakespeare Company in their recent production as any more creditable to the artists concerned and to audiences of our time than Nahum Tate's 'happy ending' is to us, or whether the treatment recently accorded to *Much Ado About Nothing* by the National Theatre Company will appear to be any less regrettable than Dryden's 'improvements' on *A Midsummer Night's Dream*, in *The Fairy Queen* or D'Avenant's versions of *The Tempest* and *Macbeth* seem to be to actors and scholars today.

I do not seek to argue that actors and directors should deny themselves the right to bring their own creative imaginations to Shakespeare production in the interests of historicity or an academically orientated approach; but I think they can reasonably claim to be better artists if their own creativity grows out of a fully informed picture of the background from which Shakespeare and his contemporaries themselves drew their inspiration and their dramatic technique.

Essays 10 to 15 all seek to investigate some aspect of this dramatic technique and to suggest the sources in the mediaeval and early Tudor theatrical tradition from which it may possibly have been derived. Essay 14, *Coriolanus*: Shakespeare's Tragedy in Rehearsal and Performance, is reprinted from *Stratford-Upon-Avon Studies, 8: Later Shakespeare*, ed. J. R. Brown and B. Harris, published by Edward Arnold in 1966, where it is accompanied by a wider range of pictorial illustrations. The first sub-section of Essay 12, *Hamlet*, and of Essay 13, *Macbeth*, are also reprints: 'Notes for an Actor in the role of Hamlet' appeared in a volume of tributes to Nevill Coghill edited by John Lawlor and W. H. Auden under the title of *To Nevill Coghill From Friends* (Faber and Faber, 1966) and 'Hellcastle and its Door-keeper' is now reprinted from *Shakespeare Survey 19*, ed. Kenneth Muir, 1966. All the other studies appear here for the first time.

My thanks are due to H. D. F. Kitto, Nevill Coghill, William Melnitz and to all the editors and publishers who have kindly allowed me to reprint material originally prepared for them. I would also like to thank the managers, actors and designers whose confidence and artistry have given me the chance to gain an insight into the dramatic techniques of Mediaeval, Tudor and Shakespearean playmakers by preparing most of the plays discussed in this book for presentation to audiences in the theatre.

Glynne Wickham

Section One

The Mediaeval Heritage
of Shakespearean Drama

I

Drama and Religion in the Middle Ages

I F we are to attempt to understand what drama meant to the mediaeval mind or to assess the approach adopted by men and women of the Middle Ages to dramatic entertainment, our first step must be to make several large adjustments in our own current attitudes to both the theatre and religion. Because so much of mediaeval drama was a product of Roman Catholicism, we have got to make allowance not only for the vast blanket of Protestant prejudice in which it has been smothered since the Reformation, but also for the more recent critical pre-conceptions which have their roots in anti-clericalism and scientific scepticism. One or more of these creeds has underlain almost every historical account of the origin and development of drama in the Middle Ages written during the past hundred and fifty years. It is hardly surprising therefore that to the student of today the words 'mediaeval drama', if they mean anything at all, carry with them images of quaint pageant-wagons, of crude devils with black faces and fireworks exploding out of their bottoms and of little alliterative playlets suitable for Sunday School but irrelevant to either life or the theatre in the twentieth century: nor have teachers, whether in schools or Universities, helped to dispel these deeply contemptuous and ingrained notions by persistently treating mediaeval drama as if it were at best some primitive, gothic prologue to Shakespearean drama which only merits a place in a curriculum of English studies because it happens to provide some useful Middle English texts for analysis. Needless to say the Latin antecedents of these texts have been almost wholly ignored. The idea has thus taken root that a latin drama of genuinely religious origin grew up in the early Middle Ages, was banished from the church to the market-place, was translated into the vernacular, secularized and vulgarized with superstitious and idolatrous accretions until it died in the late Middle Ages of its own obesity. The Penguin *Short History of English Drama* supplies an admirable example of this thesis in the form it has taken at popular level.

In general [reads this text, pp. 19–20], it would seem that the plays began in the choir, and from the choir went to the nave, and from the nave to the outside of the church. When the crowds outside the church became too unseemly for the holy precincts the play moved to the market-place, or joined a succession of plays which were shifted from one position to another in procession around the city. The change illustrates the desire of the clerical authorities to be less intimately associated with the drama, and it is obvious that once the play was in the market-place, and in competition with other forms of entertainment, its character would increase in secularity.

The first noticeable change in these basically Victorian attitudes can, I think, be directly attributed to the revivals of the York and Chester Cycles of Miracle Plays which were presented in those cities in 1951 to mark the Festival of Britain. Since then there have been several subsequent revivals of both these Cycles; the Towneley Cycle has been presented in a London theatre and at Bretton Hall, the Christmas and Easter sequences of the *Ludus Coventriae* have been revived in Tewkesbury Abbey, and the New York 'Pro Musica' has toured the latin liturgical music drama, *Ludus Danielis*, in America and Europe. The impact of these productions upon the public has been great. Confronted with one of the most moving dramatic experiences of their lives, audiences have paused to ask how it came about that they should never have been told what they might expect of these mediaeval plays, or why it was that they

4

had been so seriously misled by historians and critics. These questions have been pursued, and in some cases answered, by many scholars during the fifteen years that have elapsed since the Festival of Britain. One scholarly book, however, had at least suggested that a thorough-going reappraisal of contemporary attitudes to mediaeval drama was long overdue some five years before the first revival of the York Cycle: this was Father F. C. Gardiner's *Mysteries End*. In this monograph Father Gardiner advanced the startling idea that the religious theatre of the Middle Ages did not peter out towards the end of the fifteenth century because audiences were bored with it, or scandalized by its childishness, ribaldry or increasing production costs, but was conscientiously suppressed as a matter of government policy between 1530 and 1580: Chester lost the right to perform its Cycle with impunity in 1574, York in 1575, Wakefield in 1576 and Coventry as late as 1581.

Father Gardiner's admirably argued and lavishly documented monograph was definitive in at least one respect: it charted in a new and refreshing manner the closing years of the Catholic religious stage in England. This achievement sufficed of itself however to reopen to speculative enquiry all other areas of the subject which formerly had seemed to have been so firmly closed by the publication of Sir Edmund Chambers' *The Mediaeval Stage* (1903) and Karl Young's *The Drama of the Mediaeval Church* (1933).

The next person to extend the vistas opened initially by Gardiner's work was Professor F. M. Salter with his book of essays, *Mediaeval Drama in Chester*, published in 1955. This dropped a timely bomb upon the cherished notion of compilation of cyclic drama by means of translation from latin into vernacular texts with the addition of an occasional original play here and there. Nevertheless, reactionary opinion was to be substantially reinforced a year later by the publication in 1956 of Professor Hardin Craig's *English Religious Drama*, which despite some novel ideas (especially those relating to the *Ludus Coventriae*) reiterated the traditionally accepted patterns of development from latin devotional and didactic texts to extended vernacular and secularized cycles. This was a view I felt

5

bound to challenge in 1958 when I published the first volume of *Early English Stages*, since it squared neither with Gardiner's nor Salter's findings on the one hand, nor with my own instinctive reactions to the performances I had witnessed in Chester and York and actually presented in Tewkesbury Abbey on the other. The question that was uppermost in my mind, and to which neither Chambers', Young's nor Craig's account of the origins and development of mediaeval religious drama gave any satisfactory answer, was why there should be so obvious a difference *of quality* between latin liturgical music-drama and vernacular cyclic drama. To define this difference of religious feeling and artistic atmosphere was more than I could fully accomplish at that time; but I did sense a parallel in dramatic terms to what, in architectural parlance, we have come to describe as Romanesque and Gothic—a recognizable difference of style which in the nature of things was to be explained by a corresponding difference in creative motivation. I therefore ventured to suggest that we should

admit the likelihood of two dramas of single Christian origin but independent motivation: the drama of the Real Presence within the liturgy and the imitative drama of Christ's Humanity in the world outside. The one is a drama of adoration, praise and thanksgiving: the other is a drama of humour, suffering and violence, of laughter and sorrow. Where the former remains ritualistic, the latter carries within it the germs of tragedy and comedy.[1]

I was soundly rebuked by Hardin Craig in the columns of *Speculum* for my presumption and folly in advancing these views, and for drawing attention to the co-existence of a secular tradition.[2] However, notwithstanding this magisterial admonition, these views appear to have found some favour with more recent writers and to have provided the basis for the three most substantial volumes to have appeared on the subject of mediaeval drama during the present decade: Emily Prosser's *Drama and Religion in the English Mystery Plays* (1961), O. B. Hardison's *Christian Rite and Christian Drama* (1965) and V. A. Kolve's *The Play Called Corpus Christi* (1966). Indeed, it is not too much to say that Hardison's and Kolve's books between

---

[1] *Early English Stages*, i, p. 314.　　　　[2] *Ibid.*, Chs. V and VI.

them go far towards proving that latin liturgical music-drama and Corpus Christi vernacular drama are as different in spirit and character as are the plays of Shakespeare from those of Ibsen or O'Neill. The time has come therefore to ask some searching questions of the traditionally accepted accounts of the origins and growth of religious drama in the Middle Ages.

Let us then take the question of origin first. On one point at least everyone is agreed. The first recognizable manifestation of the existence of drama within the Christian Church is to be found in a ceremony associated with the Introit which was used to begin Mass on Easter Sunday in the Roman liturgy of the tenth century and which was initiated in the monastic churches of Northern France and Southern England.

> *Quem Quaeritis in sepulchro, O Christicolae?*
> *Jesum Nazarenum crucifixum, O coelicolae!*

Historians, however, who were working on the nineteenth-century assumption that effects must be explained in terms of causes and who viewed events as items in an evolutionary process which moved from small beginnings to bigger and thus to better things, seriously misunderstood the significance of this Introit and the dramatic manner in which it was presented by the celebrants of the Mass in question. Looking back over their shoulders through historical time they viewed this ceremony as *the* beginning of just such an evolutionary process (which it was not), and interpreted its advent causally as an attempt to teach biblical history to illiterate congregations. The questions which ought to have been put to this proposition and were not are:

1 If instruction of an illiterate laity is the prime objective, why do this in Latin?
2 Why chant it and not speak it?
3 Why do it in monastic churches for the benefit of clergy who were the schoolmasters and university dons of the time?

Ask these questions, and whatever else the primary objective of the Introit ceremony may have been, it clearly cannot have been a teaching exercise. Had that been the intention, a simple, spoken vernacular text would have been used, and parish churches chosen for the performance of them. The most that can be harvested from approaching the Easter Introit ceremony of the tenth century in the name of didacticism is an admission that representation of the visit of the three Maries to the tomb illustrates as well as ornaments the liturgical ceremony proper to the occasion.

Where the beginnings of the vernacular drama of the fourteenth and fifteenth centuries are concerned, a very similar situation pertains in respect of critical approach. Historians who were wedded to the idea that the historical past should be analysed in terms of scientific methodology and of the evolutionary concept, were predisposed to force a direct and organic connection between the early latin plays of the eleventh and twelfth centuries and the fully developed vernacular cycles that have survived to us. The ideal hypothetical means by which to effect such a process and on which to base such a thesis of development lay to hand in the supposition that latin originals were translated into the vernacular, coalesced with one another and were then augmented with any portions still missing. The question which ought to have been asked of this thesis (and was not) was why Christ's crucifixion was never dramatized in latin liturgical form at any time between the tenth and thirteenth centuries? Another question which might have been asked (and was not) was why this same subject augmented by the betrayal on one side and the harrowing of hell in the other should have lain at the very heart of the vernacular drama from its inception. There is a lacuna in the orthodox argument at this point of crucial importance and which cannot be glossed over since it represents a major difference of substance affecting both the form and content of the two types of play.

There is one other question that must be asked of the standard textbook account of the origins and development of religious drama in the Middle Ages. It is noticeable that the vernacular plays associated with the Feast of Corpus Christi coalesced naturally into a single dramatic Festival from the outset, whereas the latin liturgical plays remained isolated from one another throughout their history, each being particular to its appointed

Calendar day and continuing to be presented in this context until Roman Catholicism ceased to be the accepted religion of the country; and this notwithstanding the advent of the Feast of Corpus Christi and the vernacular plays associated with it. Why then, we must ask, did the Corpus Christi vernacular plays coalesce into what we term Cycles when no hint to this end was offered by latin liturgical precedent, and indeed while the latter obstinately refused to do so?

If all these questions that I have been asking are looked at collectively, the damage that results to the orthodox nineteenth- and twentieth-century accounts of the history of mediaeval drama is virtually irreparable: for the standard narrative is assaulted and breached at its beginning, in the middle and at its end. What remains is hardly worth trying to patch up and repair. There is, however, one factor which is common to all those questions the asking of which has occasioned this destruction and which warrants close attention since it may supply the basis for a new approach to the subject and thus to a more accurate reconstruction of events: this is the religious and artistic considerations which moved men of the Middle Ages to express themselves in drama.

If we ask ourselves why the earliest liturgical plays of the tenth and eleventh centuries were chanted in Latin in monastic churches instead of being spoken in the vernacular in parish churches, if we ask ourselves why the Corpus Christi vernacular plays coalesced immediately into large cycles embracing the history of the universe from Creation to Doomsday when their latin predecessors had remained short and isolated from one another and had avoided any treatment of the Crucifixion, if we ask ourselves why the Corpus Christi cycles and vernacular Morality Plays did not expire naturally but had to be censored and suppressed by the central government in Elizabethan London, we at once find ourselves obliged to give precedence to religious and artistic considerations in our thinking about these problems. And if we are to get to grips with these religious and artistic questions we shall have first to involve ourselves with a number of subjects which at present have little or no place in the normal school or university curriculum. No intelligent

beginning can be made, for instance, without a working knowledge of the forms of Christian worship practised in the years
preceding the advent of liturgical drama. And since so many of
these ceremonies made extensive use of the arts (notably the
fine arts, music and mime) a sound grounding in Byzantine
and Romanesque achievement in the arts is another basic tool
for such an enquiry. This knowledge in its turn must be
supplemented by a concern with subsequent Church history;
for how else are we to understand why it was thought necessary
to institute a new Feast in 1311, the Feast of Corpus Christi, or
to supplement existing monastic Orders with those of the
mendicant friars whose sermons were to provide the basis for
the vernacular Morality Plays, or to use Royal Proclamations
and Acts of Parliament to ban all overt discussion of religion in
the English theatre? Yet where today has the average student
of English, History or Divinity any chance of acquiring this
knowledge? Indeed it is more normal to find students arriving
at Universities without having made the acquaintance of such
archetypal figures as Cain and Abel and without knowing what
is meant by such words as Epiphany or Pentecost. Much the
same, of course, may be said of latin, music and fine art, the
verbal and visual languages within which most of the information about mediaeval drama that we are seeking is couched.
I say this, not to depress the old and enrage the young, but in
order that no one may underestimate the difficulties which
await the student of English or History who would like to
enquire into the origins and development of a drama that was
once great, but who finds that some sixteen years of so-called
higher education has failed to provide him with any of the
tools he needs to begin his task. He needs Latin, he needs
an historical and aesthetic appreciation of Romanesque and
Gothic art and architecture, he needs some knowledge of
plainsong and early polyphony, he needs—however repellent
the prospect—a working knowledge of the forms and content
of the Roman liturgy between the eighth and sixteenth centuries. Without these basic tools he cannot expect to produce
much by way of new contributions to knowledge. Even so, if
he is aware of the general directions in which modern enquiry

is moving he may be encouraged to acquire the tools by recourse to further study.

In trying to sketch what I take these directions to be I shall probably commit myself to generalizations about developments in England which I may not wish to defend in a continental context and to a degree of dogmatism that would not be warranted if more factual evidence were available: I would only ask the reader to remember for his part that more texts have perished than have survived and that the historical period under review is itself as wide as that which separates us from the later Middle Ages. Both of these facts inevitably place as high a premium upon our powers of imaginative reconstruction as on our normal powers of reasoning. That said, I suggest that we direct our attention to three particular aspects of mediaeval drama where religious thinking and artistic expression appear to be inextricably intertwined: the origin of dramatic performances within the Mass, the advent of the Feast of Corpus Christi and its plays and the genesis of the Morality Play.

Where the origins of liturgical music-drama are concerned, if we are abandoning the concept of a didactic drama designed to bring scriptural narrative to life for illiterate congregations, then we must also abandon the accompanying image of ecclesiastical committees sitting round a table like the local Parish Council, discussing how this objective should be effected. Rather must we turn our attention to liturgical ritual itself, to the musical conventions in which it was clothed and to the architectural shapes and spaces in which it was contained. If we do this we can begin to discern that the '*Whom seek ye in the sepulchre?*' Introit for Easter Sunday and the '*Whom seek ye in the cradle?*' Introit for Christmas Day are integral parts of the form of worship appropriate to those particular moments in the Church's commemoration of its own history. They happen to carry with them dramatic overtones, partly because the text of these Introits takes the form of question and answer and partly because these texts were chanted antiphonally—that is to say by two voices, or groups of voices, the one responding to the initiative taken by the other. If, in this instance, monastic brotherhoods assembled for Mass on Easter Sunday happened to make a mental equation between the deacons and the cantors of the antiphon and the angels and the Maries respectively whose words before Christ's tomb now formed the subject of the antiphon before the altar, they were doing no more than the liturgy required of them: for this Introit, ornamented musically by melismatic plain chant divided between two groups of voices, was part of the Proper in the Mass, not of the Ordinary.

In other words, this particular Introit was unique to Easter Sunday, fitly introducing the historical event and the article of faith that was being commemorated on that particular day in the Church's Calendar. It thus invites equation between the celebrants of the Mass for the day wherever it happens to be celebrated and the people and words of the first Easter as recounted in the gospels.

Once we have grasped this idea we can extend our vision of the circumstances attending the birth of Christian drama to include the larger and more important concept of historical time mirrored in ritual time. This enables us to see the Church accommodating the linear concept of historical time within the cyclic concept of seasonal or annual time, thereby enabling itself to relive every important moment of Christian history repeatedly on the recurring basis of the agricultural year. The significance of this premise to the nature of the liturgical ceremonies adopted is that each ceremony, while repeated annually is unique to the occasion commemorated. Thus it comes about that all liturgical ceremonies carry with them an element of representation of actual historical event which will inevitably become dramatic as soon as the ceremony in question has been elaborated to a point where the ritual representation of the historical event involves impersonation of figures associated with that event. On the other hand, once a ceremony has acquired dramatic overtones by these means, its purpose rivets enactment firmly to its own particular place in the Calendar of ritual time. Thus the Easter or Christmas *'quem quaeritis'* Introit remains particular to the proper occasion whether the form that the ceremony happens to take is dramatic or not. This applies with equal force to those other liturgical ceremonies with dramatic qualities particular to Epiphany, to Palm Sunday or to Whitsunday. The paradox that we must learn to accept is that while there was nothing to stop items within the liturgy for most Feast Days in the Calendar acquiring dramatic qualities by process of ornament and elaboration over the years, there was an absolute bar to the merging of any one of these dramatic representations of historical event into another. Ritual time itself precluded such coalescence: Christmas Day was Christmas Day and it was meaningless to perform liturgical rituals particular to the Annunciation or to the Epiphany within the liturgical context of Christmas Day itself. This paradox applies with equal force, whether the language of the liturgy is latin or the vernacular: it can be extended, moreover, from events in Christ's ministry to Festivals commemorating notable Saints and Martyrs. Translation therefore of liturgical plays like the *Quem quaeritis in sepulchro* or the *Ordo Stellae* into the vernacular could not of itself result in coalescence, since the order of service for each day was strictly prescribed and respected, and any attempt to link several liturgical plays together for performance on one day would have required a radical break with traditional precedents. And it was not until the start of the fourteenth century when an entirely new Feast was instituted within the liturgical Calendar—the Feast of Corpus Christi—that there was any opportunity to make a change of this sort.

Before transferring our attention to this new Festival, there is one other aspect of liturgical music drama that requires some attention, the fact that the Crucifixion failed to receive ritual treatment of the fully dramatic kind accorded to Easter Sunday: and without such treatment a further barrier existed to the coalescence of plays or even groups of plays into a full Cycle. To us it may seem strange, not to say extraordinary, that an event as strikingly dramatic as the Crucifixion should have escaped dramatic treatment in its liturgical commemoration. Yet this is only so if we persist in regarding liturgical music-drama as the direct product of a self-consciously didactic purpose. If, instead, we transfer our attention to the nature of the liturgical commemoration and its artistic and ritualistic

expression, the reason for this neglect is self-evident and is seen
to be deliberate. Liturgically, Good Friday was not viewed as
a self-contained moment in historical time, but as the climax to
a series of events which Professor Hardison has described as
'the Lenten Agon' and which began seventy days before Easter
on Septuagesima Sunday.[1] For members of the early Church
the arrival of this day in the liturgical Calendar signalled the
start of that period of reflection, self-denial and personal pen-
ance which was to become obligatory for all at Ash Wed-
nesday and ever more strict and severe in its observances
as Good Friday approached. It was, moreover, the period
ordained both for the preparation of converts to the Christian
faith for Baptism and for sinners who had strayed from the
narrow paths of the true faith to prepare themselves for reunion
with Christ: both the penitents and the converts were received
into the congregation on Easter Sunday. In this way the morti-
fication of the flesh could be contrasted in the sharpest possible
manner with the ensuing renewal of life for the soul. Artistically,
the significance of these liturgical ceremonies was expressed in a
self-conscious stripping away of ornament, of light and of all
other outward expressions of joy. Nothing therefore could, of
itself, be more dramatic than this deliberate contrast between
death and life, darkness and light, sacrifice and thanksgiving;
yet, if the dramatic quality of this concept is to be appreciated,
it must be viewed whole and not piecemeal. The liturgical
ceremonies from Septuagesima to Good Friday thus formed a
progressive sequence of increasing sorrow and gloom which
reached its climax in the mimetic ceremony known as the *Ordo
Deposito Crucis* which involved the physical removal of the cross
from the altar and its emblematic 'burial'. This is no moment
for the decoration of rituals, either musically or dramatically,
the whole purpose of which is to bring the participants to feel
worthless and forsaken: by the same token, celebration of the
Resurrection on Easter morning provides all the incentive
imaginable to release feelings so long under constraint in an
outpouring of joy, praise and thanksgiving made manifest in
every form of artistic expression the human heart and mind is

[1] See O. B. Hardison, *Christian Rite and Christian Drama*, pp. 87 *et seq.*

PLATE I

1 COSTUMES OF THE BYZANTINE EMPIRE

The Empress Theodora, wife of Justinian, and her attendants. Mosaic in the Church of St. Vitale Ravenna, executed and installed A.D. 547. The extreme formality and severity of these rich, imperial garments supply a good idea of the style of costume used in liturgical music drama. Note the Adoration of the Magi embroidered on the foot of the Empress's purple cloak.

2 COSTUMES IN THE GOTHIC MANNER

The Way of the Cross as represented in the York Festival production of the York Cycle, June 1966.

Photo: Yorkshire Post

PLATE II

3　EVERYMAN
Stage setting for a 'modern dress' production in the Drama Studio,
University of Bristol, 1964. The setting is a free adaptation of the
Fouquet miniature of the Martyrdom of St. Appolonia.
Production: Glynne Wickham　Photo: Derek Balmer

4　FULGENS AND LUCRES
The jousting scene in Medwall's Interlude as presented in the
Reception Room of Bristol University, 1964.
Production: Karl Eigsti　Photo: Derek Balmer

capable of achieving, including dramatic re-enactment. Thus Christ's Passion came to be relived by priest and congregation alike throughout Lent in the early Middle Ages, but not to be ceremonially re-enacted by physical representation of the Crucifixion within the order of service prescribed for Good Friday itself.

It is only in the late Middle Ages that the Crucifixion comes to be represented on the stage and then in the vernacular and not in Latin. How may we account for this change? If not in terms of translation from non-existent Latin originals, then how? Hardly in terms of secularization (which is the other prop of the orthodox account of events) since there is no reason to suppose as yet that anyone other than the priest-celebrants of Mass had anything to do with these liturgical music-dramas. In short, if we are to find an answer that fits the facts of the situation both artistically and liturgically, we must abandon the evolutionary hypothesis and seek out some nucleus for a fresh start. One such lies obviously enough to hand in the Feast of Corpus Christi instituted by Pope Urban IV in 1264 and promulgated for observance throughout Christendom by his successor Clement V in 1311. Historians have never doubted that there was some connection between this Festival and the performance of religious plays for the simple reason that civic records from all over the country make mention of such plays in the context of the Feast from the end of the fourteenth century until the Feast itself was suppressed in 1548. It is typical however of the way in which Protestant and Humanist prejudice has operated in the writing of mediaeval English history that no one investigating the development of mediaeval drama should have bothered to carry out any serious enquiry about the circumstances prompting the institution of this new Feast. Professor Hardin Craig, writing as recently as 1956 in *English Religious Drama*, was the first person to notice any correspondence between the artistic nature of the Miracle Cycles and the religious nature of the new Feast.

The service of Corpus Christi [he says] is theologically and ritualistically a consummation of the entire plan of salvation, and the Grand Cycle of religious themes from the Fall of Adam to the

Ascension of the Saviour . . . [was] an objectivization of the same grand theme (p. 133).

But having got that far he let the matter drop. Had he pursued it further and enquired into the ecclesiastical thinking which prompted Popes Urban IV and Clement V to create this new liturgical celebration and to impose it on to the liturgical Calendar on the Thursday following Trinity Sunday he would have seen that the artistic, structural pattern of the cyclic plays faithfully mirrors the religious purpose of the Feast and that these are altogether different from those informing the advent and development of latin liturgical drama.

To put first things first, we are here dealing with events in the thirteenth and fourteenth centuries instead of with events in the ninth and tenth centuries; and the three centuries which lie between mark a great change both in the Church's own situation in Europe and in the relationship of its priesthood to the laity. These changes were large enough for us to be able to recognize their architectural manifestations in terms of the shift from the Romanesque to the Gothic style, and we ought logically to pursue them into other aspects of Christian thinking. This of course opens up a vast subject and I cannot do more here than single out two or three points of special significance. The first of these is the change in the Church's attitude to its own nature and function in Christendom. The great tide of missionary fervour which had driven it north and west from the Mediterranean between the fourth and the seventh centuries had spent itself by the eighth century and was replaced by a long period of consolidation and introspection. There was no loss of energy; only a deflection of energy from basic evangelism towards elaboration and decoration of established liturgical procedures, of which the advent of liturgical music-drama was one of the more important products. With the passing of time however this introspection degenerated into narcissism and while the Church admired its own navel its converts drifted away from the true faith and towards heresy or a relapse into paganism. Language changed, commerce expanded and a rich Church as often appeared to the layman to be corrupt as holy. By the end of the twelfth century the more earnest and farsighted churchmen were beginning to view this situation with alarm and to urge strong counter-action upon the Pope in Rome. Slowly ecclesiastical authorities began to heed these warnings and to gird up their energies for a massive evangelistic campaign to impress the relevance of Christianity to daily life upon peasant, merchant and feudal lord alike. Leading this crusade were the Orders of mendicant friars established by St. Francis and St. Dominic at the start of the thirteenth century who had dedicated themselves to preaching Christ's humanity and the redemptive power of his self-sacrifice on the cross. This shift of emphasis from the miraculous nature of Christ's Nativity and Resurrection in which the divine quality of his being was revealed towards the human quality of his ministry and the atonement for original sin which his Passion represented, prepared the way for the vernacular cycles in much the same way that the musical and mimetic elaboration of the Proper in the Mass had prepared the way for latin liturgical drama. The catalyst required to effect the release of this new drama was the institution of the Feast of Corpus Christi.

The *raison d'être* for this innovation is to be found partly in the general change of emphasis in Christian thinking that I have been discussing and partly in the particular change of attitude adopted towards the Eucharist at this same time. In 1215 the famous dogma of Transubstantiation was promulgated: thenceforth Christians were required to believe that Christ manifested himself in the bread and wine of the Eucharist whenever Mass was celebrated. This is a miracle on a par at least with those of Virgin Birth and physical resurrecton from the dead: yet within the liturgical Calendar of annual commemoration of outstanding historical events, it lacked recognition adequate to its importance. True, it was not altogether neglected since the Last Supper itself was commemorated on Maundy Thursday; but the placement of both the event and the day within the frame of the Lenten Agon militated against an appropriately joyful festival of thanksgiving. Coming late in the long sequence of penitential liturgies prescribed for Lent and serving as the prelude to introduce the grimmest day in the Calendar, the sorrow of farewells and impending betrayals inevitably coloured the Maundy Thursday ceremonies: nor could they be allowed to anticipate and thus detract from the joy of Easter. If then the miraculous quality of the Eucharist and its redemptive grace was to be properly observed in ritual terms, this aspect of the Last Supper must be accorded independent celebration and at a more appropriate time. This inevitably involved dislocation between the commemoration of the historical event and the place hitherto accorded to it in ritual time. The solution found to this problem was to leave commemoration of the Last Supper *per se* in its appointed place on Maundy Thursday and to institute a new festival in an otherwise relatively quiet and uncrowded part of the liturgical Calendar to give thanks for the redemptive power of the Eucharist itself. A clear and simple statement to this effect lies in the latin text of Pope Urban's Bull announcing the new Feast of Corpus Christi: the source itself supplies the probable explanation of its neglect by English historians. Here, in V. A. Kolve's English translation, is the crucial passage. Speaking of the Eucharist, Pope Urban says:

For on the day of the Supper of our Lord—the day on which Christ himself instituted this sacrament—the entire Church, fully occupied as she is with the reconciliation of penitents, the ritual administration of the holy oil, the filling of the commandment concerning the washing of feet, and other matters, does not have adequate time for the celebration of this greatest sacrament.[1]

Since the mood is wrong and the time is inadequate on Maundy Thursday, Pope Urban goes on to prescribe another Thursday, the first Thursday after Trinity Sunday, when the Church is not preoccupied with 'other matters', for the sounding forth of 'hymns of joy at man's salvation'.

These words and phrases of Pope Urban IV lead us directly to the heart of the mystery surrounding the origin and development of the Corpus Christi plays: for the treatment to be accorded to the Eucharist on the occasion of this new Festival is not to be commemoration of the historical event of the Last Supper—(that is already looked after on Maundy Thursday)—but thanksgiving for man's salvation. Thus we are taken out of ritual time and into universal time; for the Eucharist has no

[1] See V. A. Kolve, *The Play called Corpus Christi*, pp. 44 *et seq.*

significance in the context of man's salvation without looking back to the Fall of Adam on the one hand and forward through Christ's Harrowing of Hell on the other to Doomsday itself when man himself is to be judged. Here then, in the purpose and nature of the Feast, we have the dramatic structure of the plays which were so closely associated with it as to carry its name. Beginning, middle, end—doctrinally and dramatically they are the same—the Fall; Last Supper, Crucifixion and Harrowing of Hell; Judgement.

That said, we can at once see that an entirely different set of circumstances surrounds the advent of the vernacular Corpus Christi plays from those surrounding latin liturgical music-dramas at any point in their development. No question of translation or coalescence arises: they are possessed of what we term cyclic form from their inception. Artistically, the nucleus of the Corpus Christi Cycles is a triptych: the focal centre and climax of the drama is Christ's redemptive sacrifice introduced by the Last Supper and concluded by the defeat of Satan in Hell, and this is flanked by plays representing the fall of Lucifer, Adam and Cain, and by that representing the general resurrection and judgement of souls. Dramatized versions of stories lying between Adam's fall and the Crucifixion and between the Crucifixion and Doomsday play can of course be added or interpolated. These can include translations of stories already dramatized in liturgical form. Inclusion, however, of additional material from any source will now depend not upon random choice or particular Calendar Festivals but upon a selective principle—the relevance of the material in question to the doctrinal purpose of the drama: for, unlike the ornamental music-drama of the latin liturgy, this vernacular drama was selfconsciously and overtly didactic. Just as the Host was carried in procession on Corpus Christi day from the Church through the streets of countless cities and back into the Church again as an outward symbol of the relevance of Christianity to daily life, so the Corpus Christi drama was designed to explain God's purposes to man (for the benefit of everyone who lived in or near these cities): the laiety were thus encouraged to participate in the performances as well as watch and listen to them, and the market place was to be preferred to the Church precincts as an environment for their performance.

The overriding evangelistic purpose of Corpus Christi drama therefore itself supplied the regulator for determining the subject matter to be included and the treatment to be accorded to it. By transposing historical events into a context of universal time, the pioneers of these plays invited a deliberately anachronistic approach to the characters and settings of biblical narrative and placed a premium upon typological relationships between material selected from Old and New Testament sources. Thus Pontius Pilate of the York Cycle is at once the Roman pro-consul of the first-century Judea and the Knighted Justice of the Peace of the mediaeval city of York, and the anachronism implicit in this treatment is not a naïve misconception of historical character, event and environment, but a necessary signpost to their abiding significance for the beholder. Similarly, since Christ's crucifixion is an obligatory scene, Abraham's sacrifice of his son Isaac deserves to be included in the Cycle since the former is prefigured in the latter. Once these attitudes and approaches to the writing of the Corpus Christi plays begin to become apparent we can see readily enough that the new vernacular drama had a clear-cut beginning, middle and end where each latin liturgical play treated only of one isolated event, that dramatic treatment of the Last Supper and Crucifixion was the *sine-qua-non* of the Corpus Christi Cycles where liturgical music-drama had neglected these subjects and that the Corpus Christi plays were written in the vernacular and performed in the city *ab initio* where the liturgical plays began life in Latin and were performed in the Church or within its precincts. In short, the Corpus Christi Cycles are a product of the Gothic spirit where the liturgical plays are Romanesque. In drama, as in architecture or in fresco, the differences are both recognizable and similar and have their common origin in religious life and thought. (See *Plate I*.)

Two awkward problems remain to be taken into account; a number of early plays which at first glance fit into neither of the two categories we have been discussing, and the Morality Play—which also cannot be grouped with either liturgical music-drama or the Corpus Christi Cycles. Among the former are such plays as the Anglo-Norman *Mystère d'Adam* and *La Seinte Resureccion*, the so-called Shrewsbury fragments, the *Jeu de Saint Nicholas* and the Cornish *Ordinalia*. In one way or another all these plays may be said to combine elements of both the liturgical and vernacular play types and thus to support the orthodox theory of development by translation, addition and coalescence. Professor Hardison advances a theory of a development of the liturgical tradition in the twelfth century in two directions, complex Latin and simple vernacular: Miss Prosser and Mr. Kolve ignore the problem. I have no solution to offer beyond the suggestion that if each be approached separately, and in terms of local circumstances that include clerical minstrelsy as well as liturgical practice of the time where these are known, rather than collectively as a group under an evolutionary umbrella, answers will be found that make sense from every viewpoint, religious, artistic and historical.[1] In the meantime it will be as well if we remember that these problems still await solution and that so long as they do we cannot afford totally to reject Chambers', Young's and Craig's accounts of the origins and development of mediaeval drama, even though we may view them more sceptically than hitherto.

The Morality Play poses a different sort of problem. Historians who have espoused the evolutionary hypothesis of origin and development ask us to regard the Morality Play as an extension or offshoot, rather late in time, of the vernacular cycles. Once again, however, this view is only tenable if all religious and artistic considerations are either ignored or suppressed. Even the comparatively simple question of historical co-existence of Morality Plays and Corpus Christi Cycles is hurtful to this thesis: for if *The Castle of Perseverance* can be dated c. 1410, and if the *Creed* and *Paternoster* plays (of which no texts survive, but about which we do have some descriptive notices[2]) of the late fourteenth century are taken into account as bearing a much closer resemblance to Morality Plays than anything else, there is little or no historical evidence for regarding the

---

[1] See G. Wickham, *Early English Stages*, i, pp. 201–2 and 230–1.
[2] See Chambers, *The Mediaeval Stage*, ii, pp. 120, 130, 154, 341, 378 and 403–6.

Morality Play as of substantially later provenance in point of chronology than the vernacular Corpus Christi Cycles the earliest recorded reference to which is of the year 1377.[1] Again, from any serious religious or artistic standpoint, apart from a basic Christian ritual pattern of fall from grace followed by a reversal admitting the regaining of lost grace, it is the differences, not the similarities, between the Cycles and the Moralities which are striking. Where religious thinking is concerned, the subject-matter of the Cycles is drawn from biblical history and discusses the impact of Christ's birth, death and resurrection upon human history; the Morality Plays are concerned with Christian ethics, discuss personal conduct in the light of Christian revelation and derive from the vernacular sermon, *not* from the latin *lectio* or 'reading' from the Vulgate. Artistically, the same correspondences may be seen in the respective forms in which these two sorts of plays are fashioned. The precedence given to historical narrative in the Cycles is reserved for theme or argument in the Morality Play. The Morality Play is thus structured on contention or debate and not on progressive, typological narrative; and it is no coincidence that such secular institutions as the Tournament and the legal or academic Disputation are accommodated within Morality Plays while finding no place within the Cycles. For the same reason the Morality Play could as easily be stretched to accommodate discussion of social and political conduct as personal conduct and thus to include in its *dramatis personæ* a much wider range of character than was admissible within the Cycles. Indeed, in the sixteenth century, as plays like Skelton's *Magnyficence*, Sir David Lyndsay's *Ane Satyre of the Thrie Estaitis*, or Bale's *Kyng Johan* demonstrate, the Morality Play, having been stretched in these directions, ran into trouble with officials of both Church and State and brought first censorship and then suppression down upon the whole religious stage.[2] Nevertheless, as we are slowly coming to realize, the structural patterns, philosophical and artistic, evolved in the religious theatre of the Middle Ages did not die with the suppression of the texts,

[1] See Chambers, *The Mediaeval Stage*, ii, pp. 339 and 399.
[2] See Essay 2, pp. 35–8 below.

but survived the Reformation to provide Shakespeare and his contemporaries with models for their own play-making. The grand cosmic pattern of Fall, Redemption and Judgement provided by the Cycles, the equally impressive ethical debate between Vice and Virtue for the souls of men and of nations provided by the Moralities and the groundswell of a ritualistic pattern within which both were framed give the structural strength and forcefulness of expression to the Chronicles, comedies and tragedies of the Elizabethan and Jacobean theatre which have made them the envy of posterity throughout the world.

2

Dramatic Qualities of the
English Morality Play and Moral Interlude

I T is a truism of orthodox accounts of the history of English
drama that a theatre which took its genesis from the worship
of the Catholic Church 'became secularized' upon its migration
from Church precincts to city streets and market-places:
rarely is credit given to the possibility that a secular dramatic
tradition could have come into existence independently of the
religious tradition and grown up alongside of it. Yet if man is
instinctively religious, he is also a predator and a procreator,
his instincts to protect his territory and to perpetuate himself in
his family being at least as strong as his fear of death and his
reverence for the supernatural. In almost any organized society
therefore, the arts of courtship and of self-defence beget their
own rituals which are at least as compulsive as those of worship; and the greater the stability, complexity and sophistication of the society, the more elaborate and highly ornamented
will these rituals become.

In the early Middle Ages self-defence was still a personal
affair (bombardment with the aid of gunpowder being unknown) and the soldier, whether infantryman, archer or
equestrian knight learnt the arts of war through the experience
of the many forms of combat provided at Tournaments. Since

it was in the nature of the Tournament to stress virility by distinguishing the man with most strength and skill in arms from the man with less, its rituals were always likely to become related to those of courtship if women were admitted as spectators: once women are allowed to initiate Tournaments and arbitrate between contestants, as was the case in the thirteenth century, the process of marrying the rituals of these battle-schools to the rituals of courtship has already begun.

Holidays and Festivals, by providing lesisure, also provided the most favourable opportunities for social intercourse and thus for the pursuit of love and arrangement of marriages. To the initially simple, amateur diversions of dancing and singing which served to introduce and familiarize young men and women, the more sophisticated pastimes of entertainment provided by professional performers could at any time be added. In mediaeval society, at least by the thirteenth century, this function was provided by the minstrel troupe who offered recitations from Romance poetry, recitals of music, conjuring, tumbling, mimicry and the antics of performing animals. Thus there evolved in the great Halls of the nobility at Christmas and other holiday seasons that sequence of rituals grounded on dance, song and divertissements known as the Revels. The rituals of the Revels met and fused with those of the Tournament in the ceremonies of the prize-giving when the heroes of the daytime 'battlefield' were rewarded for their prowess by the ladies in the Hall at night, the followers of Mars receiving their jewelled trophies from the attendants of Venus.

Certainly religion informed all aspects of mediaeval life and thought, and in the environment of the Hall it provided the actual occasion of the festivities decorated by the Revels— Calendar Holidays and the sacramental celebrations of birth, marriage and death. However, we must be careful not to confuse the religious inspiration of the occasions with the shape or nature of the festive rituals associated with them. The organizers of the Revels were clearly free to borrow entertainments evolved from within the theatre of worship, but only on terms that accorded with the *raison d'être* of the Revels themselves and would not disrupt their own rituals. A dramatic entertainment

25

which complied with these conditions was the Morality Play. Borrowed from the Church and tailored to fit the Hall it was transformed at the hands of professional entertainers in the fifteenth century into the Moral Interlude, and paved the way in Tudor England for a new drama that was to rival that of Greece and Rome.

For the most part these plays have received a quite unwarranted neglect from historians and critics: since few of them can claim to contain the sustained studies in character or the lyrical, poetic qualities of Elizabethan comedy and tragedy, they have been dismissed as pedestrian curiosities about which it suffices to know only that they existed within a period of historical time lying *between* mediaeval and Shakespearean drama. Students who worship the modern Morality Play with a veneration bordering upon idolatry as a theatre of commitment are encouraged to dismiss the mediaeval and Tudor Moralities as alarmingly academic and boring relics of the historical past. Those who would rather run a mile before breakfast than read *The Castle of Perseverance* or *The Conflict of Conscience* for pleasure are as often as not the very same students who clamour to study Brecht or Miller or to produce the plays of Durenmatt, Frisch, Osborne or Wesker. Yet I doubt whether there ever was a drama more wholehearted in its commitment to concepts of moral order than the mediaeval Morality Play or more overtly critical of political institutions and social injustice than the Moral Interlude of Tudor England. The didactic drama of modern times, although rooted in German Expressionism, has branched out to assume many distinctive national characteristics in both Europe and America; but it is neither as new as its champions sometimes think, nor, as I believe, more effective from a theatrical standpoint than its mediaeval precursor. On both counts therefore, teachers, students and actors today have some cause to examine afresh the dramatic as opposed to the literary qualities of a drama that has the imprint of both the Middle Ages and the neo-classical Renaissance upon its form, content and style.

The strength and long life of this type of entertainment is in my view directly attributable to the rock-like foundations upon which it was built. In an age of faith, and within a liturgy chanted in a foreign tongue, no instruction could have had a wider appeal or a more profound relevance to the individual than the vernacular sermon. Whether as an exposition of Scripture or as a commentary upon it, the sermon provided every individual with an ethical yardstick by which to measure his own conduct and, by extension, social and political conduct within the nation at large. Canons of right and wrong were absolute, black and white in colour, diabolic and angelic in motivation, tragic and comic in effect. The teaching implicit in the sermon was presented in the form of debates in which these antithetical extremes were shown to be in a state of perpetual conflict: it could thus be simple and brief or long and complex as the occasion and intellectual standing of the congregation suggested.[1]

The doctrinal basis of the sermon moreover provided both preacher and congregation with a common ritualistic approach to the ethics discussed. The baptized and confirmed Christian, although born innocent, is Adam's heir and will inevitably fall from grace; but, unlike Adam, the mediaeval Christian had Christ's example to bring him to repentance and thus to a reversal in his way of living or a spiritual rebirth which would open the way to a reconciliation with God. Mercy tempering wrath in the hour of judgement, if it does not preclude punishment, does preclude damnation as the companion of death. This pattern can be presented figuratively as a war between God and Lucifer in which Lucifer and his diabolic allies lay seige to God's children.

By codifying and personifying these extremes as Vices and Virtues mediaeval preachers made it easy to dramatize the supernatural struggle for the soul of man both imaginatively and pictorially. In doing so they happened also to provide actors with an urgent incentive to represent these imaginary struggles upon the public stage.[2] Precedent was conveniently to hand in the Tournament, which, as I have remarked, although in essence a battle-training school, had already by the fifteenth

[1] See G. R. Owst, *Literature and Pulpit in Mediaeval England,* 1933.
[2] See Essay 1, p. 22 above.

century been decorated with overtones of romance and allegory allied to the rivalries of courtship. The struggle for the soul of *Humanum Genus* represented in *The Castle of Perseverance* is not far removed in spirit (even if it is in character) from that of the struggle to win the favour of the *Sauvage Dame* in the *Pas d'Armes de la Sauvage Dame*.[1] The 'Pas' and the 'Castle', as the objects to be defended, are to all intents and purposes one and the same from a scenic viewpoint and in the eyes of the spectator. The jousting in Medwall's *Fulgens and Lucres* is an even more overt borrowing from the Tournament. In an age moreover when acting is just beginning to be enjoyed for its own sake, whether as actors or as spectators, a prime necessity for further development is an adequate supply of new scenarios. To the minstrel troupes who lived by entertaining their masters and their masters' friends at Feasts, nothing could have been more opportune than the sort of dramatic scenario developing within the vernacular sermon, and the precedent for dramatic enactment of a warlike struggle for precedence than that already formulated within Tournaments of the Round Table variety, where singing, dancing, heraldic disguise and elementary scenic units were already assembled to embellish the nucleus of human courtship with artistic ornament.[2] (See *Plate II*, no. 4.)

If the sermon served as the ethical cornerstone of the Morality Play, the *chansons de geste* of the trouvères and the comic antics of the jongleurs served to supply a source of romantic narrative and comic fantasy that was just as fruitful. Both the Troy story and that of Geoffrey of Boulogne's siege of Jerusalem appear to have been adapted from romance poetry and re-enacted mimetically in Paris before the end of the fourteenth century, while in England a farcical debate between hen-pecked husbands and nagging wives was acted out before the King at Hertford early in the fifteenth century. Lydgate's 'Mumming at Hertford' strikes me as especially important in this context as it anticipates the direct involvement of audience with players which forms so notable a feature of Medwall's *Fulgens and Lucres* and many later Moral Interludes.[3]

[1] See *Early English Stages*, i, pp. 24, 42 and 44.
[2] See *ibid.*, pp. 13–50 and 179–90.   [3] *Ibid.*, pp. 191–228.

The last general observation of an introductory kind that needs to be remarked is the comparative freedom which the Morality Play enjoyed in respect of formal ties to ritual time. Where early liturgical music-drama was so closely tied to the specific liturgical commemoration of historical event as to be unable to coalesce, and where the vernacular miracle cycles were so tightly harnessed to the Feast of Corpus Christi as to be unable to move intact to any other season of the year, the Morality Play was only tied to Calendar holidays in a very loose sense; moreover it could be pressed into service to decorate festivals of a private and occasional kind—weddings, christenings and other family parties of a sort that made something more jovial than a sermon desirable by way of recreation, and it could serve equally well to secure remuneration for actors on occasions of abnormal public assembly like trade fairs and carnivals at any place or time. It was thus a much more serviceable commodity both to actors and to audiences than either liturgical sequences or large-scale cyclic drama, yet could borrow features of both, and in addition gave to the deviser, inventor or maker of such plays much greater freedom of action in respect of both plot material and construction: for this very freedom from the restrictions of ritual time, combined with society's sanction to use ethical debate in conjunction with romance poetry as material for dramatic dialogue, opened the way to the playmakers to draw upon both modern history and classical drama should they ever be minded to do so. By the end of the fifteenth century audiences, actors and playmakers alike were evidently ready to experiment in both of these directions.[1]

So much then for historical background. I hope I have said enough to make one general point about the dramatic qualities of the Morality Play acceptable: the wide-ranging nature of the narrative and the plot material that was allowable within the genre. I believe this to have been one of its greatest strengths: for it enabled the authors and the actors to develop their crafts experimentally little by little, while depending for their

[1] For a modern bibliography of Morality Plays and Interludes, see T. W. Craik, *The Tudor Interlude*, 1958, pp. 142–52.

broad effects upon well-tried routines with which their audiences were already familiar. These are the conditions which pave the way to virtuosity in any art. They are the conditions with which, a century later, William Shakespeare and Richard Burbage were to be confronted as members of the Lord Chamberlain's and King's Companies at the Globe. They are the antithesis of those conditions of shock and sensationalism in which twentieth-century exponents of didactic drama from German Expressionism to the Theatres of Cruelty and the Absurd have tried to gain acceptance for the modern Morality Play. This, however, is a point which I will need to qualify later on.

To make my next points I must be parochial and refer to the special programme of plays produced under the aegis of the Bristol Old Vic Trust by the Company, the Theatre School and the Drama Department of the University in 1964 to mark the Shakespeare Quatercentenary. Fifteen plays were presented collectively within the space of a three-week festival: *Everyman, Fulgens and Lucres, Kyng Johan, Respublica, Nice Wanton, Gammer Gurton's Needle, Ralph Roister Doister, Mother Bombie, Edward II, Love's Labour's Lost, Henry V, The Fair Maid of Bristol, Volpone, Othello, The Two Noble Kinsmen.*[1] Of these *Everyman*, the three Shakespeare plays and *Volpone* were comparatively familiar to the public. Of the other eleven virtually none had been seen before and some of them not even read. One result of this juxtaposition of the hackneyed with the unfamiliar was to cast an entirely new light on both: Shakespeare and Jonson seemed much less original than our audiences had supposed, while the Moral Interludes seemed far more vital and entertaining than any critical commentary upon them had led one to imagine. Nowhere, perhaps, was this paradox more startlingly illustrated than in the coupling of *Everyman* with *Fulgens and Lucres*. *Everyman* was familiar enough both as a text and in performance to warrant expectation of a rewarding evening—at least for those predisposed to enjoy 'religious drama'. *Fulgens* by contrast was so obscure and unknown a quantity as to warrant dire

---

[1] For photographs and commentaries see *New Theatre Magazine*, vol. v (1964), no. 2.

PLATE III

5   BALLET COMIQUE DE LA REINE

Emblematic settings for an entertainment at the French Court, 1582. The scenic units represent: 1. Circe's Garden; 2. A fountain; 3. A sky-palace; 4. An arbour. The arches of Circe's 'garden' were constructed in perspective with a scenic cloth behind the centre one. The balustrade around it was ornamented in gold and silver, and animals can be seen within. The whole unit was artificially illuminated with oil lamps. Immediately in front of the garden on the left of the picture is the fountain. (Negative reverse printed for greater density.) For details greatly enlarged see G. Wickham, *Early English Stages*, vol. 1, Plate 28.

PLATE IV

6   SCENIC EMBLEMS

The Courtyard of the Pitti Palace, Florence, prepared for festivities marking the wedding of Christine of Lorraine and the Grand Duke of Tuscany, 1589. The yard was roofed over with red satin and the 'barrier' for jousting stands in the middle. At the far end are two scenic emblems: a 'city' in the form of a painted cloth before which is set a three-dimensional 'battlement' or 'castle'.

7   The same with the 'Naumachia' or water tournament in progress. The 'castle' and the 'city' are here defended by the Turks. Water was specially pumped into the courtyard for this engagement between the Christian and Turkish fleets.

forebodings of an evening of educational theatre at its grimmest. In the event, *Fulgens* turned out to be one of the most entertaining items in the festival and directly comparable with *Love's Labour's Lost* in terms of the pleasure derived from it, notwithstanding an undergraduate company and an American producer for Medwall's play in the University in contrast with a professional company and director for Shakespeare's play in Britain's oldest theatre. Yet it was accorded as strictly 'historical' a presentation as was imaginable. The Reception Room of the University with its panelled walls and ceiling, its screen and gallery above, provided an almost ideal replica of a Tudor Hall. Not quite ideal because the screen only contained one door instead of two. However the basic setting was virtually the same as that envisaged by Henry Medwall. Within it were set refectory style tables laid with a sufficiency of food and wine. Audiences were startled, to say the least of it, to find themselves seated at these tables lining the walls of the hall and looking back at the screen and gallery. Thereafter the play proceeded exactly as written with all references to the meal within the text made relevant by the food on the tables and with provision for eating it made in the interval, again as specified within the text. The lack of a second door in the screen was remedied by placing an artificial screen six feet within the hall in front of the single door, thus making two entrances to left and right of the artificial screen. The hall and tables were lit with candles, and a small concession to modern times was made in the provision of a few concealed spotlights, to place actors' faces in relief in the central floor area, which was of course the main acting area. Against this setting (or should I say within this environment) two unexpectedly dramatic qualities of the play revealed themselves with startling clarity. First, those two dauntingly drab ciphers of the printed text, A and B, proved themselves to be among the most engaging of stage characters. Moving ambivalently between the audience and the players with the sophistication of Pirandello's mouthpieces—speaking at one moment for the players and the next for the spectators—these two characters in their role of servants swiftly seized the attention of the audience and thereafter manipulated their victims as suited them and their author. By this means, ancient Rome is brought out of antiquity and into the Tudor present. Incident and character are thus given a contemporary significance; and with these aids a moral that is of itself unpalatable to such an audience is made both unmistakable and entertaining if not acceptable. With A and B acting as servants to both audience and actors at one and the same time, the author is enabled moreover to employ them as agents for the advancement of his plot. It is a brilliantly economical stage device.

The second dramatic quality of importance which performance served to reveal was the artistry with which the debate between the two suitors for Lucres' hand is introduced and sustained. The near obscene parody of this contest in the jousting between A and B for the favours of Lucres' maid Joan is farcical and very funny to watch.[1] The dumb-show, the recourse to music and choreography, elevates the same theme to that of romantic chivalry. Thus the actual verbal contest between Gaius Flamineus and Cornelius, when it comes, contrasts sharply in its realistic commonsense with both the romantic and farcical treatments of a similar situation already imprinted on the audience's minds. The audience's perceptive faculties are thus prepared and heightened to receive the full impact of the debate itself. Told that birth and wealth of the sort boasted by Cornelius are of small consequence compared to modesty, honesty and a will to work as exemplified by Gaius Flamineus, members of the audience must determine for themselves whether this is just a fable from the Roman past or an image of things to come in Tudor England. The fact that in performance it is so evidently both at once is the true measure of Medwall's dramatic skill. It is ironical that the message can still ring true today.

Everyman, by contrast, cannot hope to make as great an impression, since it is too familiar to occasion the same degree of surprise. For all that, it serves as an example of a substantial group of plays that are overtly religious in intention, some of which like *Mankind* or *The Croxton Play of the Sacrament* survive,

[1] See *Plate II*, no. 4.

but the majority of which were destroyed at the Reformation. Production of it in Bristol with an Everyman dressed in jeans and reefer jacket, who is first seen placing his nickel in a juke-box and idling on to the stage to the strains of 'I've got a lot of livin' to do' from *Bye-bye Birdie*, and Death dressed as a Marine Commando with face blackened and armed literally to the teeth with knife, dynamite, napalm and lasso, proved that the fabric of the play was tough enough to survive transposition to the twentieth century and to impress non-Christians sufficiently to acknowledge its impact upon their emotions.[1] Closer examination, however, reveals that the secret of this appeal lies partly in the directness of the message and partly in the rhetorical device of direct address by which it is communicated. Everyman, as protagonist, imparts his own anguish to his audience in the form of successive rhetorical questions which in their cumulative effect invite personal answers from every individual spectator, and thus involve everybody present in the action of the play. This technique is particularly apparent in Everyman's soliloquies which punctuate his several encounters with other characters. Thus whatever one's personal religious persuasion, it is virtually impossible to shirk giving a personal answer to the question, 'Where do I stand in the face of death?' One's own answer may or may not be an orthodox Roman Catholic answer; but that's beside the point. Dramatically speaking, the play has succeeded in sucking the spectator into its own magic by involving him personally in the predicament of the protagonist. Fellowship, Kindred and Cousin, Strength and Discretion may all be abstract personification and, as such, contemptuously dismissed as shadows rather than characters by some literary critics of mediaeval Morality Plays; but each is characterized broadly and firmly enough for the imaginative actor to fill in just enough detail to endow the character with a personality. The spectator can then easily take the last step and equate this personality with a real-life character of his own acquaintance. In this sense, the characters possess a reality during the actual performance which can appear to be more vivid and three-dimensional than many naturalistically documented characters

[1] See *Plate II*, no. 3.

of modern plays and novels. The possibility, therefore, of self-identification with both characters and action in the religious Morality Play is just as easy as in the secular Morality of the *Fulgens and Lucres* type; only the techniques of involvement are different. Yet in both types the responsibility for arresting the spectator's attention lies squarely with the actor.

This point is so important that I must try to illustrate it from the director's angle. In both types of play, religious and secular, the audience must never be allowed to sit back and watch the play. The director's first duty is to trust his actors; his next is to encourage them to seize every opportunity provided in the text to draw the audience into the action. Since many of the spectators will be reluctant to expose themselves in public in this way, this task requires an enormous degree of self-confidence on the part of the actors. They must regard themselves as hypnotists if they are to succeed. Any nervous mannerisms —trembling hands, shaking legs, twitching faces—that betray hesitancy or doubt will be spotted at such close quarters and embarrass the audience. Similarly, the need to move in and out of character, dictated by both the technique of direct address and by physical proximity to the audience, demands of the actor a very accurate sense of audience psychology, and a very relaxed approach. Never must any hint be given of speaking lines *as lines*; at the same time an iron grip must be maintained upon the rhythms within the lines since it is in these rhythms that the mechanics for spinning the hypnotic confidence trick upon the audience lie concealed. The actor, therefore, while appearing to be neither more nor less natural than any member of the audience, must have a complete command of those technical skills required to manipulate the audience as a whole and draw them out of themselves and into the essence of the moral argument.[1] It is these skills which translate sermons into plays, lectures into entertainments: the touchstone of success is the handling of the lyrical passages within these

---

[1] The archaic nature of the language does present a difficulty; but this can easily be exaggerated since the actual language of the text is as much an artificial convention as any of the more obvious scenic and costume conventions and acceptable as such to audiences.

plays when they occur. They are rare; but if properly introduced, they can be sublime. A magnificent example is Everyman's penitential prayer beginning:

> O eternal God, O heavenly figure,
> O way of rightwiseness. . . .

This speech of twenty-seven lines is the climax of the play and soars out of the surrounding dialogue like a love-duet in Italian opera. It is profoundly moving, capable of reducing the spectator to tears; but this cannot happen unless the actor in the role of Everyman has prepared his audience by bringing them step by step with him on his hapless quest for friends and moved them to pity in the course of it for his abject loneliness. In these circumstances his decision to cast himself upon the mercy of God, and his plea to the Virgin to act as intercessor, are then recognized as being as dramatically appropriate as they are doctrinally correct. It is this fusion of the two which produces a moment of sublime art.

I remarked earlier on that the makers and players of interludes enjoyed a social and intellectual environment conducive to virtuosity in artistic achievement—a relationship between artist and audience distinguished by mutual understanding and respect; but I said I would need later to qualify this general observation: the time has come to do so now. I think this statement holds—at least in England—until 1530 or thereabouts. Thereafter, deliberate use of the Morality Play as an instrument of propaganda, first *for* the Reformation and then *against* it, distorted it artistically and served to divide actors and audiences into hostile factions. As a vehicle for the discussion of so highly charged a polemical issue as the Reformation, the Morality Play in both its religious and secular forms was ideal: not only did it possess a didactic focal centre and invite controversy in its form, but its very popularity could be reckoned to secure a wide hearing for any religious and political viewpoints debated within it. The idea of injecting this new wine into old skins seems to have originated in Germany, but to have been taken up and developed very quickly by the leaders of Church and State in both England and Scotland with alarming results: for the controversial nature of the subject-matter, when presented in so emotional a context as the stage, was transmitted by the actors into the auditorium. The resulting sense of shock and outrage relieved itself in physical violence. The degree of violence and the dangers of its consequences are well enough attested to in the letters sent by Henry VIII to his magistrates in Yorkshire and Suffolk and by his Act of Parliament of 1543 forbidding discussion of doctrinal matters on the stage. This Act was subsequently repealed by Edward VI in 1549 and was immediately followed by a new flood of controversial plays and further violence. The return to Roman Catholicism under Queen Mary only reversed the tide of argument, giving Catholics a chance to retaliate in kind to what they had endured from the pens of their opponents.[1]

As examples of these polemical moralities, we chose in Bristol in 1964 to present the anonymous, Catholic, *Respublica* and an edited version of John Bale's *Kyng Johan* originally commissioned by Henry VIII's Protestant Chancellor, Thomas Cromwell. No one seeing either play could mistake its ancestry. The four daughters of God that walked the stage in *Respublica* and the personifications of the three Estates who, as single characters, strutted before the audience in *Kyng Johan*, were at once recognizable as recreations of the *dramatis personæ* of *Everyman*: King John himself, Cardinal Pandulphus, Stephen Langton and the Vices of *Respublica* were just as recognizable as reincarnations of the cast of *Fulgens and Lucres*. The one big difference was that the distinct religious moral of *Everyman* and the equally distinct political and social moral of *Fulgens and Lucres* were now wholly merged into one another in both *Respublica* and *Kyng Johan*. This blurring of the centre of focus, itself a product of the times, while calculated to heighten both tension and tempers in the mid-sixteenth century, serves in retrospect to deprive both plays of the directness and simplicity of their predecessors. The language of *Kyng Johan* is still shocking in its grossness, the wit of *Respublica* is still astringent in its mockery; but the fire of emotional shock has burnt itself out. *Respublica* remains the better entertainment of the two

[1] See G. Wickham, *Early English Stages*, ii(2), pp. 54–97.

because it is more compact in construction and less dependent upon historical event in its narrative: but the fact remains that both are rooted in politics of the time which cannot now be of more than historical and academic interest to an audience in the theatre—with the possible exception of audiences in Dublin and Belfast respectively. I believe that *Kyng Johan*, presented by a company of Ulstermen in Dublin on St. Patrick's Day, or *Respublica* presented by students of a theological seminary from the Irish Republic on Orange Day in Belfast could still provoke notable riots in both cities![1] Be that as it may, in England they cannot—as we proved in 1964 when both pieces, from a polemical standpoint, fell flat on their faces. But that, happily for the audiences concerned, was not the end of the matter: for both plays in revival offered audiences of today a bonus they could never have held for their contemporaries— a remarkable insight into the dramatic imaginations of Marlowe, Shakespeare and Ben Jonson. Despite the anchor chains rooting *Kyng Johan* and *Respublica* to earlier Moralities, precedents for the Elizabethan Chronicle play and the Comedy of Humours are startlingly self-evident in performance. The Vice Avarice, the satirical lynch-pin of the anti-Protestant *Respublica*, is a clearly defined prototype for Volpone. By the same token, the wretched figure of King John, blackmailed by his barons of Church and State and murdered by seditious subjects, leads the spectator's mind forward to the oppressed figure of Marlowe's Edward II. Just as significant, the obvious association of King John with Henry VIII in the allegorical disguise of Imperial Majesty shows how natural it was for a dramatist like Lyly to translate such figures as Endymion, Cynthia and Tellus into mouthpieces through which to conduct a discussion of Queen Elizabeth's relations with the Earl of Leicester and Mary Queen of Scots.[2]

Thus in both plays, *Kyng Johan* and *Respublica*, one becomes vividly aware during performance of the high degree of skill in

---

[1] It might be objected that the native Irish sense of humour would preclude such a reaction: on the other hand the reception Sean O'Casey encountered for his plays in Dublin suggests that it might not.

[2] See Essays 10 and 15 below.

both plot-construction and characterization that is present in these early works and on which the Elizabethan and Jacobean masters did not improve very noticeably except in terms of variety. What is missing is the poetic imagination of the later plays. There is no lack of ideas in the Moral Interludes of the middle period, but there is a serious deficiency of notable language in which to clothe them. In performance therefore the same heavy burden rests upon the technical virtuosity of the actor as in the Moral Interludes of the early period. If *Hamlet* or *Twelfth Night* can be made tolerably enjoyable experiences for an audience at the hands of school and college students, this is because the sustained poetic quality of the language acts as a safety net for their technical failings as actors. The Moral Interludes provide no such safety net.

The last of the Interludes revived in 1964 for which my own Department was responsible was *Nice Wanton*. This is both short and very funny. The moral is as stark as a temperance tract, and, as a play, the piece invites comparison with that most famous of Californian theatrical enterprises, *The Drunkard*. It is a stunning vehicle for clowns and the more straight-faced it is played the funnier it is. It is impossible (at this distance in time away from the play) to determine whether this ambivalence was deliberate on the part of its author. If the prayer for the Queen at the close is taken as a formal and obligatory gesture required by protocol at the time and thus divorceable from it, I am myself inclined to regard the play as an entertainment within the tradition of the Feast of Fools and the Lord of Misrule, and thus as a piece of debunking of parental, scholastic and judicial authority at least as deliberate as Shakespeare's treatment of Holofernes and Sir Nathaniel or of Malvolio and Justice Shallow.

However this may be, what *Nice Wanton* does illustrate is an obvious way out of the impasse in which the English Moral Interlude was in danger of finding itself as a result of embracing religious and political polemic to its bosom in the middle years of the sixteenth century. Threatened with extinction by censorship in the 1560's and 1570's, it escaped the fate of the Miracle Cycles by its ability to develop the farcical element already there and with the aid of it contrived to absorb and anglicize an older and foreign tradition of Latin origin and Italian provenance. In this it was greatly assisted by the swelling tide of academic enthusiasm for dramatic performances in the Universities and the schools. Many of the latter were new foundations and many others had reformed their statutes making provision in the process for the performance of plays in both Latin and English.[1]

The clearest evidence of the impact of these changes in academic thinking upon the Moral Interlude is to be seen in the two Interludes presented by the Bristol Old Vic Company during the 1964 festival, *Gammer Gurton's Needle* and *Ralph Roister Doister*. Both have moral comments to make on elements of Tudor society but neither are likely to get author or actor in trouble on account of religious or political controversy. Both are lighthearted farces which reflect their mediaeval and renaissance ancestry in parasites who are nevertheless still Vices, and in the reliance placed upon the inventive virtuosity of the clowns: the female characters are much funnier if played by men (like pantomime Dames) than if played by women. Of their abiding dramatic vitality, suffice it to say that a professional company had no box-office regrets for having revived both plays in a double-bill for a two-week run in 1964; and what was done then can be done again at any time. Given an intelligent understanding of the historical background to the original staging methods and a group of actors talented enough to arrest and maintain the interest of their audiences, I see no reason to think that this would not be true of any other Moral Interlude.

I have discussed the plays presented in Bristol in 1964 at some length because this festival provided one of the rare occasions for assessing the comparative strengths and weaknesses of the Morality Play and the Moral Interlude from the experience of performance; and this experience was at least as revealing in its own way as recent revivals of the York, Chester and Wakefield plays have been where criticism of the Miracle Cycles is concerned. Among the more important new factors that criticism

[1] See T. Vail Motter, *The School Drama in England*, 1929.

39

must consequently learn to accommodate are first, the extreme intimacy of the relationship between actors and spectators which was more akin, in its own style, to cabaret than to the full-length play of the modern playhouse. Scarcely less important was the use made of all visual aspects of the performance to signpost and underline the significance of particular actions and their relevance to the theme under discussion. For the most part, scenic emblems—items of furniture, trees, huts and so on—sufficed to identify the locality of the action, and to make it easy for the players to present the same play in many different environments, while the disguises of stage costumes were used with extraordinary flexibility and economy both to identify character and to present in counterpoint (and thus to make explicit) the contrasts and contradictions between an actor's words and his actions. These points may be conveniently illustrated by Everyman's changing of his own clothes for the cloak of Contrition provided by Knowledge, or by the Vice Avarice in *Respublica* whose sober-looking cloak contains a multiplicity of pockets in the lining, or of the placement of Virtue in the stocks by Vice as is the case with Chastity in *The Satyre of the Thrice Estatis*. All these devices were later to be taken over and put to new use by Shakespeare: the change of clothes in *Coriolanus*, the emblematic cloak for Rumour in *Henry IV* (Pt. 2) and the setting of Kent in the stocks by Regan in *King Lear*.

Scholars have often deplored the paucity of information that survives to us about acting and production techniques in Elizabethan and Jacobean public playhouses: yet much, if not all, of this information still exists to be consulted within the surviving but neglected scripts of Moralities and Interludes. If schools and universities could bring themselves to devote some of the energies habitually expended on reviving Shakespeare's plays to experimental revival of those plays in which he and his contemporaries were themselves schooled, I think we should quickly learn to accord to Morality Plays and Moral Interludes a greater degree of critical respect than has been customary hitherto, and might even contribute something concerning dramatic and theatrical techniques of interest and value to playwrights of our own time who in seeking to free themselves from the tyranny of picture frames around their stages find it difficult to come to terms with any other form of theatre.

3

Genesis and the Tragic Hero: Marlowe to Webster

THE dramatic concept of the tragic hero was one of the genuinely original and creative contributions of Elizabethan actors and playmakers to the theatre of their time. I use the word 'Elizabethan' here in the strictest historical sense of the last four decades of the sixteenth century, 1559–1603, the span of the great Queen's reign: for where tragedy is concerned this period begins with *Cambises* (Thomas Preston, 1561) and *Gorborduc* (1562) and ends with *Hamlet* (1601) and *Sejanus* (1603).

The difference is astonishing, but nowhere more remarkable than in the treatment accorded to the title roles. Some part of the explanation for this change must lie with the acting companies themselves, since the period encompasses their transformation from small groups of itinerant entertainers into tightly organized companies of professional players based on London and performing regularly on weekdays as well as on public holidays.[1] By the time that the Queen died Edward Alleyn was firmly established at the head of the Lord Admiral's Company at the Fortune Playhouse and Richard Burbage at the head of the Lord Chamberlain's Company at the Globe. These actors, who were revered by their public at Court, in

[1] See M. C. Bradbrook, *The Rise of the Common Player*, 1962.

the City of London and throughout the provinces, were expected to appear in roles commensurate with their reputation as performers; and, as the paymasters of their playmakers, they could bring some pressure to bear on the actual choice of subject-matter and the treatment to be accorded to it for stage purposes. The copyright in the play in any case passed into their hands as soon as the script had been paid for and had gone into rehearsal. To these actors therefore must go some of the credit for fashioning a new concept of the tragic hero in the theatre.

For all that, whether we are discussing *Cambises* or *Hamlet*, *Gorborduc* or *Sejanus*, it would be stupid to suppose that the poet was not in ultimate control of the shaping of both plot and tragic hero. The poet's own reading and the use he made of it, whether in Horace and Ovid or in Chaucer and Lydgate, is thus clearly a factor of great importance to the development of Elizabethan and Jacobean tragedy; but we must, I think, be careful to temper our speculations in this direction (as the poets were themselves tempered) by taking the forces of popular taste and theatrical conservatism into our reckoning. And here the actors, by providing the playmaker with his market, stood between any obsessive concern with literary and academic aspirations on the part of the poet and a desire for vulgar, banal or spectacular entertainment on the part of the populace at large. Where tragedy and the fall of the hero were concerned, I believe that this delicate balance between playgoers, actors and playmakers in Elizabethan England served to make the Book of Genesis a far more potent influence upon plot and character than either Horace's *Ars Poetica* or the plays of Seneca: for where knowledge of Aristotelian precept in matters of dramatic theory was reserved to the learned few, the stories of a tragic fall from divine grace recounted in Genesis were familiar to all from constant repetition in Church and from repeated theatrical representations of them within the Miracle Cycles.

For the orthodox Elizabethan, whether of Anglican, Roman Catholic or Puritan persuasion, there was no question but that evil in the world was attributable to the Fall of Lucifer and Adam's first disobedience. Everyone acknowledged that these

43

errors had been atoned for by Christ's Passion, that Adam, Eve and the Patriarchs had been redeemed by Christ's harrowing of hell, and that sinful mankind of more recent time had the means, through Holy Scripture, to attain salvation and eventual return to Paradise himself. Yet, given this happy issue out of affliction, the very idea of tragedy, when defined as a fall from prosperity into adversity, becomes difficult to sustain since it is within man's own reach to avoid the fall or, having fallen, to attain forgiveness through Grace. It is thus one of the more fascinating aspects of Elizabethan and Jacobean drama that it should bring these commonplace beliefs of audiences of the time into direct conflict with those newly resuscitated Graeco-Roman concepts of tragedy and comedy which made no allowance for Christ's nativity, ministry, passion and resurrection. This conflict of viewpoint focuses itself upon the question of the Fall and raises in its turn a host of related questions. What sort of a Fall? What reasons for it? What moral repercussions?

The line of thought which I wish to develop in this essay relates to the varying ways in which the major writers of tragedy for Elizabethan and Jacobean acting companies faced up to and answered this challenging question. What sort of a person was their ideal tragic hero or heroine? Which was to be preferred as a model, Cain or Oedipus? Eve or Phaedra? Lucifer or the Borgias? In *Hamlet* Shakespeare tells us Claudius' crime had 'the primal eldest curse upon it, a brother's murder'. Tourneur in *The Atheist's Tragedy* develops the same theme at much greater length: it is 'Black Beelzebub and all his hell hounds' who escort the ghost of a murdered brother before D'Amville's distracted eyes and strip him of everything he has—his wealth, his power, his hopes in posterity, his peace of mind. Marlowe, Cambridge scholar that he was, appropriately sees Paradise set in a library rather than in a garden, and substitutes necromantic books for the apples that ruined Adam, as the bait that is to destroy his Faustus. It is the serpent in the Garden of Eden whom the Evil Angel is quoting in saying 'Go forward, Faustus, in that famous art / Wherein all Nature's treasure is contained; / Be thou on earth as Jove is in the sky, / Lord and commander of these elements.' The serpent's words in Genesis are:

> Ye shall not surely die:
> For God doth know that in the day ye eat thereof, then your eyes shall be opened, and ye shall be as gods, knowing good and evil.

Still more important, at least in its subsequent influence on drama, is Marlowe's treatment of Barabas in *The Jew of Malta*: for here Lucifer himself is reincarnated in stage-terms, via Machiavelli, in the person of the non-Christian, avaricious Barabas. It is Machiavel, as Prologue, who presents Barabas and his story to the audience. It is his servant Ithamore who declares (III, 92).

> The devil invented a challenge, my master writ it, and I carried it.

The link between Barabas and Lucifer is egotism. 'Ego mihimet sum semper proximus,' says Barabas. This is Lucifer's state of mind before the fall, as represented repeatedly in the Miracle Cycles; Barabas' advice to Ithamore (II, 297–8)—

> First, be thou void of these affections,
> Compassion, love, vain hope and heartless fear—

represents Lucifer's state of mind after the Fall just as faithfully.

This preoccupation with monstrous villainy begotten of an extremity of pride and knowing no bounds to its destructiveness leads directly through a sequence of villain-heroes to Milton's extended portrait of Satan in *Paradise Lost*. It takes its dramatic beginnings from the Miracle Cycles—especially the quality of general malevolence. The Chester Satan soliloquizes explicitly enough.

> Ghostly paradise I was in,
> but thence I fell through my sin.
> Of earthly paradise now, as I myn,
> a man is given mastery.
> By Belzabub! shall I never blyn
> tyll I may make him by some synne
> from that place for to twyn
> and trespace as I did . . . (*Creation*, lines 169–76)

45

> they shall fare both, as did I
> be banished both of that vallye
> and their offspring for aye. (lines 202–4)

We should not be surprised therefore to find Webster taking care to place the malevolent Flamineo in *The White Devil* together with Brachiano and Vittoria in a verbal, poetic context which enables his audience to view them simultaneously in Rome and in the Garden of Eden. Webster's instrument is Cornelia, Vittoria's mother, who, when she obtrudes upon her daughter's adulterous encounter with Brachiano (I, ii) declares,

> Never dropped mildew on a flower here
> Till now—

and again,

> O, that this fair garden
> Had with all the poisoned herbs of Thessaly
> At first been planted; made a nursery
> For witchcraft, rather than a burial plot
> For both your honours!

It is Flamineo who completes the image for us in his declaration, 'We are engaged to mischief, and must on' and in his determination to pursue it by imitating, 'The subtle foldings of a winter snake.'

In sharp contrast to these echoes of scriptural archetypes is Ben Jonson's bald title and dedication to his tragedy *Sejanus*. The play's title is quite simply 'Sejanus: His Fall'. The dedication to Lord Aubigny starts with the terse sentence: 'My Lord, —If ever any ruin were so great as to survive, I think this be one I send you, The Fall of Sejanus.' Very interestingly Jonson continues, 'It is a poem that . . . suffered no less violence from our people here, than the subject of it did from the rage of the people of Rome.' In other words, the tragedy failed with the public, either because it was not properly understood or because it is a bad play. Much the same is true of Jonson's other venture into tragedy *Cataline: His Conspiracy*. Since Jonson makes no bones about the deliberateness of his attempt to imitate classical precept in the construction of these plays, it seems important to me that we should try to ascertain whether Jonson's rejection of specifically Christian prototypes of tragic hero and of the allegorical convention for the discussion of his fall should have had any bearing on the failure of his tragedies in the estimation of their audiences: after all, Shakespeare's Roman plays from *Titus Andronicus* to *Coriolanus* were no less popular than his other tragedies so far as we know.

Before examining this question further, however, there is another aspect of the direct influence of Christian concepts of the Fall upon Elizabethan and Jacobean drama which must first be considered in general terms. This is the inescapable relationship between the Christian concept of the Fall and its counterpart of the Redemption which, in drama, finds its expression in comedy or, at its darkest, in tragi-comedy. In *Measure for Measure*, for instance, Angelo falls no less culpably than Adam or Webster's Brachiano; yet Angelo is forgiven and reprieved, and the play ends in general rejoicing. *The Tempest* provides an even more extreme example, where a banished Duke works his way back to his Dukedom by reconciling himself to his enemies through forgiveness in his own generation and through the marriage of their respective children in the next. This reflection pinpoints, in appropriately dramatic manner, the size of the gulf separating the English traditional playmaker from the avowed neo-classical poet where the construction of tragedy is concerned in the Elizabethan and Jacobean theatre. Once this has been remarked, it becomes evident that any further investigation of the nature of this difference of approach should begin in a comparison of the respective sources of inspiration. In both cases there is a dramatic and a literary precedent: for the reactionary playmaker the *exempla* for tragedy were to be found in the Miracle Cycles and in Lydgate's *The Fall of Princes*: the innovators stood just as firmly by the plays of Seneca and the critical writings of Aristotle and Horace. This division in basic attitudes, of course, did not preclude informal borrowing by each group from the other; but here the innovators were at a distinct disadvantage since their dramatic model was virtually untested outside Italy while their literary model took no cognizance of a Christian ordered society. To put the matter baldly and in concrete terms, Marlowe, Kyd, Shakespeare, Tourneur, Heywood and

Webster, by choosing to echo if not to follow traditional precepts in the construction of tragedy, placed themselves in a much stronger position vis-à-vis their audiences in the public playhouses than those dramatists who tried to divorce themselves from it like Chapman, Beaumont and Fletcher and especially Ben Jonson.

That said, I want now to look more closely at several different attitudes to and treatments of the story of the Fall. A necessary preface to this discussion must be some reference to Lydgate's *Fall of Princes*. Students today can be assumed to be familiar with Willard Farnham's chapters on the subject in *The Mediaeval Heritage of Elizabethan Tragedy* and I want only to stress two particular points arising. Posterity has rated Boccaccio's *De Casibus Virorum Illustrium*, from which Lydgate (via Laurence Premierfait) adapted his own poem, far more highly than Lydgate's work; but most literate Englishmen of the fifteenth and sixteenth centuries held Lydgate's poem in much higher esteem than Honours Schools of English Literature do now. The two most striking features of Lydgate's version are, first, the extraordinary hotch-potch of biblical, classical and more modern historical figures whose falls are recounted, and secondly his sharp criticism of the particular vices to which his Princes owe their fall. As Dr. Bergen pointed out in his edition of the work,[1] murder, slander and accompanying credulity, covetousness and ingratitude, materialism, deceit and tyranny are all singled out for special attention in the l'Envoys. The recurring threnody of the whole work is that men reap what they have sown. The adaptation was prepared for a special audience and as such is generally conservative in outlook; but, very importantly, Lydgate does recognize that, 'nobility is by the grace of God and not by blood, and poverty is no bar to royalty: nor can anything good ever come out of an evil stock'.[2]

Obviously, these sentiments have considerable importance for anyone who himself happens to be preparing to write a tragedy, more especially when most of the notable figures of past history who might qualify as candidates for the role of tragic hero pass

[1] For *The Early English Text Society*, 1924, p. xx.   [2] *Ibid.* .p. xxi.

in review through the pages of Lydgate's vast work. Here we meet Adam and Isis, Oedipus and Hercules, Deborah and Lucrece, Dido and Cleopatra, Julius Caesar and King Arthur, Robert of Normandy and King John of France. Over them all broods Dame Fortune, raising and jettisoning Princes on and off her wheel with indifference bordering on contempt. When, from Chaucer's day to Shakespeare's, tragedy was by definition a story of a great man plunged from prosperity into adversity, no one who read this work and sought to write tragedy himself whether in the form of epic narrative or dramatic dialogue, could hope to escape its influence: and the more of the poem one reads the more evident does it become that, despite the arbitrary nature of Fortune's mutability, it is *moral weakness of character*, as judged by Christian standards, which precipitates each and every Prince from Adam to King John of France towards his or her ruin. This puritan streak is Lydgate's own. The seven deadly sins are as manifest as agents of destruction within this poem as they are in any Morality Play. This heavy, moral flavour is, by contrast, a quality conspicuously absent from Aristotle's discussion of 'harmartia': misfortune according to Aristotle is brought upon the tragic hero *not* by vice and depravity but by some error of judgement. As the late Humphrey House pointed out in his discussion of *The Poetics*, 'The phrase "tragic flaw" should be treated with suspicion. I do not know when it was first used or by whom. It is not an Aristotelian metaphor at all. . . . Bywater and Rostagni agree on this point, and I think I can safely say that all serious modern Aristotelian scholarship agrees with them that "harmartia" means an error which is derived from ignorance of some material fact or circumstance' (*Aristotle's Poetics*, 1956, p. 94). In other words, 'harmartia' is directly related to 'hubris' and results in 'nemesis', but is not necessarily related to moral turpitude. No one reading Lydgate's *Fall of Princes*, however, could avoid adding to 'error of judgement' the Christian concept of sin and thus explain the error in terms of moral failings. For instance Othello's error of judgement is to trust Iago—that is his 'harmartia'—but his jealousy (with its fatal results for himself and Desdemona) is a sin, and it is this black jealousy which brings him to despair: by despair I mean two crimes expressly forbidden by God—murder and suicide. This distinction therefore between the true Aristotelian concept of the tragic fall and Lydgate's interpretation of the mediaeval *De Casibus* theory is a large one and must be borne in mind when considering such different writers of tragedy as Shakespeare and Jonson. Before leaving *The Fall of Princes* there is another aspect of its impact on Elizabethan and Jacobean playmakers that merits attention. Lydgate's version follows Laurence's softened and extended French adaptation more closely than Boccaccio's Latin original: any sixteenth- or seventeenth-century writer who chose to by-pass Lydgate and revert to Boccaccio's Latin text would notice the dedicatory epistle to Mainardo dei Cavalcanti, virtually omitted by Lydgate. Boccaccio chose Mainardo because of his own contempt for all princely patrons, and in his preface he declares that as a result of their pride, their laziness, greed, licentiousness and vindictiveness, justice, honesty and all private virtues were mocked; by their example, they corrupt the rest of society. His work is thus a bitter and scornful attack on Princes, not written to flatter or even to advise them, but to stir them out of indolence, vice and folly and thus to benefit the community as a whole. This attitude to Princes was destined to win wide approval among radical divines and men of letters in Geneva, Edinburgh and London before the close of the sixteenth century, and to find its European apotheosis in the English Puritan sect who described themselves as the Levellers. It finds its clearest echoes in the Jacobean theatre, not in Shakespeare but in Middleton and Webster. In *The White Devil* Cornelia castigates Brachiano with scorching sarcasm on surprising him in Vittoria's arms.

> The lives of princes should like dials move
> Whose regular example is so strong
> They make the times by them go right or wrong. (I, ii)

Bosola, after the murder of the Duchess of Malfi, rounds on Duke Ferdinand in the same vein:

> Your brother and yourself are worthy men:
> You have a pair of hearts are hollow graves
> Rotten and rotting others. (IV, ii, 387–9)

It is not so much the fall of the prince that interests Webster in his tragedies as the effects of his falling on the society over which the prince presides. This is a state of mind which he shares with Calvin and John Knox and which both of them share with Boccaccio.

If we turn now to the dramatic precedent of the native tradition—the Miracle Cycles—we find a third and equally potent variant of the story of the fall, typological or prefigurative juxtaposition. The Cycles begin uniformly with a triple fall—Lucifer, Adam and Cain. It has been common practice among literary critics for a long time to regard the Cycles as loosely constructed sequences of playlets, the subjects of which were chosen, if not wholly at random, then at best for expedient rather than artistic reasons. I would challenge this view: my own reading of mediaeval religious drama suggests quite otherwise. If this were true, why then are so many stories, in themselves highly dramatic, uniformly left out of the Cycles—Samson and Delilah, Absolom, Jonah and the Whale—to cite only a few of the most obvious? The answer, I think, is twofold.

Structurally, the Cycles are built on the three Advents of Christian belief and the three corresponding falls.[1] God deals with man by three decisive interventions in human affairs—as Creator, as Saviour and as Judge: these events provide the beginning, climax and conclusion of the Cycles. Choice of material from the Old Testament for inclusion is governed in part by structural necessity and in part by its ability to prefigure New Testament material. The author of the Townley Cycle for example starts his play of the Annunciation as follows. God is speaking.

> I will that my son manhede take,
> ffor reson wyll that ther be thre,
> A man, a madyn, and a tre:
> Man for man, tre for tre,
> Madyn for madyn; thus shal it be. (lines 30–4)

Another example of the same technique but in visual rather than

[1] See G. Wickham, *Early English Stages*, 1958, i, pp. 315–22, and V. A. Kolve, *The Play Called Corpus Christi*, 1966, pp. 60 *et seq.*

in verbal terms is provided by the baby in swaddling clothes cradled in the branches of the tree of knowledge within the Paradise garden of the Cornish Cycle. Nothing could be more explicit. As audience we look back as we look forward. In this way Lucifer's Fall is made to prefigure Adam's and both serve to prefigure Christ's Temptation in the Wilderness: Cain's murder of Abel prefigures Judas' betrayal of Christ just as Abraham's sacrifice of Isaac prefigures the Crucifixion. The importance of these episodes, liturgically and dramatically, is that they stand for events greater than themselves—sometimes for several events. In asking our students today to read single playlets from the Cycles as samples of dramatic writing before Shakespeare, we do their authors a violent injustice since we destroy the context and thus make them appear quaint and trivial. But we do more damage than that; we blur if not destroy our own approach to Elizabethan drama. Tudor audiences saw the Cycles whole: after seeing the Fall of Lucifer, the Fall of Adam, Cain's murder of his brother Abel and Noah's Flood in swift succession, mediaeval and Tudor audiences could hardly miss the significance of this sequence of disasters in relation to the Crucifixion, the Harrowing of Hell and Dooms-day plays. Those that did so were helped by the authors to repair the omission. I have already illustrated the method from the Townley Annunciation. The York Cycle provides another where, as Mr. Kolve notices, God's speech at the start of the Judgement play directly echoes his speech before the play of the Flood: there is one important difference: it lies in the fact that where before he found Noah, now there is no one.[1] The end of the Cycle is thus declared to lie in its beginning. This is some-thing we must understand before we can begin to appreciate the Miracle Cycles as drama, and the way in which the tradi-tional conventions of the Cycles are carried over into Elizabe-than dramatic structure. Berthold Brecht in our own day has taught us that prefiguration and juxtaposition can be success-fully used as dramatic devices: Elizabethan audiences did not need to be taught this lesson as they were heirs to a poetic and dramatic tradition that took it for granted. When therefore in

[1] *Op. cit.*, p. 68.

The Tempest Prospero, with every third thought devoted to his grave, bequeathes his island to Caliban, a creature compounded of the impure elements of earth and water, and releases Ariel, a spirit compounded of the pure elements, fire and air, before setting sail himself for Milan, Shakespeare's vision of the soul parting company with the body at death and setting forth on its journey to paradise regained was not a hard one for the spectator to grasp. The book of necromantic art which brought Faustus to ruin has here been used to better purpose and is finally buried 'deeper than ever plummet sounded'. Disobedience has been atoned for by love and forgiveness. All that remains is a requiem mass.

> Now I want
> Spirits to enforce, art to enchant;
> And my ending is despair
> Unless I be reliev'd by prayer.

This romantic view of the fall, epitomized for mediaeval and renaissance Europe by Dante in *The Divine Comedy*, had its bourgeois counterpart in the mundane crime story of the news-reporter. Mediaeval audiences had been taught from their pulpits and their stages for generations that if a Prince could fall from prosperity, so could his subjects, Everyman and *Humanum Genus*. By Christian standards, a descent from a well-ordered, if simple, mercantile or farming life to viciousness and crime was no less reprehensible, and therefore tragic, than such conduct in a king. Indeed it is the very possibility of a fall from virtue that makes us brothers in one another, notwithstanding degree, and of one substance with both Adam and Christ. St. Paul provides the classic text—'for as in Adam all die, so in Christ shall all be made alive'. The subject, like the sovereign, in the parlance of the preacher or of the Moral Interlude, reaps what he sows. If he repents he may yet make a good end and, in the manner of his dying, atone for his bad deeds; for Abel's murder has been absolved in Christ's. A contrite heart, made manifest in public confession and repentance, is necessary to the dramatic expression of this notion. Comparison is useful here between Chapman's Duke of Biron and the

criminals of the anonymous *Arden of Faversham*. Duke Charles
dies with defiance on his lips, not contrition. Seneca provides
the model. Towards the end of the last Act, Vitry accompanies
the Duke up on to the scaffold and chides him for his arrogant
behaviour towards the executioner.

Vitry: My lord, you make too much of this your body,
　　　　Which is no more your own.
Biron: Nor is it yours;
　　　　I'll take my death with all the horrid rites
　　　　And representments of the dread it merits;
　　　　Let tame nobility and numbed fools
　　　　That apprehend not what they undergo,
　　　　Be such exemplary and formal sheep;
　　　　I will not have him touch me till I will.

Having secured the right to prepare himself physically for
execution in his own time and in his own way, he prepares to
meet it spirtually:

　　　　　　Never more
　　Shall any hope of my revival see me.
　　Such is the endless exile of dead men.
　　Summer succeeds the spring; autumn the summer;
　　The frosts of winter, the fall'n leaves of autumn:
　　All these, and all fruits in them yearly fade,
　　And every year return: but cursed man
　　Shall never more renew his vanish'd face.
　　Fall on your knees then, statesmen, ere ye fall,
　　That you may rise again: knees bent too late,
　　Stick you in earth like statues: see in me
　　How you are pour'd down from your clearest heavens;
　　Fall lower yet, mix'd with th'unmoved centre,
　　That your own shadows may no longer mock ye.

This nobility of spirit in the face of the executioner's axe shows
high courage and is expressed in a befittingly grand poetic
manner, but suggests little regard for any world or time other
than the present. Very different is the case with Mistress Arden
in that bourgeois tale of crime and punishment, *Arden of
Faversham*. The Mayor, confronting Alice with her husband's
corpse, declares:

54

Mayor: See Mistress Arden, where your husband lies;
　　　　Confess this foul fault and be penitent.
Alice: 　Arden, sweet husband, what shall I say?
　　　　The more I sound his name, the more he bleeds;
　　　　This blood condemns me, and in gushing forth
　　　　Speaks as it falls, and asks me why I did it.
　　　　Forgive me, Arden: I repent me now,
　　　　And, would my death save thine, thou should'st not die.
　　　　Rise up, sweet Arden, and enjoy thy love,
　　　　And frown not on me when we meet in heaven:
　　　　In heaven I'll love thee, though on earth I did not.

For all the cloying sentiment of her actual words, Alice Arden shares Faustus' regret for a life wasted by a foolish choice: what the vision of Christ's blood streaming in the firmament recalls for Faustus, the more material confrontation with the blood-stained clothing of her husband does for Alice. Like Faustus she admits to repenting too late. Both are bourgeois heroes and their fall is from prosperity interpreted as virtue rather than as power and wealth. It is an approach to tragedy of which, in the seventeenth century, Thomas Heywood was to be the prime exponent.[1] For Alice Arden, however, the frenzied panic of Faustus' final moments is translated by public confession and contrition into a serenity of mind more nearly resembling the assurance and fortitude of the Duke of Biron.

Alice: Leave now to trouble me with worldly things,
　　　　And let me meditate upon my saviour Christ,
　　　　Whose blood must save me from the blood I shed.

The cathartic effect of each of these deaths, therefore, is different in itself and will differ in its impact upon the spectator in accordance with his own religious standpoint. Alice meets in death the punishment for disobeying Christian rules of conduct in respect of adultery and murder; but, thanks to her public admission of guilt and repentance, opens for herself the way to salvation by grace.[2] *Sub specie aeternitatis* her end is not tragic and, for the audience, the emotional response is

[1] See Irving Ribner, *Jacobean Tragedy*, 1962, pp. 50–71.
[2] Shakespeare takes this standpoint in *T.G. of V.*, V, iv, 81: 'By penitence th' Eternal's wrath's appeased.' See also *Hamlet*, V, ii, 340, and p. 210 below.

one of joy salvaged out of fear and horror: Faustus, by contrast, has by the very nature of his pact with Lucifer, separated himself from the fount of grace and thus faces eternal damnation. For the Christian this is the only irretrievable and thus truly tragic disaster, and the emotional response demanded is sorrow, pity and fear. It is a fate Shakespeare reserves for his blackest villains, Richard III, Macbeth or Iago. In murdering others they have murdered their own consciences and thus destroyed their way to Grace: 'Conscience,' declares Richard III before Bosworth Field, 'is but a word that cowards use, / Devis'd at first to keep the strong in awe.' This is the language of the serpent talking to Eve, of the Evil Angel talking to Faustus: it is the language of Barabas the Jew talking to Ithamore. When talked by Princes this language translates society into a little Hell, like Macbeth's Scotland, where

> Curses, not loud but deep, mouth-honour, breath,
> Which the poor heart would fain deny, but dare not

replace the 'honour, love' and 'obedience' due to the Prince. All is here lost, not only in this temporal world but for eternity. Chapman's Biron, by contrast, and guilty of treason though he is, does not face death in these terms of reference. For him an after-life is something about which 'tame nobility and numbed fools' chatter and comfort themselves at a safe distance from the reality of death: the reality is 'endless exile' which must be faced as such with stoic fortitude. The emotional response demanded of the audience is admiration.

Chapman, however, in choosing a topical event of recent memory as the basic subject-matter out of which to form his tragedy restricts the freedom with which he can treat this state of mind; for Biron meets death as a representative of a Christian-ordered society. Jonson, in reverting to Roman antiquity, set himself no such limits. Conscience plays little or no part in the rise and fall of either Cataline or Sejanus. Both are men of outstanding natural ability as attested by the positions accorded them in public life: both make great errors of judgement and bring disaster upon themselves in consequence. Yet in the last analysis both plays are stories of simple treachery; the heroes' 'harmartia' to have placed trust in a woman when undertaking ambitious plans for political aggrandisement. Fulvia ruins Cataline, Livia Sejanus. Direct comparison may usefully be made here with *Macbeth* and *The White Devil*: if this is done, it will be noticed that there is a very important difference between the dramatic function of the women in these two plays and in Jonson's. Like Eve in the Garden of Eden, Lady Macbeth and Vittoria Corombona are the direct agents of disobedience for Macbeth and Duke Brachiano. In Jonson's tragedies both Livia and Fulvia are presented to us as high-class courtesans, but neither of them directly corrupt their lords: indeed both Cataline and Sejanus are impatient at having to count such light-weight commodities into their personal bills of reckoning at all.

Thus Cataline:

> What ministers men must, for practice, use!
> The rash, the ambitious, needy, desperate,
> Foolish and wretched, e'en the dregs of mankind,
> To whores and women! Still, it must be so. (III, 714–17)

Fulvia merely impinges on Cataline's circle in this context. Had Cataline bothered to ponder upon the workings of the human heart, he might have examined Fulvia and discovered that both she and her lover Curius were in Cicero's pay: that he confides in both of them is his 'harmartia'. Sejanus is more closely concerned with Livia as a woman. She is the daughter of the late Emperor Augustus, is married to Drusus and a kinsman of the Emperor Tiberius. That Sejanus, a mere gentleman's son, should seek to marry into the imperial house is his 'harmartia', for it is this presumptuousness which alerts the otherwise besotted Tiberius to set a watch upon Sejanus. Sejanus tells Livia's doctor that he loves her, but in soliloquy he tells the audience another story.

Sejanus: If Livia will be now corrupted, then
> Thou hast the way, Sejanus, to work out
> His secrets, who (thou know'st) endures thee not,
> Her husband, Drusus: and to work against them.
> Prosper it, Pallas, thou that better 'st wit;
> For Venus hath the smallest share in it. (I, 369–72)

It is this lack of personal commitment in human relationships which, in my view, provides the key to the failure of both plays. In his letter to readers of *Sejanus* Jonson gives a clear account of his purpose.

> If it be objected [he says] that what I publish is no true poem, in the strict laws of time I confess it, as also in the want of a proper chorus; whose habit and moods are such and so difficult, as not any, whom I have seen, since the ancients, . . . have yet come in the way of. In the meantime . . . in truth of argument, dignity of persons, gravity and height of elocution, fulness and frequency of sentence I have discharged the other offices of a tragic writer. . . .

He cites Horace's *Art of Poetry* as his model for construction and Tacitus, Suetonius and Seneca as his sources for the subject-matter, and goes out of his way to state that he has worked from the original 'learned tongues' and not from English translations.

There can be no question therefore that the product is a thorough-going attempt at a tragedy in the classical manner, self-consciously stripped of all Gothic and Christian accretions. Sejanus aspires to convert his domination over the Emperor Tiberius into actual possession of the imperial crown, just as Macbeth covets the crown of Scotland: but where, in *Macbeth*, the Devil in the form of three 'black and midnight hags' and Eve in the form of Lady Macbeth conspire with Macbeth to make him yield to this temptation, Sejanus knows his mind from the outset, is never tempted in any formal sense and merely uses Livia as a means to achieve an already clear-cut objective. Where Shakespeare uses prefiguration, Jonson does not. Jonson allows us to see Sejanus increasing his hold over Tiberius' mind; he admits us to the manner in which the reversal of Sejanus' schemes is planned and accomplished in the Senate; and he informs us at length in eye-witness report of the lynching of Sejanus by the Roman mob. From the whole there emerges a firm and objectively stated moral warning.

> Forbear, you things,
> That stand upon the pinnacles of state,
> To boast your slippery height; when you do fall,
> You pash yourself in pieces, ne'er to rise:
> And he that lends you pity, is not wise.

This may be true, but there is little likelihood of our pitying Sejanus when his character is presented to us in so frigid and academic a manner as to deny our interest in him as a man in the first place. Jonson succeeds in establishing Sejanus as a subject better equipped to rule than Tiberius just as successfully as Marlowe establishes Young Mortimer in *Edward II* or Shakespeare Henry Bolingbroke in *Richard II*: but thereafter he fails to develop his character in any way that can evoke the sympathy of the audience for any of his subsequent actions or confrontations with other characters. All his actions are contemptible and the other characters are bores. Nor does Jonson help himself by dismissing all low-life characters whether serious or comic from his narrative in his determination to adhere to classical precept. How much is our sympathy with Hamlet enhanced by his encounter with the grave-diggers! How greatly is our understanding of Coriolanus increased by his encounters with the citizens and soldiers of Rome and Aufidius' servant in Antium! In short, what Jonson denies us is any yardstick equivalent to a Christian conscience in action by which to distinguish between errors of judgement and emotional indiscretions, between miscalculation and instability: it is here precisely that the Christian concept of the Fall (mirrored in Lucifer, Adam, Cain and Noah) gave to dramatists who chose to make use of it an unsurpassed instrument for self-identification between tragic hero and individual spectator: 'There, but for the Grace of God, go I' is a cry that could readily be uttered by anyone seeing *Faustus, Arden of Faversham, Macbeth* or even *The Tragedy of Biron*. Identification with Sejanus is impossible because not invited: as a tragedy it has a didactic dimension, but not an allegorical one. The former quality is usually to be found in the structure; the latter, when it is present, in the behaviour of the characters to one another. Jonson is more interested in the accurate rendering of his source-material than in endowing the characters given to him by his sources with conduct that is interesting in itself: and by denying himself any use of Christian allegory in his treatment of the protagonist he deprives himself of the means to comment philosophically on the moral problems confronting his own generation.

In this Chapman is more successful: he shares Jonson's interest in neo-classicism and endows his Duke of Biron with a stoic rather than a Christian outlook on life, but depicts the society in which his Duke moves and by which he is condemned as one corrupted by original sin. A measure of Biron's tragedy therefore lies in the arrogance which leads him to see himself like Lucifer or Adam before the Fall and to deny his share of the guilt for the corruption in Church and State which he so despises. The idea, however, that natural man can exempt himself from any share of guilt for the Fall by being true to himself is more fully realized in the far more complex and brilliantly executed setting of Webster's *The White Devil*. Vittoria and Brachiano in their different ways each share Biron's arrogance, self reliance and personal integrity: they are thus the perfect instruments for Flamineo, himself both deathshead and devil, to use in reducing the fair garden of society into a desolate graveyard. Here it is not so much the fall of a single protagonist that forms the subject of tragedy, but the collapse of society itself under the strain of the cumulative effects of original sin upon every individual that corporately make up society. The orthodox Christian view of the Fall is here fused with Boccaccio's scorn for corrupt princes whose faults breed like cancers in the community at large. And here the marked affinity between this moral viewpoint and that of Puritan opinion in England should be noticed. The initial evil which Flamineo engineers—no more than an affair between a married Duke and a married woman—is seen to spread via Vittoria's dream and Brachiano's interpretation of it to double murder. This brings Marcello, Zanche, the Doctor, the Conjuror, the Duke of Florence and Cardinal Monticelso within the frame of this evil web. By the time Vittoria is required to stand trial, the heads of Church and State have become parties to the dispute, and when the justice of the law-courts has been mocked, the law of the jungle takes over with revenge pursued by hired assassins disguised as churchmen. The context within which Webster wishes his audience to interpret this horrific disintegration of society is made explicit in part by the fact that the Duke of Florence and the Cardinal-come-Pope escape punishment and in part by the repeated use of the traditional typological images of the Fall. Flamineo's initial seduction of Vittoria and Brachiano is placed figuratively, in the imagery of the verse, in a garden to recall Adam's Fall: this leads in due season to the re-enactment of Abel's death at the hands of his brother Cain and to Judas' betrayal of Jesus with a kiss. This moral vision of an inescapably corrupted universe finds its final expression in the last scene in an image of partial regeneration with marked affinities to that of Noah and the Flood. The young Prince Giovanni alone survives the annihilation of both the Orsini and the Coromboni houses which has occurred within the course of the play's action: yet he is Brachiano's son, a nephew of the Duke of Florence, and heir to their corrupted stock just as Noah, although spared the Flood, was Adam's heir—a point which Webster goes out of his way to make in Giovanni's final exchange with the dying Lodovico.

Giovanni: You bloody villains,
            By what authority have you committed
            This massacre?
Lodovico: By thine.
Giovanni: Mine?
Lodovico: Yes: thy uncle,
            Which is part of thee, enjoined us to't.

There is no rainbow in this hall of carnage when the play ends. Noah is aboard the ark: that is all that can be said. The Ambassadors, English among them, are treated to a severe Boccacian warning.

Giovanni: Remove the bodies—See, my honoured lords,
            What use you ought to make of their punishment:
            Let guilty men remember, their black deeds
            Do lean on crutches made of slender reeds.

There is nothing perfunctory in this warning. All men are guilty: crime and corruption are inescapable consequences of Lucifer's and Adam's Fall: but if society's rulers allow corruption to flourish by indulging in it themselves instead of punishing it, then black deeds will multiply to the point where only another flood can cleanse the world, sweeping the princes away with their subjects. It is a grim vision, but consistently expressed and tragic in its totality if not in respect of any single character.

When Webster wrote the play there was still a Giovanni in England, another flower of chivalry, another Hal, Henry Prince of Wales. Prince Henry's death was received as a national calamity. Thereafter things changed from a situation resembling that before the Flood to that depicted in the opening of the York Doomsday—or as the Puritan preachers put it 'The Day of Wrath is at Hand'. It was left to Ford to depict a society unable to do more than extend the range of its sympathies for human folly and depravity while awaiting the cataclysm. It was swift in coming. By 1642 the theatres were officially silent and by 1649 it was the actor-prince of *Salmacida Spolia* who walked from the Banqueting House to the stage of execution, the King himself.[1]

Not for nothing was Charles I viewed by as many people after his death as a Martyr as had regarded him before his death as a criminal; for in one sense at least he was seen to die like Christ as a sacrifice—in this case to save the nation and thus prepare the way for a new beginning.

My summary can be brief. The book of Genesis had provided the authors of the Miracle Cycles with a discussion of personal and national disaster beginning with an individual and reaching outwards, like the ripples from a stone thrown into a pond, to embrace society at large. Each of the images in terms of which the discussion is conducted is separate if related and thus enables the dramatist who consults it to choose whichever one happens best to suit his own purpose when talking to his audience about the moral basis of the important political and social issues of their own time, or to treat them collectively. Shakespeare took over this pattern in its entirety and applied it to English history, starting with the deposition and murder of Richard II and spreading outwards to the involvement of the whole nation in the misery and carnage of the Wars of the Roses.[2]

[1] See Essay 6, p. 116 below.　　　　　　[2] See Essay 10, pp. 165–71 below.

PLATE V

8   THE TEATRO OLIMPICO, VICENZA
Designed by Andrea Palladio as a reconstruction of a Roman theatre and built by him and his pupil Scamozzi between 1581 and 1585. The picture is a fresco in the Teatro Olimpico itself and represents a scene from the opening production, *Oedipus Tyrannus*, in 1585. It was painted in 1594 and is to be seen in the Odeon. (Reproduced from L. Schrade, *La Representation d'Edipo Tiranno an Teatro Olimpica*, Paris, 1960.)

PLATE VI

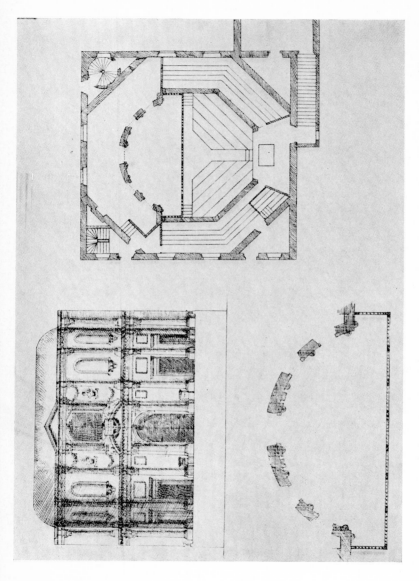

9 THE COCKPIT-IN-COURT
Inigo Jones' design for the renovation of the Cockpit-in-Court,
1630.

Library of Worcester College, Oxford

In Elizabethan and Jacobean England, despite the growing interest in Graeco-Roman tragedy and the increasing thoroughness with which the Revels Office suppressed overtly religious subject-matter from reaching the stage after 1589, Genesis continued to provide dramatists, actors and audiences with as potent a moral basis for the allegorical discussion of their own society in theatrical terms of reference as it had ever done. Indeed, as the image of the acted Cycles faded from view, the growing emphasis placed by Protestant preachers on personal reading and interpretation of the Old Testament in English translation served to renew it. The story of the Fall from Marlowe to Webster therefore is one of re-iterated echoes of Genesis and the Cycles varying from the simple and conventional theme of disobedience, as exemplified in the persons of Dr. Faustus and Alice Arden in the early part of the period, to the more pessimistic and complicated discussion in the later period of a whole society inviting another flood such as Webster contrives to inject into *The White Devil* or of a society that is still capable of avoiding such disaster by atoning for past wrongs in a present striving for grace through the exercise of *caritas* such as Shakespeare mirrors in *The Tempest*.[1] Only Jonson attempted to work wholly outside this scheme of things. In so doing he distanced himself so far from audiences that were newly possessed of a Bible in the vernacular and busily reappraising their religious and social positions in the light of it, as to forfeit both their interest and their applause. He dismissed their censure as deriving from ignorance and folly; the verdict of badly schooled and fickle plebeians 'whose noses are ever like swine spoiling and rooting up the Muses' gardens'. But in this he misjudged them. For them, harmartia in itself was not enough; and posterity has cause to be glad that they were greedy enough to ask for more.

[1] See Essay 15, 'The Winter's Tale: A Comedy with Deaths', pp. 249–65 below.

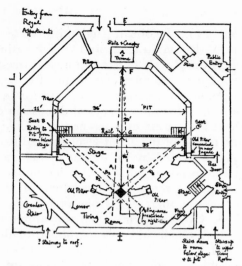

Fig. 1   The Cockpit-in-Court; simplified ground-plan.

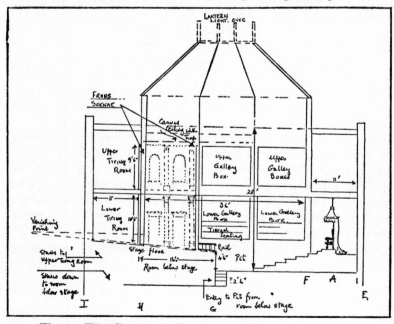

Fig. 2   The Cockpit-in-Court; simplified cross-section.

Section Two

Reformation and Renaissance

4

Neo-Classical Drama and the Reformation in England[1]

'Seneca cannot be too heavy, nor Plautus too light.'
POLONIUS, *Hamlet*, II, ii.

I

DRAMA today is studied and discussed either as an aspect of literature or as the end-product of theatrical creative skills, seldom as both. Curiously, much the same may be said of drama in the sixteenth century. The multitude, whom Shakespeare was to compare to Cerberus, whether flocking to the sacred Miracle Cycles of pre-Reformation days in country towns, or packing the public playhouses of Elizabethan London, regarded drama as a festive recreation. The educated minority regarded it quite differently: to them it was a means of education, a form of poetry embodying moral philosophy in

[1] Reprinted from *Classical Drama and its Influence*, essays presented to H. D. F. Kitto, B.A., D.-ès-L., F.B.A., F.R.S.L., Professor Emeritus of Greek at the University of Bristol, edited by M. J. Anderson, pp. 157–73 (Methuen & Co. Ltd., 1965).

emblematic manner or, alternatively, an object for contempt, being morally and politically subversive.

In adopting these attitudes most English divines, schoolmasters and university dons took their cue from continental example; the apologists from current opinion among scholars and artists in Italy and France, the opponents from the precepts of religious reformers in Germany and Switzerland. Unfortunately the debating of viewpoints derived from these conflicting attitudes on the continent could hardly be carried on in a cool and rational manner in a country that was itself divided on the religious issue. The English apologist for drama, in advocating the writing and acting of plays on grounds of classical precedent in a country that had so recently abjured the rule of Rome in matters ecclesiastical, inevitably found himself at loggerheads with either Church or State or sometimes both.

At the start of the Tudor epoch interest in Roman and Greek antiquity was widespread in government and academic circles and was quickly reflected in artistic achievement ranging from architecture to literature. The interlude of *Fulgens & Lucres* (1497), the work of Cardinal Morton's private chaplain, Henry Medwall, is the first surviving memorial to the effects of this new interest on dramatic art in England.[1] It is to be noted, however, that knowledge of Roman theory and practice advanced much more rapidly than knowledge of Greek equivalents. This is not surprising since Latin was still a living language, used throughout Europe not only by the Church but by government officials in diplomatic, judicial and even domestic affairs: Greek as a language was dead. Those men who read and spoke it like Erasmus, Dean Colet or Sir Thomas More were rare spirits; provision for acquiring a knowledge of it in English schools and universities at the start of the sixteenth century was poor. The quest therefore for Greek and Latin manuscripts which threw light on Greek and Roman attitudes to life was not matched by corresponding skills in translation and interpretation. By the middle of the century, despite rapid improvement in the mastery of

---

[1] See Essay 2, pp. 30-2 above, and *Plate II*, no. 4.

Greek, the lead of Latin studies over Greek was so marked as to give Roman thought and practice a virtually unbeatable supremacy. This linguistic pre-eminence of Latin over Greek was paralleled in Western Europe at least by such physical monuments of the two civilizations as remained for the eye to see and the excavator to uncover. The Romans as imperial colonizers had everywhere left evidence of their way of life ranging from ruined but still standing structures as striking as the Colosseum to fragments of pillars or of mosaic pavement and the bric-à-brac of deserted armouries. Not having crossed the Alps, the Greeks had left no visible and tangible memorials to their way of life in Northern and Western countries. Thus, although scholars recognized that much of Roman art was derived from Greek example, even the best of them were not equipped to discern how plagiaristic and debased this derivation was. As a result the worship of false gods became widespread, Horace, for example, ranking higher as a dramatic theorist than Aristotle, Seneca ranking higher as a dramatist than Sophocles, Roman theatres and amphitheatres (in strangely confused amalgam) assuming a greater authority than the genuine θέατρον at Delphi or at Epidaurus. It is these confusions which led directly to the imitations of Terence in Italian, French and English with their curious illustrations, to the building of the *Teatro Olimpico* at Vicenza and the naming of a public playhouse in a dissolved Priory in Shoreditch as *The Theater*. Polonius, although a figure of fun to Hamlet and Horatio, was very much in the academic *avant-garde* in acting the part of Julius Caesar in his university dramatic society and in praising Seneca and Plautus as 'the only men' for 'the law of writ and the liberty': Sir Philip Sidney and Ben Jonson would have agreed with him. How then did Shakespeare dare to risk making these sentiments the cue for laughter? Only because he knew the multitude knew little of them and cared less.[1]

II

Perhaps the most startling consequence of the discrepancy in the pace at which studies of Roman and Greek drama advanced in

[1] See Essay 5, p. 101 below.

Italy itself during the sixteenth century was the genesis of what we now term opera. Accustomed as we are to the vast musical forces (and complementary financial subsidies) associated with the operas of Verdi, Wagner or Richard Strauss, it requires a substantial imaginative effort to see any connection between the music dramas of the modern opera house and performances of Latin comedies and tragedies in Florence, Ferrara and Rome: the link is in Florentine efforts of the 1590's to solve in musical terms the problems posed by the Chorus in Greek tragedy.[1] Scarcely less startling to the modern mind is the pre-eminence accorded to the landscape-painter's art in Italian revivals and adaptations of Latin plays which to us appears to involve flat contradiction of Aristotle's views on the place of spectacle in drama. Both of these phenomena derive from the pre-eminence which Latin comedy enjoyed over tragedy coupled with the pre-eminence which all Latin drama enjoyed initially over Greek; for knowledge of Latin drama embraced not only the texts of plays but Vitruvius' remarks on the architecture of Roman theatres as well. When painters and musicians who were themselves men of genius, like Raphael, Leonardo da Vinci or Monteverdi, assisted with these revivals, the original academic course of these studies was submitted to a greater strain than it could bear without shifting its direction. Comedies by Plautus and Terence were being performed in Rome, in Florence and in Ferrara when Henry, Duke of Richmond, defeated Richard III and founded the Tudor dynasty in England: Henry VII had been succeeded by his son before the first Latin tragedy (Seneca's *Hippolytus*) was performed for the edification of audiences in Rome and Ferrara. Although this revival of the *Hippolytus* was an undoubted *succès d'estime* it did not encourage the immediate revival of other tragedies, whereas the repertoire of comedies was steadily expanding, and

---

[1] A group of musicians, poets and nobles known as 'the Camerata' used to meet in Florence during the 1580's to discuss how best to imitate and revive Greek tragedy, and in particular the relationship of lyric poetry to music in production. Initially it was admitted that the music must be subordinate to the verse, but by the end of the century this attitude had changed. See H. Leclerc, *Les Origines italiennes de l'architecture théâtrale moderne*, Paris, 1946, pp. 121 *et seq.*

several of them were being translated out of Latin into Italian.[1]

Greek studies in Italy began to make some headway early in the fifteenth century as princely bankers began to commission their oriental agents to import Byzantine manuscripts along with other merchandise. In 1423 Giovanni Aurispa returned from Constantinople with a collection of books that included six plays by Aeschylus and seven by Sophocles. Further plays arrived in subsequent consignments, but it took nearly a century for any of them to become available in print. Nevertheless it is worth noticing that at most twenty years separates the publication of the first edition of *Senecae Tragoediae* (1480–90) and that of the works of Sophocles (Venice, 1502). May not this fact account in some measure for the evident lack of enthusiasm for Senecan tragedy in performance that followed the revival of the *Hippolytus* in 1509? It is at least significant that in the first published excursion into tragedy in the Italian vernacular, *Sofonisba* (1515), the author, Giangiorgio Trissino, leans more heavily on Sophocles than Seneca in his handling of the Chorus. *Sofonisba* earned Trissino a striking literary reputation, but the play was not performed until 1562, twelve years after his death. Leo Schrade adopts the view that the advent of published editions of Greek tragedy (Sophocles, 1502; Euripides, 1503; Aeschylus, 1518) was at least partially responsible for delaying practical experiments based on Senecan tragedy either in Latin or in the vernacular in Court theatres.[2] The first tragedy in the Italian vernacular to appear on a stage was Giraldi Cinzio's *Orbecche* (Ferrara, 1541). Cinzio himself declared Seneca to be more deserving of imitation than the Greek authors, but the general trend of academic thinking on dramatic theory and practice was gradually moving in the opposite

[1] Ariosto's *I Suppositi* was performed in Ferrara in 1509 and Cardinal Bibbiena's *La Calandra* in Urbino in 1513.

Machiavelli's *Mandragola* was performed in Florence in 1513. The latter, although constructed in the Roman manner, is wholly his own creation in respect of plot and characters. Raphael provided a backcloth for the production of *I Suppositi*, and *La Calandra*, when revived in Rome in 1518, was presented in a setting designed by Perruzzi.

[2] L. Schrade, *La Représentation d'Edipo Tiranno au Teatro Olimpico*, C.N.R.S., Paris, 1960, pp. 11–33.

direction. The final triumph of Greek tragedy over Latin was bodied forth in the performance of Orsatto Giustiniani's *Edipo Tiranno* with Choruses set to music by Andrea Gabrielli in the *Teatro Olimpico* at Vicenza on 2nd March 1585.[1] The text was published that same year, the *Canto Chori in Musica* three years later. The title page of the former is explicit: '*Edipo Tiranno di Sofocle . . . in lingua volgare ridotta. . . .*' Giustiniani's dedication is to Sophocles himself. A dedicatory epistle to Signor Veniero explains the translator's aims and comments on the difficulties encountered.[2] And yet . . . and yet . . . posterity must be excused for harbouring doubts. The *Teatro Olimpico* with its painted ceiling, its Roman style of auditorium and orchestra, its scenic streets modelled in receding perspective and its batteries of oil lamps in coloured glass, still stands to testify to any scholar who cares to visit it that the Latin spirit rather than the Greek was pre-eminent in that notable performance of 3rd March 1585. Was it not, one must ask, a desire to dignify Italian literature by harnessing the Greek antecedents of Roman antiquity to the modern language rather than a determination to let Greek culture speak for itself that had prompted both this 'translation' and all its predecessors? This must remain an open question; but it is certain that the related problems of style and versification were those on which academic discussion centred. This of itself suggests a wish on the part of the translators to refine Italian verse forms by recourse to Greek example.[3] Greek tragedy in Greek (or comedy for that matter) was not attempted either indoors or in the open air. Both Greek and Latin tragedy in Italian failed to find a popular following. Patrons, aided and abetted by their architects and painters, moved away from the derivative style of the *Teatro Olimpico* towards a stage of pictorial illusion: actors, perplexed by the problem of finding a rhetorical style appropriate to the

---

[1] See *Plate Three*, no. 6.   [2] Schrade, *op. cit.*, pp. 85–9.

[3] Schrade (*op cit.*, p. 24) says of Lorenzo Valla's translation of Demosthenes' *De Corona* following swiftly upon Leonardo Bruni's translation of the same work: 'Le motif d'une telle rivalité n'était pas le désir de donner une traduction plus fidèle, mais l'ambition de polir avec une habileté encore plus grande ce qui avait déjà été porté à un haut degré de raffinement. Ces traductions prouvent clairement que la rhétorique latine les préoccupait davantage que le sens intime des lettres grecques.'

recitation of archaic texts in translation, moved away from recitation and towards a combination of intoned declamation or '*stilo recitativo*' and melody or '*aria*'. The problem of the abrupt change from passages for individual actors to those for Chorus was met if not solved by a borrowing of the traditional 'Entries' from the masks and intermezzos of Court festivities, themselves already an excuse for lavish spectacle.[1] The practical realities of stage performance thus came to combine with renaissance theatrical taste to swamp the original objectives of the learned translators (or possibly to expose both the mixed motives and the theatrical sterility of those objectives) and to provide Italians of the seventeenth century with a theatre that was vocally and scenically more elegant than any other in Europe, but which was about as far removed in spirit from the austere simplicity of Greek tragedy as it could be.

III

In one form or another this pattern imposed itself during the course of the seventeenth century on every country in Europe from the Tagus to the Volga. My concern here is with the English variant. The generalization which has dominated school text-books on both historical and literary aspects of this topic is that the renaissance followed the same pattern in England as in Italy but, being an imported commodity, at a later date. This view seems to me to ignore altogether the impact which the Reformation in England had upon higher learning throughout the country and its repercussions on academic life. You cannot, for instance, dismiss the Latin Bible of the Roman Catholic Church and substitute for it an English version which draws its inspiration from Greek originals without dragging the two languages in question into the wider issues of metaphysical polemic. In other words, as a convinced

---

[1] See H. Leclerc, *Les Origines italiennes de l'architecture théâtrale moderne*, Paris, 1946, and Enid Welsford, *The Court Mask*, Cambridge, 1927. On the Florentine *Intermezzi*, see A. M. Nagler, 'Theater der Medici', *Maske und Kothurn*, IV (1958), no. 2/3, pp. 168–98, and A. Beijer, 'An Early 16th Century Scenic Design in the National Museum, Stockholm, and its Historical Background', *Theatre Research*, IV (1962), no. 2, pp. 85–155.

Roman Catholic you find yourself obliged to defend Latin whatever your personal feelings may be about the Greek authors: for the convinced Protestant there is a similar but opposite compulsion to denigrate Latin as the language of superstition, and to defend Greek as the language of the Evangelists and the Early Fathers. Ample evidence survives from the middle of the sixteenth century to show how adoption of these rival standpoints retarded the progress in both languages which had been made earlier in the century. The damage done to the advancement of classical studies in England during the reigns of Edward VI and Mary I on this account however was small compared to that resulting from the extreme extension of the Protestant standpoint under Elizabeth I: personal inspiration and enthusiasm were elevated to a point where it became a virtue to abrogate academic degrees and dismiss *all* disciplined study as of small consequence when compared to the direct revelations vouchsafed by the Deity to the self-appointed 'saved'. Whole libraries were stripped and destroyed by these zealots, including the MSS. of religious plays.[1] When the effects of this attitude to manuscripts and books are considered in conjunction with those resulting from the earlier dissolution of the monasteries it may readily be seen that the revival of interest in classical learning in England could not possibly follow the course of such studies in Italy. For one thing, no steadily evolving programme of humane studies lavishly and consistently patronized within sheltered academies could be contemplated after 1531. Once Henry VIII had broken with

---

[1] T. Warton, *History of English Poetry* (ed. 1778–81), pp. 607–27, discusses the effects of the Reformation on university life at Oxford and Cambridge with particular reference to the fortunes of Greek and Latin studies. He concludes: 'The study of the classics, together with a colder magic and a tamer mythology [i.e. than those of Gothic times], introduced method into composition: and the universal ambition of rivalling those new patterns of excellence, the faultless models of Greece and Rome, produced that bane of invention, IMITATION. Erudition was made to act upon genius. Fancy was weakened by reflection and philosophy. The fashion of treating everything scientifically, applied speculation and theory to the arts of writing. . . . The lover of true poetry will ask', he says, 'what have we gained by this revolution?' This question and his own answer to it have a special urgency in the twentieth century. 'We have parted with extravagancies that are above propriety, with incredibilities that are more acceptable than truth, and with fictions that are more valuable than reality.'

Rome, pursuit of classical studies had either to be conducted publicly in an atmosphere of propagandist debate not unlike that which surrounds diplomacy as conducted today in the General Assembly of the United Nations, or else carried on by isolated individuals in privacy, semi-secrecy and even in exile: the better part of half a century separates the break-up of Sir Thomas More's circle and the re-establishment of free intercourse among humanists in the circle centred on Sir Philip Sidney.[1]

English interest in the revival of Greek and of classical latinity had begun early. The mediaeval passion for pilgrimages to the Holy Land ensured that some contact at least was maintained with Hebrew, Arabic, Greek and Latin during the fourteenth century: and in the fifteenth century, despite the social and political insecurity that accompanied the Wars of the Roses, determined efforts were made by many Englishmen to acquire in Italy itself the knowledge which could not be obtained in English schools and universities. The reward for this enterprise and industry was high preferment in the Church at Papal hands. Two examples from the middle of the fifteenth century are Robert Fleming and John Free. Fleming acquired Greek, is said by Leland to have compiled a Greek–Latin Lexicon, became prothonotary to Pope Sixtus and was appointed by him to the Deanery of Lincoln c. 1450. Free, who was born and bred in Bristol, was similarly favoured by Pope Paul II, being appointed in 1465 to the bishopric of Bath and Wells. He earned this preferment by translating, among other Greek authors, the works of Xenophon; and his Latin was so good that he received an invitation to compose an elegiac epitaph for Petrarch's tomb. These men and others like them copied, bought, imported and donated MSS. to English libraries in much the same way that Italian princes were enriching their own libraries.

When Henry VII seized the throne in 1485, he quickly recognized the worth of these pioneer efforts and encouraged further initiative by giving Italian artists and men of letters incentives to work in England. Latin received the greatest impetus by virtue of the commission accorded to Polydore

[1] See G. Wickham, *Early English Stages*, 1300–1660, ii(1), pp. 13–53.

Vergil to reside at Court and write an official History of England.[1] Greek however began to be a matter of public as opposed to purely private interest when William Grocyn began to lecture on it at Oxford, albeit on a voluntary basis: with the establishment of a chair at Cambridge shortly afterwards, and the appointment of Erasmus to that chair, all was set for a revival of humane studies in England as vigorous and enlightened as that progressing in Italy. It was in England, we might note, that Erasmus completed his translation of two of the plays of Euripides. No less important for classical studies in general and dramatic art in particular was the reorganization of St. Paul's School by Dean Colet in 1512 and the appointment of William Lyly as High Master.[2] Lyly had spent five years in Rhodes acquiring Greek and as long again in Rome working in the learned company of Pomponius Laetus and Sulpitius, both of whom were actively concerned with the earliest representations of Latin plays in Italy.

Where Henry VII had moved cautiously, setting an auspicious eye on the efforts of others, Henry VIII and his Chancellor Wolsey vied with each other in bestowing liberal endowments on humane studies in both schools and universities.[3] But here they were acting without reckoning on the forces of reaction, the dons and churchmen who viewed this mad career to new disciplines with ever-increasing alarm. Their riposte, when it came, was deadly. 'What men are these' they asked 'who pour scorn on the old scholastic curriculum in divinity and philosophy, if not heretics and even pagan idolators?' We in our turn and at this distance in time may fairly ask what sort of men were those who reproachfully stigmatized Erasmus as *Graeculus iste* and cautioned young priests under instruction: *Cave a Graecis ne fias haereticus!*

In this way the ground was prepared for the forces of academic reaction to rally to the cause of Roman Catholicism with its Latin liturgy immediately Henry VIII had vested in his own

[1] See Denys Hay, *Polydore Vergil, Renaissance Historian and Man of Letters*, 1952.
[2] On the significance of Lyly's appointment, see L. B. Campbell, *Scenes and Machines on the English Stage*, 1923, p. 83 *et seq.*
[3] See Warton, *op. cit.*, pp. 608–10.

person the headship of the Church in England. The dissolution of the monasteries which proceeded piecemeal throughout the last decade of his reign paradoxically strengthened the hand of the reactionaries, for it deprived the provinces of all centres of higher learning other than Oxford and Cambridge. The full effects of this took time to make themselves felt, but were evident enough twenty years later when the Anglican Church of Elizabeth discovered that it lacked sufficient clergy to fill its livings who could be trusted to construct a sermon in English, let alone claim a command of the classics. It is this aspect of the decline in literacy which is touched on by Shakespeare in the character of Sir Nathaniel who is rebuked by Holofernes for saying *bone* instead of *bene* (*LLL*, V, i, 30).

At Oxford and Cambridge the classics had come to stay, but pursuit of them there was severely disrupted. Roger Ascham notes with satisfaction that under Edward VI the works of Homer, Sophocles and Euripides were normal reading for undergraduates, but wonders how long this can last and deplores the state of Latin studies in the schools. The founder of Trinity College, Oxford, particularizes in his statutes which Latin authors are to be read and to what end: yet when encouraged by the liberal Cardinal Pole to make better provision for Greek, replies: 'This purpose I lyke well; but I fear the tymes will not bear it now.'[1] Much of the ground made up was, however, quickly lost again under the attacks of the Calvinist exiles on their return to England following the accession of a Queen who prided herself on her command of Greek. It is this type of fanatical ignoramus whom Ben Jonson satirizes in the person of Zeal-of-the-land-Busy who stigmatizes quotation from Horace as 'lists of Latin, the very rags of Rome, and patches of Popery'. To have small Latin and less Greek therefore on leaving school was possibly no bad thing if one had chanced to be born in 1564 and wished to adopt a truly objective standpoint when depicting human nature in dramatic dialogue in the England of Elizabeth I.[2]

To have had no reading knowledge of either Greek or Latin

---

[1] See Warton, p. 622; also F. S. Boas, *University Drama in the Tudor Age*, 1914, pp. 7–8.   [2] See Essay 5 below.

at a time when the Italian *novella* and the literature out of which it was born was being imported into England from so many quarters would have been a crippling disadvantage to any aspiring artist, especially a poet. Yet to have acquired an authoritative mastery of either or both carried with it not only the risk of being branded as a heretic, an atheist or a political revolutionary, but the certainty of isolation from the mainstream of popular attitudes and thought. Heresy and atheism were closely associated with necromancy and witchcraft, papists with political subversion: excessive enthusiasm for Greek or Latin, like the mark of Cain, served to advertise these criminal tendencies and invited investigation. Only following the execution of Mary of Scotland and the defeat of the Armada were these suspicions relaxed, by which time a formidable attack was being mounted on the theatre in all its aspects. The religious stage had already succumbed:[1] both the popular and the academic stage were fighting for their lives.

IV

The facts relating to the revival of Roman and Greek plays in England during the course of the sixteenth century are well known and are clearly set out by F. S. Boas, *University Drama in the Tudor Age* (1914) and by T. H. Vail Motter, *The School Drama in England* (1929). Neither of these scholars concerns himself directly with plays performed by the young lawyers at the Inns of Court, and neither of them devote much attention to the physical conditions in which the plays they discuss were performed. Both of these aspects of the subject, however, are treated by Miss L. B. Campbell, *Scenes and Machines on the English Stage* (1923). Where staging is concerned I have myself felt unable to agree with Miss Campbell in some of her deductions and have argued an alternative case in *Early English Stages* (vol. ii, chapter VII). A full bibliography of documents relating to drama at the Inns of Court is shortly to be published by D. S. Bland.

With so much information of a factual kind so readily

---

[1] See Essay 1, p. 5 above.

PLATE VII

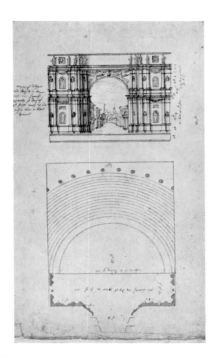

10   DESIGNS BY INIGO JONES
Design for a theatre in Inigo Jones' copy of Palladio now in the
Library of Worcester College, Oxford.

PLATE VIII

11   Design prepared by Inigo Jones for the Lord Chamberlain, 1639.
Chatsworth House

available it is pointless to retail it here: on the other hand theatre research in recent years has caused us to alter many of the assumptions which served as a background to these earlier surveys of the surviving evidence. Accordingly a case exists now for drawing the reader's attention to those aspects of the subject which appear to warrant reappraisal. In doing this we can at least start from reasonably firm ground; for no one is likely to wish to dispute the fact that during the first three decades of the sixteenth century the same passion for the revival of Roman and Greek plays as prevailed in Italy (in so far as technical mastery of the respective languages allowed) was given free rein in England. It is with the start of the Reformation that development of this interest in Italy and in England began to part company. I wish to suggest that where in Italy matters of form and stylistic expression began to assume an overriding importance, in England questions of pedagogical content took precedence. I attribute these developments in part to a sharp divergence in attitude to the virtues of Latin as a language, in part to a marked difference of approach to the religious stage inherited from the Middle Ages and above all to the impact made on both Latin studies and the religious stage by advances in the command and understanding of Greek.

In the early years of the century the study of Roman plays and of Greek plays in Latin dress recommended itself to educationalists as much as a training in the *speaking* of Latin as for the extended knowledge of vocabulary, syntax and grammar that accrued.[1] It was on these grounds that schools and university colleges when given the opportunity to reconstitute themselves or when newly endowed by private benefaction chose to include the annual performance of a play or plays in Latin in their statutes.[2] No such immediate or obvious *vocational* benefit

---

[1] A notable English work in this context was Nicholas Udall's *Floures for Latine spekynge*, 1534–5, culled from three of Terence's plays.

[2] Westminster School, set in order by Elizabeth I in 1560, is particularly important in this respect, Ben Jonson having received his education there. Sir James Whitelock who entered Merchant Taylors' School in 1575 says, 'I was brought up at school under Mr. Mulcaster. . . . Yeerly he presented sum playes to the court, in which his scholers wear only actors, and I on among them, and by that meanes taughte them good behaviour and audacitye.' T. H. Vail Motter, *The School Drama in England* ,1929, pp. 85–104 and 110.

was to be gained by performing Greek plays in Greek. The Reformation, however, occasioned a sharp reappraisal: for with the Latin liturgy and Bible, together with any other overt demonstration of dependence on Rome, translated into subjects of contention, continued performances of Latin plays could scarcely be justified on these grounds alone except by reactionaries.

The dilemma confronting Protestant humanists on this account was resolved by a dawning realization that Greek plays were possibly to be preferred to Latin ones (at least as texts for reading if not for acting), and by the performance in Germany of Thomas Kirchmeyer's violently anti-Catholic play *Pammachius*, written and performed in Latin in 1535 and presented at Christ's College, Cambridge, ten years later.[1] As a piece of Protestant propaganda, this play suggested that the traditional Miracle and Morality plays could be reformed on lines which combined humanist ideals in respect of scholarly style and education with Protestant ideals in respect of theological and moral content. Such an idea, if carried into action, could not but divorce subsequent development of neo-classical drama in England from its counterpart in Italy; for, in effect, it changed the motive underlying the study and revival of classical plays from being a straightforward desire to imitate and thus refine personal style into one of purifying and thus improving the moral and philosophical content of English drama at large.

Steps in this direction were swiftly taken with the performance at Oxford, c. 1540, of Nicholas Grimald's *Christus Redivivus*. This play opens with the burial of Christ, makes Caiaphas the villain, includes a quartet of comic Roman soldiers and a spectacular Harrowing of Hell, and ends with doubting Thomas's confession of faith. Grimald was a friend of John Bale who was not only a dramatist himself but enjoyed the patronage of Cranmer and Cromwell in turning the religious stage into an

[1] This performance created a scandal involving a sharp exchange of letters between the Chancellor, Bishop Gardiner, and the Vice-Chancellor, Matthew Parker, Master of Corpus Christi College. The accompanying investigation only served to draw the maximum degree of attention to the play. See Boas, *op. cit.*, pp. 22-3.

instrument of Protestant polemic in the German manner. This of course was a game at which two could play. At Cambridge Thomas Watson and John Christopherson retaliated in defence of the old religion in Latin and in Greek respectively; Watson with *Absalon* (c. 1540) and Christopherson with *Ἰεφθαε* (c. 1544).[1] Both authors found life difficult under Edward VI, Christopherson going into exile, Watson into prison; both were restored to grace and office under Mary, but were ruined with the return to power of a Protestant monarch.

The Latin polemical play, whether Roman Catholic or Protestant in spirit, was doomed however like its vernacular equivalent on the professional stage, once the government of Elizabeth I had determined that the security of the realm did not permit of any plays on religious subjects being performed in public or circulated in print. This ban on religious plays of every kind, which was launched shortly after the excommunication of the Queen in 1570, had become fully effective by 1590. The academic stage had therefore to look at itself again and re-examine its *raison d'être*. This it did in the form of violent internal controversy. The question at issue was whether plays, Greek, Latin or English, should be countenanced at all in centres of learning. It was particularized in the exchange of letters between John Rainolds and William Gager at Oxford in 1592–4 which is treated in full by Boas (*op. cit.*, pp. 220–51). In effect Rainolds brings all the arguments unleashed by Puritan opponents of the professional theatre to bear upon academic performances. Gager counters with the old argument of the training in rhetoric which such performances provided, coupled with the innocent and profitable recreation which they offered to both performers and spectators. Rainolds's letters found their way into print but not Gager's replies or those of his supporters. As public property, the former provided enemies of the professional playhouses with a rich assortment of arguments for their suppression which quickly found their way into sermons, pamphlets and broadsheets and played their part in the ultimate closure of the theatres in 1642.

---

[1] These two plays are discussed by Boas, *op. cit.*, pp. 43–68. On the subject of performances in Greek, see Boas, pp. 16 and 17, and Campbell, *op. cit.*, pp. 86–8.

What then did the English humanists of the Tudor epoch, who risked imprisonment, exile and death to champion a renewed interest in Greek and Roman drama, achieve? Unquestionably they brought a vivid interest in Terence, Plautus and Seneca, derived as much from performance as from textual exposition, into the academic curriculum of the two universities and of all the leading schools. Unlike their Italian counterparts, however, they appear to have lost interest in the problems of stylistic refinement which arose when the verse forms of Latin plays were compared with those used by the Greek dramatists. The Chorus of Greek drama which in Italy aroused the fiercest academic disputes, and which there engaged the attention of musicians as well as scholars, failed to provoke any startling developments in England. A similar lack of concern is noticeable in England in respect of the structural and scenic problems occasioned by strict observance of the unities of place and time which were exercising architects, painters and dramatists in Italy. In this connection it should be noted that where Vitruvius' *De Architectura* was translated into Italian and French early in the sixteenth century, English scholars interested in the Roman theatre had to content themselves with these translations or the original Latin text. No attempt was made to comment on it in English.[1] On the other hand, the English humanists, by adapting Latin plays to meet conditions created by the Reformation, greatly reinforced the didactic element of traditional religious plays inherited from the mediaeval past. In doing this they brought the refinement of their own style, grounded in study of classical models, to bear upon historical narrative and ethical disputation. New characters like the title role of Plautus' *Miles Gloriosus* began to colour the cast-lists of English plays: abstract personifications like those in the early Moralities were softened and given distinctive personali-

---

[1] The first English work on architecture was Sir John Shute's *First and Chief Grounds of Architecture* published in 1563. He acknowledges his debts to Vitruvius and to Philander's commentary of 1544–5, but confines his attention to the five orders. It was 1611 before Serlio's work found its way into English translation.

Vitruvius' *De Architectura* was published in Latin in 1486, in Italian in 1521, in French in 1547 and in Spanish in 1602. An abridged translation into English appeared in 1692.

ties constructed from the human predicament in which the character was situated. An Interlude like *Ralph Roister Doister* thus looks forward to Falstaff, while the Vice, 'Avarice', of *Respublica* forecasts Volpone: in more serious mood, the deposition scene in Bale's *Kyng Johan*, although conducted by abstract characters, looks forward just as unmistakably to a similar scene in *Edward II* or *Richard II*. These processes of influence and adaptation paved the way for a professional, secular drama to replace the religious stage in Elizabethan England without losing sight of traditional stagecraft and without losing touch with popular audiences. Revolution, when it came in the next century—scenic and operatic—was not a native product but a specifically Italian import.[1] In its arrival it swept poetry out of the English theatre and replaced the scenic emblems of mediaeval and Tudor stages with pictures, painted in perspective and properly framed by an arch above the stage or proscenium.

[1] See Essay 6, pp. 107–11 below.

5

Shakespeare's 'Small Latine and Less Greeke'

I

This familiar catch-phrase pin-points a clash of philosophies and aesthetic values which lie at the heart of the Elizabethan drama, and which are of as much interest to the actor and producer attempting to interpret it to audiences, as to scholars attempting to explain it to pupils or readers.

This clash is conveniently typified for us in Shakespeare's and Ben Jonson's respective conceptions of dramatic art: its nature in Jonson's two familiar strictures on Shakespeare.

> Shaksperr wanted Arte,[1]

and

> . . . thou hadst small Latine, and less Greeke.[2]

In consequence of these two remarks poor Ben has been—and in some quarters still is—accused of envy, spleen, malice and all uncharitableness towards his rival.

---

[1] All quotations from Ben Jonson's works are given from the edition by C. Herford & H. Simpson, *Ben Jonson*, 1925–52, 11 vols. See vol. I, p. 133.
[2] *Ben Jonson*, VIII, p. 391.

Edmund Malone, writing to his friend Mr. Walley in 1782 observed,

> . . . I shall with great pleasure add my mite of contribution to your new edition of Ben Jonson. . . . At the same time I must honestly own to you that I have never read old Ben's plays with any degree of attention, and that he is an author so little to my taste that I have no pleasure in pursuing him. . . . I agree with you entirely that no ridicule was intended against Shakespeare in the Poetaster. . . . But notwithstanding this, I think I have brought together decisive proofs of Jonson's malignity and jealousy of Shakespeare. . . .[1]

It is not surprising therefore that others should have followed so scholarly a lead. Yet I would maintain that this view is only tenable if one equates the Elizabethan and Jacobean era with the arrival of the high Renaissance in England. This, I know, has often been done; but I regard it as a false assumption because it is grounded on a number of assumptions equally false. The first is that the Middle Ages came to an abrupt close with the Reformation. The second is that the Renaissance, the New Learning, or, if you prefer, the revival of ancient classical learning, replaced mediaeval culture with equal abruptness. The third—as Congreve's Mrs. Marwood observed—is that nothing could be ruder than Gothic. There is a grain of truth in all this. It is the picture of sixteenth-century thought in England which emerges if one confines one's attention exclusively to the utterances of such avowed champions of classical antiquity as Erasmus, Polydore Vergil, Sir Philip Sidney or Ben Jonson. This is very easy to do because these men were so vocal and explicit. But such a picture is grossly oversimplified— a sort of strip-cartoon—for it omits altogether the mental outlook of the majority of the English people who certainly did not share the views of their intelligentsia any more than they do now. And this is, surely, a matter of considerable relevance to any theatre management? For, if a management hopes to attract anything wider than a coterie audience, it must offer drama which mirrors a broader view of life, thought and manners than the latest modes and fancies of the intelligentsia. The Royal Shakespeare Company at Stratford-upon-Avon, for

---

[1] W. Gifford, *The Works of Ben Jonson*, 1838, p. 31.

example, continues to set its productions beneath a proscenium arch (and, note, an empty seat is virtually unknown) despite the exhortations of learned authorities to revert to sunlit Globes and rain-drenched apron-stages.

A much more accurate picture of sixteenth-century thought is one of constant struggle for predominance between two rival philosophies of life. On the one hand there exists in all the European countries that went to make up Christendom, a popular, native tradition that is fundamentally mediaeval and which amongst peasant peoples in countries bordering upon the Mediterranean is by no means extinct today. On the other hand a group of intellectuals closely associated with those responsible for the government of countries newly awakened to a sense of nationhood are attempting to force a complete divorce from this 'barbaric' native tradition in favour of a new marriage with 'civilized' Hellenistic culture. The latter won the day gradually and piecemeal. Italy, where the struggle originated in the fifteenth century, capitulated first. There are clear signposts for the historian: revivals of Plautus, Terence and Seneca, first in the original Latin, then in translation, treatises on perspective scenery, the Teatro Olimpico at Vicenza, opera. Late in the sixteenth century France and Spain follow suit. But the countries of the Protestant North do not capitulate till late in the seventeenth. In England, theatregoers of Shakespeare's generation (except for the few privileged to attend Court Masques after 1605) knew nothing of stage-scenery as we understand that word. First use of the word in that sense is attributed by Dr. Johnson to Dryden, a whole century later. Not only that: at James I's accession Homer had not yet supplanted Chaucer as the usual source of information on the Trojan war and even Geoffrey of Monmouth could still have counted on some champions for his account of British conduct under Roman rule as against that given by Caesar, Livy or Tacitus.[1]

Most of the theatregoers who first saw Shakespeare's and Jonson's plays were still happily settled within a fundamentally Anglo-Saxon tradition inherited from the Middle Ages and either ignorant or careless of strictures passed upon it by

[1] See E. A. Greenlaw, *Studies in Spenser's Historical Allegory*, Baltimore, 1932.

Sidney and his like. What hope then had Ben, educated at Westminster under the tutelage of William Camden,

> . . . most reverend head, to whom I owe
> All that I am in arts, all that I know, (viii, 31)

determined to model his plays on classical precept,

> The lawes of time, place, persons, he observeth,
> From no needfull rule he swerveth. (v, 24)

What hope had such a man of persuading such an audience that his plays were necessarily the most admirable because the best constructed? If you don't know 'the rules' it is not a matter of great concern whether they are kept or broken. In short, Jonson was born half a century before his time. He was the intellectual companion of Ariosto, of Molière, Racine and Dryden, who, in their turn, were the companions of Euripides, Aristotle, Terence and Horace. Few Elizabethan playgoers had much footing in such company.

Once these facts are grasped, Jonson's strictures on Shakespeare are revealed in their proper light. They spring not so much from malice, as from frustration, the words of a man whose vision of the future makes him impatient of the present. Where subjective judgements are concerned, proof is hard to come by. But here a glance at Jonson's relations with another dramatist, John Fletcher, is helpful.

In 1608 (?09) Fletcher's play *The Faithful Shepherdess* (the first English pastoral on the Italian model) was hissed off the Globe stage. Jonson wrote to Fletcher:

> The wise, and many-headed *Bench*, that sits
> Upon the Life, and Death of *Playes* and *Wits*,
> (Compos'd of *Gamester, Captaine, Knight, Knight's man,*
> *Lady,* or *Pusil,* that weares maske, or fan,
> *Velvet,* or *Taffeta* cap, rank'd in the darke
> With the shop's *Foreman,* or some such *brave sparke,*
> That may judge for his *six-pence*) had, before
> They saw it halfe, damd thy whole play, and more;
> Their motives were, since it had not to do
> With vices, which they look'd for, and came to.

> I, that am glad, thy Innocence was thy Guilt,
> And wish that all the *Muses* blood were spilt,
> In such a *Martirdome*; to vexe their eyes,
> Do crown thy murder'd *Poëme*: which shall rise
> A glorified worke to Time, when Fire,'
> Or moaths shall eate, what all these Fooles admire. (viii, 370)

I find this letter remarkably helpful: for not only does it give us a vivid picture of an audience at the Globe, but states the perennial argument between the play of good intent and 'the box-office success'.

But what light does it shed on jealous, malicious Jonson? Surely his rival Fletcher's fall should have delighted him? Yet he sympathizes and commends. At the close he even risks a prophecy which was happily fulfilled some twenty years later when *The Faithful Shepherdess* was revived before Charles I and Henrietta Maria at Whitehall with outstanding success.

This side of Jonson's nature has, to my mind, been grossly overlooked, and most misleadingly. His generous praise of Shakespeare is ignored while accusations of spite abound. In that same memorial poem, for instance, where the stricture on having 'small Latin and less Greek' reposes, there also lie such phrases as,

> Soule of the Age!
> The applause! delight! the wonder of our Stage!

or,

> Sweet Swan of Avon! what a sight it were
> To see thee in our waters yet appeare. (viii, 391–2)

Indeed in a poem which totals eighty lines, one only—that on scanty knowledge of the classics—can be construed as anything but praise of Shakespeare. A case therefore exists for thinking that if Jonson had some hard things to say of Shakespeare at least they did not originate in spite. We must look a little further and a little deeper. And if we do, the results I think are rewarding. What is more, they are just as pertinent to the theatre of our own times as they are to Shakespeare's and Jonson's.

88

II

The key to the whole matter, as I have already remarked, is the audience. The Elizabethan audience happened to prefer what Shakespeare gave them to what Jonson told them they ought to like. Modern television audiences similarly appear to prefer what Commerical T.V. gives them to what the B.B.C. and the best-established critics tell them they ought to like. Now Jonson conveniently left behind him ample evidence of what he considered audiences *ought* to like.

> Now, luck yet send us, and a little wit
>> Will serve, to make our play hit;
> (According to the palates of the season)
>> Here is ri'me, not emptie of reason:
> This we were bid to credit, from our *Poet*,
>> Whose true scope, if you would know it,
> In all his *poemes*, stil, hath been this measure,
>> To mixe profit, with your pleasure;
>> (Eight lines omitted)
> From his owne hand, without a co-adjutor,
>> Novice, journey-man, or tutor.
> Yet, thus much I can give you, as a token
>> Of his playes worth, no egges are broken;
> Nor quaking custards with fierce teeth affrighted,
>> Wherewith your rout are so delighted;
> Nor hales he in a gull, old ends reciting,
>> To stop gaps in his loose writing;
> With such a deale of monstrous, and forc'd action:
>> As might make *Bet'lem* a faction:
> Nor made he his play, for jests, stolne from each table,
>> But makes jests, to fit his fable.
> And, so presents quick *comoedie*, refined,
>> As best Criticks have designed,
> The lawes of time, place, persons he observeth,
>> From no needfull rule he swerveth. (v, 23–4)

These lines were written to be spoken by an actor by way of prologue to Jonson's best known play, *Volpone*. They leave one in no doubt of the author's theatrical likes and dislikes, comprising the dramatic theory of a man schooled in 'the classics', whose models for comedy are Aristophanes and Terence. The emphasis is clearly laid on formal unity. Form is the cardinal virtue. Within it profit and pleasure may and should be mixed. Sir Edward Herbert described Jonson as 'the Horace of our times', but little good it did him. For, alas, an appreciation of form in art is granted only to the best educated and the most civilized of men. The Athenians attained it; Rome in its best days; the Italy of Michelangelo and Leonardo; Louis XIV's France; Restoration and Augustan England; since when it has not been much in evidence; nor is it likely to be as we beat our daily retreat into neo-barbarism. Jonson lived at the right time but in the wrong country (or at the wrong time in his own country) for his theory to receive any general acceptance. It is this sense of form which Jonson terms 'Art'.

Good poets, he says, are 'made, as well as born' and the process of 'making' is a hard one. As he says to William Browne,

> I wou'd
> More of our writers would like thee, not swell
> With the *how much* they set forth, but th' *how well*. (viii, 392 and 386)

This is the 'art'—the ability to tailor the raw cloth of nature and give it shape, an ability the ancients possessed in such high degree—that Jonson thought Shakespeare lacked. How could a man who never revised or 'blotted' a line he wrote possess it? How could a man with only small Latin and less Greek model himself upon the ancients? English translations of Greek plays did not exist: and if translations of some Latin authors were readily obtainable, others were not. Moreover, the main sources of classical dramatic theory, Aristotle and Horace, were only available in Latin (or Italian) until Ben Jonson himself gave his countrymen an English version of the latter's *Art of Poetry*. The store he set by these authorities is best assessed in his own words.

The third requisite in our *Poet* . . . is Imitation . . . To make choise of one excellent man above the rest, and so to follow him, till he grow very *Hee*: or, so like him, as the Copie may be mistaken for the Principall . . . Not, to imitate servilely . . . but so to master the matter, and Stile, as to shew, hee knowes, how to handle, place, or dispose of [the history or argument of a poem] with *elegancie*, when need shall bee . . . among whom *Horace*, and (hee that taught him) Aristotle, deserve to bee the first in estimation. (viii, 638–40)

Jonson, however, in having read the classics in the original language was almost unique among his fellow dramatists. This by no means implies that even his interest was superficial. His grasp was sufficiently thorough for him to absorb and then originate. The most startling example of this I know is a passage in the Prologue to *Everyman out of his Humour* which seems, surprisingly, to have escaped the notice of literary critics. Here he antedates Dryden by some fifty-odd years in one of the ideas central to his famous *Essaie of Dramatick Poesie*—the plea that 'modern' writers should make 'the unities' their servants rather than be their slaves.

If those lawes you speake of, had beene delivered us, *ab initio*, and in their present vertue and perfection, there had beene some reason of obeying their powers: but 'tis extant, that that which we call *Comoedia*, was at first nothing but a simple, and continued *Song*, sung by one only person, till SUSARIO invented a second, after him EPICHARMUS a third; PHORMUS, and CHIONIDES devised to have foure Actors, with a *Prologue* and *Chorus*; to which CRATINUS (long after) added a fift, and sixt; EUPOLIS more; ARISTOPHANES more than they: every man in the dignitie of his spirit and judgement, supplyed something. And (though that in him this kinde of *Poeme* appeared absolute, and fully perfected) yet how is the face of it chang'd since, in MENANDER, PHILEMON, CECILIUS, PLAUTUS, and the rest; who have utterly excluded the *Chorus*, altered the property of the persons, their names, and natures, and augmented it with all liberty, according to the elegancie and disposition of those times, wherein they wrote? I see not then, but we should enjoy the same licence, or free power, to illustrate and heighten our invention as they did; and not bee tyed to those strict and regular formes, which the nicenesse of a few (who are nothing but forme) would thrust upon us. (iii, 437)

No wonder Dryden admired Jonson so greatly. He was, indeed, with the possible exception of Bacon, the finest scholar of his age. But this very scholarship was enough in itself to divorce him from most of the Globe audience, an audience that knew next to nothing about the models Jonson prized so dearly—and cared less.

> Come leave the loathed stage,
> And the more loathsome age:
>
> . . . .
>
> Say, that thou pour'st them wheat,
> And they will acornes eat:
> 'Twere simple fury, still, thy selfe to waste
> On such as have no taste! (vi, 492)

Arrogant, perhaps; but I would hazard quite a large sum on most authors, producers and actors of integrity in the theatre today having entertained at some time in their careers such feelings towards an audience. I only wish to add further that these Philistines whom Jonson censures are those whose 'palate's with the swine' and not necessarily groundlings only but 'brave plush, and velvet-men'. And, 'no velvet suit you wear will alter kind'.

III

From this point of view Shakespeare's ignorance of classical precept served him well. His approach to drama was as traditional as that of his audience. Polonius, with his jig and a tale of bawdry was a more typical playgoer than Hamlet. To that audience Shakespeare gave songs and dances in profusion: while, as for tales of bawdry, generations of schoolmasters and mistresses have laboured mightily to obliterate them and with as much success as that accorded Sisyphus.[1] Songs, dances, tales of bawdry, fantastic stories, passionate romance, duels, torture, a mingling of gay and tragic; all these things Shakespeare gave his audience, all these and something more, something which I can only depict in a word now much out of fashion—soul. It is in this respect above all others that Shakespeare's approach to the writing of plays is as traditional as that of his audience. Like theirs, and unlike Jonson's, it was still fundamentally mediaeval. Reformation or no Reformation, man's world was still thought to be a copy in little of God's

[1] See Essay 13, p. 214 below.

Kingdom and man himself 'the abridgement' between angel and beast.

In comedy Shakespeare is primarily concerned with telling a story. He gives the emphasis, as also in history and tragedy, to narrative that Jonson reserves for form. To the neo-classical enthusiast Shakespeare's plays inevitably appear shapeless. No shred of concern about 'the unities', about 'the rules'! Flagrant anachronisms and absurdities! Seas crossed with the aid of Chorus: generations bridged by Time! Yet if Jonson's realism had no room for Shakespeare's romance, Shakespeare's romance was but slightly concerned with Jonson's realism. Accused of wanting art or form, anyone writing within the mediaeval tradition would have replied, 'my narrative is my form. I am telling a story and that story, for those with eyes to see, ears to hear and hearts to feel, has several meanings. Besides the letter of my narrative, there is what is signified by the letter; and in this significance lies my art.' The matter is summed up by Jonson's latest and best editors as concisely as can be.

> We must not seek in the hard, categorical veracity of Jonson's art, the kind of truth by which supreme artists like Dante or Shakespeare in interpreting a country and an age interpret also universal humanity. (i, 126)

Jonson, with his great Latin and considerable Greek, modelling himself deliberately upon the ancients, is essentially a satirist in comedy. His sense of form and the economy of means which that implies enable him, at his best, to sweep away all bounds of incredulity in his audience and present them with visions of human greed, hypocrisy and guile so extravagant as to dazzle and delight.

Nowhere is the difference between the classical and mediaeval conception of comedy better exemplified than in *The Comedy of Errors*. As Mr. Nevill Coghill first demonstrated, Shakespeare borrowed Plautus' *Menaechmi* for his plot, but then altered the story drastically to conform with accepted custom.

> Few comedies, one might suppose [I quote Mr. Coghill], could reach a preposterous conclusion that started with a man being seriously

led out to execution. Yet this is what happens to the Merchant Egeon in the first scene of *The Comedy of Errors*; and Egeon is the father of the Antipholus twins, a major character in fact. This gambit is not in Plautus, and the style in which it is introduced is as high as tragedy could wish it to be. Execution on Egeon is deferred; but it is not remitted. He remains (albeit off-stage) in anticipation of immediate death until the last scene. That death is then about to be inflicted on him when from an improbable Abbey (in Ephesus) an even more improbable Abbess appears and is most improbably discovered to be Egeon's long-lost wife, and the means of his deliverance. She is also Shakespeare's invention, and turns the catastrophe to general joy.[1]

Death and laughter, ever strangers on the classical stage, had been companions on the English stage long before Shakespeare wrote for it. In the Wakefield Miracles, Mak the Shepherd steals a sheep on the night of the Nativity and Roman 'torturers' jest with one another as Christ dies. This mingling of genre, the purist Jonson could not abide. But for those to whom it was acceptable, as it was to Shakespeare, the proportions could be varied within the formula. Hence the wrangling about the 'dark' or 'tragi'-comedies. For Shakespeare and his like they were simply comedies with rather more emphasis upon the sorrow than the joy. For Sidney, Jonson and their like they were bastard products without classical precedent, neither comedy nor tragedy but 'mongrel tragi-comedy'. Echoes of such argument come to us in Polonius' introduction of the players to Hamlet.

The difference of approach to comedy, thus far considered, applies with equal force to tragedy. If we accept tragedy to mean what Jonson, Dryden, Boileau or their classical masters define it as meaning, then Shakespeare never wrote a tragedy: he wrote melodramas. In classical tragedy, according to its theorists, plot precedes character so that the inevitability of the action may be apparent. A compact action was of paramount importance and the poet ought to discipline himself in terms of locality and time-span to this end. To Jonson this self-discipline was 'arte'. Christian thinking, however, tended to reverse this

[1] 'The Basis of Shakespearean Comedy', *Essay and Studies*, 1950, p. 9.

order of precedence. As I have demonstrated in an earlier essay, tragedy, to the mediaeval mind, was quite simply the Fall of Princes.[1] Responsibility for the fall was of course complicated by the idea of what I may call 'a suffering to the point of death' and hence concerned pain. Why do we have to suffer pain? How ought we to suffer it? What do we get out of it? How can we rise above it? These, surely, are the fundamental questions which provoke the desire to write, to act, to read or to see tragedies at any time anywhere. In the Middle Ages they were answered in terms of Sin, the archetypal patterns being supplied by the Book of Genesis, and to some extent still, in classical terms of Fate—usually thought of as Dame Fortune with her Wheel, but increasingly as Divine Providence. The two are easily mingled. Chaucer makes the point explicitly in the opening stanzas of 'The Monkes Tale'.

> (1) I wol biwayle in maner of Tragedie
> . . . .
> (2) At Lucifer, though he an angel were,
> And nat a man, at him I wol biginne;
> For, thogh fortune may non angel dere,
> From heigh degree yet fel he for his sinne
> Down in-to helle, wher he yet is inne.
> Now artow Sathanas, that maist nat twinne
> Out of miserie, in which that thou art falle.
>
> (3) Lo Adam, in the feld of Damassene,
> With goddes owene finger wroght was he,
> And nat bigeten of mannes sperme unclene,
> And welte al Paradys, saving o tree.
> Had never worldly man so heigh degree
> As Adam, til he for misgovernaunce
> Was drive out of his hye prosperitee
> To labour, and to helle, and to meschaunce.

The Fall of Princes, therefore, could be attributed either to enemies within or to enemies without or to both in combination. Emphasis could vary in any given story, a factor which differentiates the mediaeval theory of tragedy from its classical

[1] See Essay 3, pp. 48-51 above.

antecedents—Shakespeare's from Jonson's. Thus, as with comedy, classical tragic theory was inherited as a literary tradition, transformed by Christian theology and pressed by Elizabethans into the service of the native drama. Tragedy still tells the story of the fall of a Prince, but with a difference. The Prince is shown to be personally responsible for his Fall. Lucifer fell by pride and so does Lear. The inevitability of the catastrophe is transferred from the plot to the character of the central protagonist. Nowhere does Shakespeare seem to be at greater pains to make this clear than in *Macbeth*. There Banquo is placed as a deliberate foil to the villain-hero. Both are presented with the identical spur to amibition, the identical opportunity to obtain it by foul means: but what Macbeth, abetted by his Eve-like wife, allows his conscience to condone, Banquo resists

> Merciful powers!
> Restrain in me the cursed thoughts that nature
> Gives way to in repose.

Both men come to a bloody end: but Banquo's integrity is rewarded in the fullness of time, through Fleance's escape, with the Union of the Scottish and the English crowns in James I.[1] The opposition of Prince Hamlet to Laertes in a play where the hero has as many enemies without as within is but a variant of this same technique: that of Antony to Caesar in *Antony and Cleopatra* another. At other times the 'flaw' is not so self-evident —as in *Romeo and Juliet*—the emphasis being squarely laid on Fate. Always, however, the dramatist working in this tradition contrives to avoid fatalism and despair by bringing the tragic hero into a state of complete self-knowledge, but only when it is patently too late to avoid the approaching catastrophe. Even atheists of the order of Tamburlaine or D'Amville in Tourneur's *The Atheist's Tragedy* come to find a power superior to themselves in death. Thus we, the spectators of the hero's fall, are brought to see him no longer at loggerheads but at one with the natural order of the universe and may say of him dead, as Hamlet does to his father,

> Rest, rest, perturbèd spirit.

---

[1] See Essay 13, pp. 230–1 below.

If, in a phrase, we seek to know what those English dramatists who 'wanted art' and had 'small Latin and less Greek' were up to when writing tragedy, I think the answer can be found, accurately diagnosed by Lear.

> Let them anatomize Regan, see what breeds about her heart. Is there any cause in nature that makes these hard hearts? (III, vi, 77–9)

—or, as D'Amville puts it in *The Atheist's Tragedy*,

> I would find out . . .
> What thing there is in Nature more exact
> Than in the constitution of myself. (V, ii)

For them the whole purpose of tragedy was to supply an answer: but neither this question nor the answers were matters of primary concern to Jonson and his followers since by their standards the dramatic product was so clearly wanting in 'arte'.[1]

IV

So much then for this clash of philosophies and aesthetic values as far as dramatic theory and play construction are concerned. I want to turn now to the related matter of vocabulary. Vocabulary is not a subject to which many of us give much attention after our first years at school—except perhaps when struggling with a crossword puzzle! Yet it is one of paramount importance to any dramatist: for his text must stand or fall on a single hearing in the theatre. He must be immediately understood—which is not to say that more cannot be gleaned on second hearing or from subsequent reading.

Shakespeare and Jonson were writing at a time when the English language was undergoing one of its several accelerations of change. And here again the two dramatists took different paths. Jonson embraced the new words of Greek and Latin stock. Shakespeare clung to the traditional vocabulary. And in so doing, he remained a popular dramatist while Jonson did not. Again this was due to the attitude of the audience and is simply understood. Let me take a blatant modern example of

---

[1] See Essay 3, pp. 56–9 above.

what I mean. Some little while ago I saw performed within a week of one another Racine's tragedy *Esther* and Molière's satiric comedy *Tartuffe*. *Esther* was performed in French and accompanied by the original music not heard, even in France, for over a hundred years. *Tartuffe* was performed in a very racy English adaptation. I need hardly say that *Esther* was performed by amateurs before private audiences and *Tartuffe* by a professional company whose box-office was open for nine weeks. The point is this. The number of people willing to pay to see a play by Racine and a play by Molière may be roughly equal: but the number of English people prepared to see the one in French is vastly smaller than that prepared to see the other in English, and simply because the majority neither speak nor understand classical French.

The situation in Shakespeare's England was roughly parallel as regards Greek and Latin. Today, so much have words and syntax of Greek or Latin origin become absorbed into our language that we scarcely ever think of how, why or when they found their way there. It is thus natural for us to assume that Jonson's language was as intelligible to Globe audiences as Shakespeare's. That it was not accounts, I think, in some measure for Jonson's failure to please. Their respective texts still provide the best evidence. Here first, is Shakespeare at his poetic best.

> *Troilus:* O virtuous fight!
>   When right with right wars who shall be most right.
>   True swains in love shall in the world to come
>   Approve their truths by Troilus: when their rimes,
>   Full of protest, of oath, and big compare,
>   Want similes, truth tir'd with iteration,
>   As true as steel, as plantage to the moon,
>   As sun to day, as turtle to her mate,
>   As iron to adamant, as earth to the centre,
>   Yet, after all comparisons of truth,
>   As truth's authentic author to be cited,
>   'As true as Troilus' shall crown up the verse
>   And sanctify the numbers.
> *Cressida:* Prophet may you be!
>   If I be false, or swerve a hair from truth,

> When time is old and hath forgot itself,
> When waterdrops have worn the stones of Troy,
> And blind oblivion swallow'd cities up,
> And mighty states characterless are grated
> To dusty nothing, yet let memory,
> From false to false, among false maids in love,
> Upbraid my falsehood! When they've said, 'as false
> As air, as water, wind, or sandy earth,
> As fox to lamb, or wolf to heifer's calf,
> Pard to the hind, or stepdame to her son,'
> Yea, let them say, to stick the heart of falsehood,
> 'As false as Cressid.' (III, iii, 183–208)

Shakespeare's source is, of course, the mediaeval version of the Troy story—Chaucer's and Lydgate's: not Homer's. The passage contains two hundred and three words. Of these a mere thirty-six contain more than one syllable: while of that thirty-six only eight have three syllables and two have four, and this in a play with a 'special vocabulary'. It is simple: it is perfect. The ratio is startling; but it is a fairly constant one. Jonson, if he wished to, could do the same.

> Drinke to me, onely, with thine eyes,
> And I will pledge with mine;
> Or leave a kisse but in the cup,
> And I'le not look for wine.
> The thirst, that from the soule doth rise,
> Doth aske a drinke divine:
> But might I of JOVE's *Nectar* sup,
> I would not change for thine.
> I sent thee, late, a rosie wreath,
> Not so much honoring thee,
> As giving it a hope, that there
> It could not withered bee.
> But thou thereon did'st onely breath,
> And sent'st it backe to mee:
> Since when it growes, and smells, I sweare,
> Not of it selfe, but thee. (viii, 106)

This song contains one hundred and two words of which only nine contain more than one syllable. Yet, again, it is both simple and perfect. Here now, by contrast, is Jonson speaking the language of the intellectuals. I quote from his Preface to *Volpone*, addressed to 'The two famous Universities'.

Never (most equall SISTERS) had any man a wit so presently excellent, as that it could raise itselfe; but there must come both matter, occasion, commenders, and favourers to it: If this be true, and that the fortune of all writers doth daily prove it, it behoves the carefull to provide, well, toward these accidents; and, having acquir'd them, to preserve that part of a reputation most tenderly, wherein the benefit of a friend is also defended. (v, 17)

The proportion of monosyllabic to polysyllabic words has here fallen to less than three to one. Jonson, as an honorary Master of Arts of both Universities, was for ever in danger of talking above people's heads, people with small Latin and less Greek. Yet of such stuff was his audience made, a fact which Shakespeare appreciated much better than he did. Jonson learnt to contain colloquialism within dramatic verse, but his eye was forever fixed on lecturing his audience. I have perhaps done Jonson an injustice in quoting a passage of literary prose rather than of stage dialogue; but I wanted first to show just how stuffily he *could* write when being consciously erudite. He is much too good a theatre craftsman ever to let his stage dialogue become quite as pompous as this. Yet it is noticeably heavier than Shakespeare's both in syntax and vocabulary. Statistics of this sort can recoil on the user's head. Mine cannot *prove* the point, but a glance at the Bible of 1611 goes far to substantiate it. To turn from the text *addressed to the people* to the Preface, *addressed to the most learned Prince in Christendom* is virtually to read two different languages. A similarly convenient point of comparison between Shakespeare and Jonson is their respective treatment of Cicero in *Julius Caesar* and *Catiline*. The latter is a five-act tragedy constructed according to classical precept complete with chorus. The play failed to please and Jonson wrote a preface of self justification, 'To the Reader in ordinary'.

Though you commend the two first Actes, with the people, because they are the worst; and dislike the Oration of Cicero, in regard you read some pieces of it, at Schoole, and understand them not yet; I shall finde the way to forgive you . . . (v, 432)

Cicero's oration, so evidently dear to Jonson, is a word for word translation of the first of his four orations against Catiline, delivered in the Senate with Catiline there. It runs out at nearly two hundred and ninety lines of blank verse. As a translation, I am assured by those better qualified to judge than I, that it is admirable. As a piece of dramatic writing, it is deplorable. Consider, by contrast, how Shakespeare handles Cicero in *Julius Caesar*.

> 'Did Cicero say anything?' enquires Cassius.
> 'Ay, he spoke Greek,' replies Casca.
> 'To what effect?'
> 'Nay, and I tell you that, I'll ne'r look you i' th' face again. But those that understood him smil'd at one another, and shook their heads; but for my own part, it was Greek to me.' (I, ii, 275-81)

Audiences today habitually receive these lines with a hearty laugh. And is there any doubt but that they were intended to? Shakespeare is surely here making capital out of his own defects. But in speaking a language closer to Chaucer's than to that of Dryden or Pope he was at least comprehensible to his entire audience. And this Jonson just as certainly was not. The closing scene of *The Silent Woman* for example (a play which Dryden singles out for its formal perfection) is a brilliant parody of legal and ecclesiastical Latin. But it is safe to say that as many people in the Jacobean audience missed its subtler points because the scene was in Latin as now miss its whole point because it is in Latin. On first performance, it is said, 'There was never one man to say plaudite to it', and the play was subsequently nicknamed 'The Silent Audience'.

In point of vocabulary and sentence structure, if we pause to think about it, this same gulf between those with higher education and those without it still exists today. Were any of us, for instance, to go into some 'pub' and use the language of contemporary literary criticism in conversation with farm hands we would certainly be unintelligible to them and probably be mocked as soon as we had left.

It may be objected that if Shakespeare and his audience were so diffident about neo-classicism, it is odd that he should have bothered to write a group of Roman plays. In choosing subjects from Roman history he may possibly have pleased the better educated section of his audience—University wits, professional men, courtiers and their ladies—and, as a member of King James I's own company of actors he may even have been commanded to prepare these plays. Primarily, however, these subjects appealed to both author and audience alike, because they made good stories. Given a good story which the meanest intelligence could follow and enjoy, the dramatist who then set to work to adorn it poetically for the benefit of the more judicious could rely on a wide social range of appreciation.

The English love of a good story is part of our Norse heritage. For centuries the saga, a story chanted to metrical accompaniment, was the staple entertainment. Later on, the trouvères of Provence opened up a vast new mine of stories unknown to the Teutonic scôp. The Church was probably the first body to give its particular brand of story dramatic expression: but the trouvères followed shortly after. To men of the late Middle Ages a good story was the first requirement of any play. Whether that story came from the Bible, English history, Roman history, from Denmark, Scotland, Italy or Illyria was wholly immaterial provided it was good. As already remarked, Shakespeare, in writing *Troilus and Cressida*, goes to Chaucer for his source and not to Homer. As a story, Chaucer's tale is the better of the two. This love of stories is essentially child-like. It is only the more sophisticated beings who scorn the simple story in favour of more complex entertainment. Jonson, one might remember, applied to Shakespeare the epithet 'gentle': and Shakespeare was never more gentle than in telling stories. Therein lay the greater part of his 'arte'.

6

The Stuart Mask

IF anything like justice is to be done within the limits of a single essay to a dramatic genre that is as often maligned as it is neglected by historians and critics, it is important to define the sort of treatment that is to be accorded to it here. One approach would be to take the actual dates which circumscribe the period—from Samuel Daniel's *Vision of Twelve Goddesses* performed in the year of James I's Coronation, to Sir William D'Avenant's *Salmacida Spolia* which gave the Court of Charles I its most expensive, glittering and mocking entertainment before Civil War disestablished the Mask as a genre—and follow its development chronologically, very much as Allardyce Nicoll has done at much greater length in *Stuart Masques and the Renaissance Stage* (1938). Another possibility would be to narrow our focus to a single Mask and, taking that as an example, make a microscopic inspection of the text and settings, as D. J. Gordon has done with Ben Jonson's and Inigo Jones' *Hue and Cry After Cupid* or *Hymenaei*, relating all its iconography to source in other literature and art of the period.[1] Yet a third approach is to try to distil the essence, as it were, of Masks of the Jacobean and Caroline period relating the blossom itself to the

---

[1] 'Ben Jonson's "Haddington Masque"': The Story and the Fable', *M.L.R.* xlii (1947), 180–7; 'Hymenaei: Ben Jonson's Masque of Union', *Journal of the Warburg and Courtauld Institutes*, viii (1945), pp. 107–45.

roots from which it sprang and to the seed which it left against the future. It is the last of these three possible approaches which I have chosen to follow here, largely because, so far as I am aware, it has not been attempted in any concise manner before.[1]

Masks are as important for historians today as they were to audiences of their own time since they reflect all the cultural pursuits of the age to a degree unparalleled elsewhere. Nearly all the poets of distinction wrote texts. All the architects and painters reckoned the dressing and setting of them to be one of their duties, while the best musicians and dancing masters vied with one another to compose scores for the songs and dances. And because Masks were occasional entertainments designed to celebrate special events with the diplomatic corps in attendance and struggling for precedence in seating accommodation they could not escape some political significance. Central to all this, the Mask was essentially the cockpit of English dramatic theory in a time of change which was as radical as it was rapid.

If it is a mistake to regard a stage-play as primarily a work of literature, it is still more misleading to think of Masks in this context: yet many critics have based their assessments on the printed texts alone, attributing such shortcomings in poetic imagination as they have found to the mischievous influence of Inigo Jones' or the audiences' debased taste for spectacle. Two other common misconceptions which stem from this assumption are that the Stuart Mask was an imported Italian product and that it had a marked influence on Shakespeare's later plays: yet as soon as the Mask is looked at as a work of art instead of as a piece of literature the absurdity of these critical judgements becomes self-evident.

The nucleus around which the Mask, as a dramatic genre, was constructed was dance, and can fairly be described as choreographic compliment. The key to any true understanding of its development is the aristocratic and amateur nature of its origin. It owes its shape to the rituals of courtship developed

---

[1] The two fullest accounts of the origins, growth and nature of the English Mask are Paul Reyher's *Les Masques Anglais*, Paris, 1909, and Enid Welsford's *The Court Masque*, 1927. A handsome and useful edition of fourteen selected Masks has just appeared prepared as a tribute to Allardyce Nicoll by his pupils and colleagues: *A Book of Masques*, ed. T. J. B. Spenser and S. W. Wells, Cambridge, 1967.

in the Middle Ages within the Revels, the particular points of growth being first Mummings and then Disguisings.[1] As inherited by the Stuarts, the structure was still essentially choreographic and only superficially dramatic in so far as it was ornamented with costumes, settings and a text. A Presenter announced (and explained) the arrival of the Maskers (disguised strangers) who first danced formally among themselves, next chose partners from among the spectators and finally danced again among themselves before retiring: each of the three principal dance sequences was introduced by a song or group of songs, and the Maskers were related to the occasion by the nature of the disguises selected. The excuse for a text was provided by the Presenter's explanatory prologue and the songs punctuating the dances. The only structural change of specifically Stuart origin was the addition of an 'antimask' which served to introduce both the Presenter and the Maskers by means of a parody of the main subject or device. Thus a Mask, considered as an entertainment, drew its inspiration from sophisticated sexual exhibitionism within an erotic musical context of song and dance and its form from attempts to transpose the actual and mundane into a make-believe world of the fabulous and exotic. Transposition could, and on occasion did, take a form that was genuinely dramatic: this, however, depended on the person entrusted with responsibility for 'the invention' or devising of subject, disguise and parody.

The first Mask presented to James I was Samuel Daniel's *Vision of Twelve Goddesses*.[2] As the title implies, it was a ladies' Mask in which the Queen and her ladies were the principal performers. The scenario contained three separate settings—a temple, a cave and a mountain—all of which were on view simultaneously, dotted around the floor space like atolls in the sea. No drawings or floor plans of this Mask survive, but an engraving of a Ballet at the French Court some twenty years earlier gives us a clear enough picture of the arrangements which should be carefully compared with Daniel's own stage

[1] See *Early English Stages*, i, chs. V and VI, and Essay 2, pp. 24–8 above.
[2] The text of this Mask with a critical introduction by Joan Rees is printed in *A Book of Masques*, pp. 17–37.

directions in the printed text.[1] The following year (1604) Ben Jonson and Inigo Jones were commissioned by the Queen for the first time to work together on a ladies' Mask for the Twelfth Night Revels. The result was *The Mask of Blackness* in which the Court had its first experience of a proscenium arch with a setting painted in perspective underneath.[2] A painted curtain across the arch concealed the setting until the Mask began, but no attempt was made to change the scene itself: for the sort of spectacle witnessed by the spectators, *Plate Eleven* (one of the settings for *Florimène*, 1636) gives a good indication and should be compared with *Plate Three*. Taken in conjunction the *Vision of Twelve Goddesses* and *The Mask of Blackness* suffice to show that whatever else Masks may have been they were not a new genre which was born, flourished and died under the first two Stuart kings. To think of Masks in that way is about as inept as to suppose that the remarkable post-World War II productions of Wagner opera at Bayreuth are similarly self-contained. At Bayreuth it is obvious enough that a man of outstanding artistic ability, the late Wieland Wagner, has used the fruits of some fifty years of experiment in techniques of stage-lighting to effect a revolution in production methods in the theatre and has applied them as an artistic synthesis to meet the aesthetic problems set by the staging requirements of *Der Ring des Nibelungen*. The Festspielhaus remains today as Richard Wagner built it and the operas as he wrote them: but the experience of seeing them in this novel staging is quite different, and indeed shocking to those familiar with earlier staging traditions. Yet what we now witness represents half a century's European discussion and practical experiment about lighting and scenery expressed through the personality of a single director who had both the vision and the opportunity to give it effect. The Swiss Adolf Appia and the Englishman Gordon Craig are to Wieland Wagner what the Italians Serlio and Palladio were to Inigo Jones. Through Jones' genius, the twin sixteenth-century problems of overcrowding in the auditorium and of appropriateness of visual appearance to spoken word found their

[1] See *Plate III* no. 5.
[2] The text is printed in Ben Jonson, *Works*, vii, pp. 161–180.

spectacular solution in the Stuart Mask: in the Mask and not the Public Theatre because both problems affected the Court more acutely than the public. But just as the Bayreuth production techniques are spreading slowly East and West across the world—labelled revolutionary of course—so the spectacular qualities of the Stuart Mask gradually spread to the public stage in England in the latter half of the seventeenth century to find its logical conclusion in the spectacular transformation scenes of nineteenth-century melodrama with its cinematic sequels.

Looked at this way—in terms of the general flow of theatre history—it becomes clear that the Mask, in its last years of a long life, translated our theatre from one of suggestion, visual and poetic, into one of verisimilitude, realistic and prosaic. Why did this happen? And why did it happen between 1604 and 1640? I have already suggested that Jones' achievement in England may be explained as a practical answer to two problems of burning moment to the English nobility. The first was the mundane but perennial one which faces anyone throwing a party. Who to invite? In any society where the right of admission to ceremonies rests on privilege, a sudden expansion of those eligible to attend creates a problem which is aggravated if the ceremonies continue to be held in the same buildings. Tudor Government had created a whole army of new officials eligible for admission to entertainments at Court. Yet very few appear to have been willing to forgo the pleasure of being able to say that they were 'among those present'! Indeed, in the early years of James I's reign, the Lord Chamberlain's white staff was no mere symbol of office but a veritable cosh to deal with latecomers for whom there was no place. Short of rebuilding the Banqueting Hall—and this didn't happen till fire destroyed the old one in 1618—the only amelioration of the seating problem possible was to annexe some of the floor space: and this could not be done without either curtailing the number of the scattered scenic units, or alternatively using much less of the available floor space for the display of these emblematic units than had been normal hitherto.

The second problem was to make the visual appearance of

the entertainment more appropriate—in every sense of the word—to the scenario. There are two clear reasons for this having become a problem when it did. One of them was that Sir Philip Sidney's *Apologie for Poetry* found a wide measure of support in Court circles; and the other was the sudden realization among poets themselves, especially those of Sidney's persuasion, that the Mask—an amateur and aristocratic diversion devoted almost exclusively to dance, song and spectacle—was worth their attention as a means of securing noble patronage. Attention from poets, practically expressed, meant a sizeable expansion of the scenario in terms of literary narrative. These pressures, in Italy and France, exploded into the famous controversy about unity of place.[1] In England they led Ben Jonson and Inigo Jones, under the direct patronage of the Royal Family, to embark on a series of experiments with a view to finding a formula that would at once permit the greatly expanded narrative content of the Mask to be grafted to its traditional components of dance, song and spectacle without giving offence to aesthetic sensibility of the sort complained of in the plays presented in the public theatres. They solved their first problem—that of extra floor space—at the first attempt. By concentrating the scene at one end of the hall under a proscenium arch—a device imported by Jones from Italy— floor space became available for additional spectators. The second problem however—that of appropriateness—defied satisfactory solution for thirty-five years, and was to involve the dissolution of the partnership. This was due largely to the nature of the solution found to the floor space problem. If the price to be paid for the concentrated scene in perspective painting was to be restriction of both the poet's freedom in narrative invention and of the audience's traditional right to variety of spectacle, it was bound to prove too high. Somehow or other, poet, architect, painter and machinist must evolve together ways and means of changing the scene on the spot and without serious time-lag. It was to this end that Jones directed

[1] On these problems in Italy and France see H. Leclerc, *Les Origines Italiennes de l'Architecture Théâtrale Moderne*, Paris, 1946, and S. W. Holsboer, *L'Histoire de la Mise en Scène dans le Théâtre Français de 1600 à 1657*, Paris, 1933.

his energies. Within ten years he had succeeded well enough to satisfy Ben Jonson. With three changes of scene (as in his *Vision of Delight* of 1617[1]) Jonson had elbow room enough for his likely narrative requirements. But Jones had other fish to fry. Nothing succeeds like success: and Jones, having started life as a joiner's apprentice saw himself on the high road to fame, security and riches. With money no object, his fertile scenic inventions had dazzled audiences with their novelty and prettiness. They wanted more and more for the sheer spectacular fun of it. What was to stop him? Did not Renaissance theories of government invite Princes to impress themselves on both subjects and foreigners with the lavishness of their entertainments? Bacon disapproved, but went unheeded. Jonson alone perceived the danger threatening the future of the drama should Jones go any further, and stood up to him. A trivial matter provoked the showdown.

Jones claimed that his name should take precedence over Jonson's on the title-page of *The Mask of Augurs* (1622) printed for circulation after the event. Jonson saw in this a direct threat to the poet's hitherto unrivalled domination of the theatre. Aristotle, Horace and the Mediaeval Church had all in their own way decreed that spectacle should serve the text, the painter serve the poet. Who was Jones—a man of sketchy education and vast pretensions—to dare to reverse their judgement? Jonson gave his answer a decade later in one of the most scorching pieces of invective in the language, 'An Expostulation with Inigo Jones'. This poem, containing the famous line 'painting and carpentry are the soul of Mask', starts,

> Master Surveyor, you that first began
> From thirty pounds in pipkins, to the man
> You are; from them leapt forth an Architect,
> Able to talk of Euclid, and correct
> Both him and Archimede . . .

and ends,

> Long live the Feasting Room. And ere thou burn
> Again, thy Architect to ashes turn!

---

[1] For the text see *Works*, vii, pp. 463–71: also *Early English Stages*, ii(1), pp. 270–1.

Whom not ten fires, nor a Parliament can
With all Remonstrance make an honest man.[1]

This poem conveniently pinpoints the crux of an artistic argument the outcome of which was to determine the nature of English drama and theatre for the next three centuries. At the centre lies the question whether words or spectacle are to take precedence in the art of drama. Jonson assumed that the protagonists in this dispute were himself and his collaborator. In this, as Andrew Sabol pointed out in his edition of *Songs and Dances for the Stuart Masque*, 'perhaps each overestimated the importance of his contribution—Jonson his fable and Jones his scenic designs, for the chief element of this form of entertainment, even in the earliest accounts, was dancing'.[2] Nevertheless, when due allowance has been made for the overriding importance of the musical element within the Mask (including the incentive which musical elaboration and contrast contributed to the development of the antimask) it is obvious that the question of the relation of words to spectacle in drama would have to be raised in the seventeenth century when every other aspect of life and thought inherited from the Middle Ages was being or was to be subjected to the scrutiny of rationalist philosophy and something approaching scientific analysis: the fact that it came into prominence in the form of a dispute between Jonson and Jones in respect of Masks only served to extend it to dramatic entertainment as a whole. That the answer given in the seventeenth century was not necessarily the right one is something which we in the middle of the twentieth century are slowly coming to recognize for ourselves as a result of the provoking contributions which such varied figures as Gordon Craig, Granville Barker, W. B. Yeats, T. S. Eliot and the pioneers of British Ballet have made to our own theatre.

However this may be, the ascendancy that Inigo Jones came to enjoy over Ben Jonson in the estimation of Charles I and his Court served in itself to settle the dispute in England in favour of the architect, painter and machinist. Jonson, after reluctantly contributing a few more texts for Masks, died in dire poverty in

---

[1] *Works*, viii, pp. 402–6, given here in modern spelling.
[2] Brown University Press, Providence, Rhode Island, 1959.

PLATE IX

12   THE COCKPIT-IN-COURT
Dankert's view of Whitehall in the reign of Charles II showing the
Cockpit-in-Court (directly above statue).

Original in Berkeley Castle

13   Reconstruction of the interior of the Cockpit-in-Court.

Drawing by Graham Barlow

PLATE X

14 HELL-CASTLE
 1 Detail, as represented on the stage for the Passion Play at
 Valenciennes, 1547.
 2 Painting by Giovanni Bellini, *c.* 1500. *Bristol City Art*
 Gallery
 3 Hearne's print.

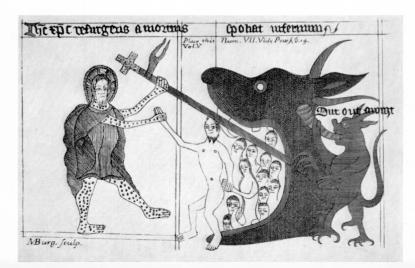

1637: Jones, secure in his sovereign's favour as Surveyor of the King's Works, found he enjoyed the trust of the Court audience and that other collaborators were to hand who were less scrupulous about either the fate of poetry or their own status. He answered the 'Expostulation' by securing the appointment of Aurelian Townshend instead of Jonson to provide the libretto of the Mask for Christmas 1631–32. Masks, in consequence and largely in terms of elaboration of the antimask, progressed from sumptuous fantasy to ever more gorgeous choreography and more costly spectacle. It was as nothing for a Mask to cost £10,000 and that for a single performance only. More machines provided more variety of scene until at length between 1635 and 1639 Jones gave the English theatre the system of changeable scenery which, in substance, is that we know today. (See *Plate XV.*)

When we come to consider why the poets should have lost the battle with the painters and musicians fought out within the context of the Stuart Masks, I think it must be conceded that they allowed themselves, in their quest for reputation, to see opportunities within Masks which were never really there, at least for them. Led by George Gascoigne late in the reign of Elizabeth I they saw in Masks a chance of obtaining royal patronage for dramatic poetry denied to them in the public playhouses. Rather ought they to have recognized that the Mask grew out of the same common stock as Italian opera and French ballet. Courtly, amateur and occasional with origins buried in the antiquity of song and dance as accompaniments to courtship, these secular diversions compounded into a distinctive entertainment in all European courts during the fourteenth century. In the fifteenth century words were added by way of prefatory exposition, and scenic decoration became usual. In this elaborate form it was known as the Disguising in England. The Italians had the happy idea that the entertainment could be rounded off more pleasantly if the performers, instead of dancing with themselves, took partners from among the spectators. With the adoption of this practice in England in 1512, the Italian name for the entertainment, *Maschera* or Mask, was taken over too. The names, Disguising and Mask, lingered as alternatives until late in the reign of Elizabeth I. Thus, at least in point of structure, the Stuart Mask is identical with its Tudor predecessor as far back as 1512 and, with the exception of the maskers taking partners from the audience, identical for 100 years at least beyond that with the Disguising. It was only in the sixteenth century that swiftly developing national characteristics asserted themselves upon this traditional recreation of the nobility. In France this took the form of additional emphasis upon the dance in the *Balet de Cours*, a development which was to lead directly to the pre-eminence of French Ballet in the late seventeenth century. In Italy both song and decoration received attention and led, via the Intermezzi and Pastoral, to opera.[1] In England, the intervention of poets schooled in the most dynamic dramatic tradition in Europe gave the genre a strong literary flavour that was distinctly English. Their primary difficulty was to strike a balance between the words which they wished to add and the music, dance and spectacle which were already there. The fact that Masks were an occasional entertainment designed to celebrate weddings, coronations, or especially festive holidays like Twelfth Night, New Year's Eve or Shrove Tuesday forced the librettist however to set a premium on topicality; and today's joker is frequently tomorrow's bore. Another factor militating against the poets was the determination of their patrons to participate in Masks as performers. The strength of the Mask, the quality that had already given it a life of more than two centuries, was its spontaneity and gaiety. Anyone who has participated in good charades has an inkling of that quality. Only after Ben Jonson added the antimask—a prelude of grotesque or comic contrast, first introduced in his *Mask of Queens* (1609)[2]—were professional actors regularly called upon to share responsibility for the performance. Otherwise the Maskers were courtiers—sometimes men (a lords' mask) sometimes ladies (a ladies' mask) and sometimes both together. A small group of people, usually not less than eight and never more than twenty-four, set out to surprise and

[1] See Essay 4, pp. 71–3 above; also *Plates III, IV* and *V.*
[2] Text printed in *Works*, vii, 265–319. See also the facsimile edition, Kings Printers, 1930.

delight their friends. By contrast, Inigo Jones thought nothing of employing 200 stage hands! Strict secrecy guarded the preparations, and the final result was as often as not parochial in theme and imagery. Jonson, trying to please a bookish king as well as indulge his own tastes, stuffed his text with a veritable glossary of abstruse classical iconography to which, in the printed edition, he himself provided the footnotes. Some of the songs from these masks can be numbered among the gems of English lyric poetry. Only rarely, however, does the full text of a Mask commend itself to the attention of posterity. Shirley's *Cupid and Death* and Milton's *Comus* are the most notable.[1] In both, the topicality of the event is allegorized with sufficient skill for issues of lasting interest to override those of the moment. Perhaps I should say rather that the moment has here been distilled with sufficient artistry for its ultimate significance to eclipse topicality.

Milton's *Comus*, for all that literary critics have said subsequently against the title 'Mask', is the single claimant to that perfection of form that Elizabethan and Jacobean poets initially aspired to when they decided to develop the Mask's literary potential. From the Attendant Spirit's prologue to his final song, *Comus* conforms in detail to the long accepted structure of the genre. Prologue—antimask—debate—resolution by divine intervention or that of divine agency—presentation of the masquers—invitation to dance and final song.

Milton only makes one major break with precedent. He greatly extends the emphasis on the debate at the expense of the presentation of the maskers—in this instance the Country Folk of Ludlow—who then present the debaters to the audience instead of the debaters presenting the maskers. To upbraid Milton, therefore, as so many critics do on the grounds that *Comus* is 'undramatic' or 'insufficiently dramatic' is to miss the whole point. No Mask can ever again be what it first was when removed in time from the event and lacking the actual participation of the people celebrated. And where now is the dramatic impact of what was once novelty in spectacle? The plain fact is

[1] The text of *Cupid and Death* introduced by B. A. Harris is printed in *A Book of Masques*, pp. 371–99. For the music for *Comus*, see Sabol, *op. cit.*, pp. 91–9.

that *Comus* is still capable of revival and is indeed revived with a greater degree of success than any other Mask: it has also provided the scenario for a notable modern ballet. If this be granted, *Comus* may be regarded as the ultimate and solitary validation of Ben Jonson's aspiration. Civil War withdrew both the occasion and the subsidy from Masks: its technical achievements were deflected into opera in the Italian manner after the Restoration. Never again could a British monarch spend £20,000 for a single evening's entertainment. In the cost, of course, lay half the fascination of the Mask. How could anything so expensive fail to be good? We might well ask the same about television which costs as much, relatively speaking, and is just as ephemeral.

Many of Inigo Jones' costume and scenic designs still survive to ravish our eye with their elegance and sensuous richness, of which a good selection are printed in P. Simpson's and C. F. Bell's *Designs by Inigo Jones for Masques and Plays at Court* (Walpole and Malone Socs., 1924). When assessing the Mask as art, however, it is easy to allow romantic nostalgia to colour our judgement and to forget that this entertainment usually followed a banquet and was intimately associated with festivals of traditional licence. Sir John Harrington with his customary wit and directness bequeathed a pertinent reminder of this aspect of Masks to posterity.

One day, a great feast was held, and, after dinner, the representation of Solomon his Temple and the coming of the Queen of Sheba was made, or (as I may better say) was meant to have been made, before their Majesties, by device of the Earl of Salisbury and others. But alass! as all earthly thinges do fail to poor mortals in enjoyment, so did prove our presentment hereof. The Lady who did play the Queens part, did carry most precious gifts to both their Majesties; but, forgetting the steppes arising to the canopy, overset her caskets into his Danish Majesties lap, and fell at his feet, tho I rather think it was in his face. Much was the hurry and confusion; cloths and napkins were at hand, to make all clean. His Majesty then got up and would dance with the Queen of Sheba; but he fell down and humbled himself before her, and was carried to an inner chamber, and laid on a bed of state; which was not a little defiled with the presents of the Queen which had been bestowed on his garments;

such as wine, cream, jelly, beverage, cakes, spices, and other good matters. The entertainment and show went forward, and most of the presenters went backward, or fell down; wine did so occupy their upper chambers. Now did appear, in rich dress, Hope, Faith, and Charity: Hope did assay to speak, but wine rendered her endeavours so feeble that she withdrew, and hoped the King would excuse her brevity: Faith was then all alone, for I am certain she was not joyned with good works, and left the court in a staggering condition: Charity came to the King's feet, and seemed to cover the multitude of sins her sisters had committed; in some sorte she made obeysance and brought giftes, but said she would return home again, as there was no gift which heaven had not already given his Majesty. She then returned to Hope and Faith, who were both sick and spewing in the lower hall. Next came Victory, in bright armour, and presented a rich sword to the King, who did not accept it, but put it by with his hand; and, by a strange medley of versification, did endeavour to make suit to the King. But Victory did not tryumph long; for, after much lamentable utterance, she was led away like a silly captive, and laid to sleep in the outer steps of the anti-chamber. Now did Peace make entry, and strive to get foremoste to the King; but I grieve to tell how great wrath she did discover unto those of her attendants; and, much contrary to her semblance, most rudely made war with her olive branch, and laid on the pates of those who did oppose her coming.[1]

Such occurrences were probably not regular. On the other hand this account serves to warn us against supposing that all the learned imagery in words, paint and needlework was assiduously followed and construed by earnest audiences bent upon cultivating their minds. Harrington's description of the junketings at Theobalds House also highlights another important aspect of the Mask—the social one. The easy intercourse between performers and spectators traditional to the Mask is something utterly foreign to us. Accustomed as we are to sitting in reverent silence through plays, concerts, opera and ballet and to applauding only at the appointed times, it takes a sizeable effort of imagination to picture an entertainment that started around 9 p.m. and was wont to last till nearer dawn than midnight: for Masks, when all is said and done, were elaborate and

---

[1] E. K. Chambers, *The Elizabethan Stage*, i, p. 172, quoting Harrington, i, p. 349.

imaginative invitations to dance. This rooted attachment to legitimate frivolity largely explains, as I see it, the inability of the Mask to rise regularly to serious themes of moral, political or social significance. Our own experience of much humbler parties should tell us that guests who use such occasions for preaching or philosophizing are quickly shunned by their fellow-guests who hasten to escape to another room!

Since Masks were normally begotten for Royalty—frequently as performers—it was inevitable that they should have a political flavour. Additional stimulus was provided by fierce jealousies over precedence among foreign embassies. Invitations to attend, admission, and, most especially, the proximity to the King's throne of the seat assigned, took on a high diplomatic significance with repercussions that were felt far outside the Banqueting Hall. It thus happens that the State Papers of Continental countries provide more information about Masks than about plays. Ambassadorial letters, however, only serve to confirm that where politics do enter the Masks it is usually under the guise of flattery. The specious hope was entertained that by telling Princes that they were perfect, they would learn to be so. Judging by the idyllic state of government and the Elysian contentment of subjects represented in Carew's *Coelum Britannicum* (1634) or D'Avenant's *Britannia Triumphans* (1638)[1] nobody would dream that Civil War was just around the corner. Even in *Salmacida Spolia* (1640) the storm clouds of the first scene are swiftly dispersed by the appearance of the King (Wisdom) and Queen (Prudence).[2] The simple truth is that Masks were never intended to reflect life as actually lived: they reflect instead a dream of life, exquisite, elegant and free of care —dangerous only when the cost becomes disproportionate to the resources of a private purse and the dream world is re-iterated often enough for the participants to equate the fantasy with the actual. Both these dangers overtook Masks.

What then should the phrase 'the Stuart Mask' convey to us?

[1] *Coelum Britannicum* is printed by Rhodes Dunlap in *The Poems of Thomas Carew*, 1949, pp. 151–85. *Britannia Triumphans* is printed by J. Maidment and W. H. Logan in *The Dramatic Works of Sir William Davenant*, 5 vols., 1872–4, ii, pp. 247–300.

[2] Printed with a critical introduction by T. J. B. Spenser in *A Book of Masques*, pp. 337–70.

In the first place, I think it should represent the development of a long-established form of entertainment as the final resolve of a privileged élite to assert its privilege; to delight its senses to the utmost regardless of cost or discretion. The value of the Stuart Mask lay in its ability to do this by grafting music, song, words, painting and costume, with system and care onto the rootstock of festive dancing. 'These Things', said Bacon, 'are but Toys.' And considered as toys they must be numbered among the most beautiful ever devised by the wit of man. The fact that they were toys made it unlikely that they could ever aspire to serious literary potentialities—a fact which the poets who undertook to write librettos either cheerfully ignored or learnt to their despair. It behoves us therefore not to persist in judging the Mask as a dramatic form by literary standards. Few are that foolish when it comes to judging opera or ballet: yet both have the same parentage. Nor, in my opinion, is the Mask as a form defunct. Rather is it sleeping until such time as human beings can again overcome their fears that anything of which the appeal rests solely in delighting the senses must automatically be sinful; for even in the austerity Britain of 1948 a Mask proved capable of entertaining both its performers and those for whom it was performed.[1]

Last, but by no means least, the Stuart Mask represents the means by which certain changes were effected in the organization and disposition of the scenic background to English drama. That the circumstances in which these changes were effected set in train the replacement of the old theatre of poetry and visual suggestion by one of prosaic, pictorial realism was a matter of chance. Nevertheless, the development of scenic decoration in the Stuart Mask, for good or evil has made our modern theatre what it is.

[1] Nevill Coghill, *The Masque of Hope*, O.U.P., 1948. See also B. Brindley and C. Leach, *Porci Ante Margaritam, or the Muses Offering*, O.U.P., 1954.

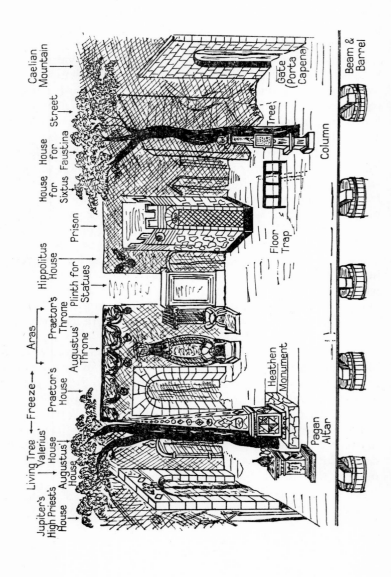

Jupiter's High Priest's House

Living Tree — Freeze — Aras

Valerius' House

Caelian Mountain

Praetor's House

Augustus' House

Hippolitus House

House for Sixtus

House for Faustina

Street

Praetor's Throne

Augustus' Throne

Prison

Plinth for Statues

Gate (Porta Capena)

Tree

Floor Trap

Heathen Monument

Pagan Altar

Column

Beam & Barrel

Section Three

Stages and Stage Directions

7

Notes on the Staging of Marlowe's Plays[1]

WHEN preparing to stage *Edward II* for the Bristol Old Vic
School in 1964 my thoughts were more immediately concerned
with the problems that the texts of Marlowe's play presented to
the actor than with those which they pose for the historian or
the critic. The first thing an actor wants to know is where and
how he makes his entrance; where and how he is to make his
exit. Confronted with a stage direction like '*Exeunt to the cave*'
or '*Enter from the cave, Aeneas and Dido*',[2] what the actor and
actress will want to know is where this cave is located on the
stage, what sort of a cave it is, how wide the opening and how
much head-room, whether it is equipped with a door or sliding
panel, and so on. An answer, of course, can be given in terms of
the set which the designer of the production in question has provided. But is this Marlowe's answer? Or, just as relevant, is the
designer rather than the director to dictate the answer? The
designer's picture, indeed the whole sequence of pictures in his
production scheme, may be admirable in its own visual context,
but it will not help the actor if it ignores or is divorced in time
and spirit from the context of Marlowe's dramatic imagination.

---

[1] Reprinted from *Tulane Drama Review*, vol. 8, no. 4, 1964, Marlowe Issue.
[2] Marlowe's *The Tragedy of Dido, Queen of Carthage*, Acts III and IV.

How are we to know what that was? We may perhaps approach an answer via reconstruction of such early public playhouses as the Theatre or the Curtain: but we have no picture of the interior of either. De Witt's sketch of the Swan is not strictly admissible as evidence since that playhouse was not built and the drawing not made until after Marlowe's death. We may perhaps approach an answer by literal interpretation of the stage directions in the printed texts: but, as modern editors are agreed that the texts, as we have them, differ from those used by the actors at first performances by reason of corruption in the course of censorship and publishing, this too is hazardous. Nor is an unfettered appeal to the director's imagination going to produce a better result, especially when the director (as is likely to be the case) is a scholar and not an artist by profession.

By whichever of these routes, therefore, we approach the problem of what stage-action Marlowe himself envisaged, we might as well be honest and admit that we shall not get very far without encountering obstacles and recognize that these obstacles must necessarily arise as a result of our own ignorance: from this point forward any calculations will be flawed by some degree of speculation.

Suppose that we make our first assault along the route offered by architectural reconstruction of stage and auditorium: how far do we get? The widest range of dates for the composition of his plays within which we can work is 1586–93. Where public playhouses are concerned, this restricts us to the Theatre (built 1576), the Curtain (built 1577), that at Newington Butts, and the Rose which was begun in 1587 and on which work was still proceeding as late as 1595. If we assume that any of Marlowe's plays were performed at the Rose in his lifetime, then the assumption must exclude the use of a throne in 'the heavens' since Henslowe himself records in the Diary that this was not installed until June 1595. Quite clearly then what we have to reckon with is a number of game-houses or play-houses, none of which was either legally or financially the exclusive property of any one acting company. The financial speculators who had lent the money needed to meet the cost of erecting these buildings shared the right to determine the nature of the entertainment presented in them: and the words 'game' and 'play' were not so circumscribed in their meaning as to imply stage-plays only.[1] A trestle-stage and tiring-room, both of which were removable and set down within a circular or polygonal 'frame' or tiered auditorium, is thus a virtually obligatory postulate. When we seek to define the appearance of this unit pertaining to the actors within the playhouse, since we lack pictorial evidence from within the period, we are forced to look either forward to 1596 and De Witt's sketch of the Swan Theatre or backwards in time to the banquet-hall stages which were the normal habitat of the professional acting companies in Tudor times. The latter provide us with a raised stage backed by a screen with one or (more frequently) two doors in it and a gallery above it.[2] Reference to the De Witt sketch provides us with a picture that resembles this mental image very closely. (See Fig. 4, p. 213.) Reference to the Revels Office Accounts or to the last decades of the religious drama indicates that actors and public alike were still familiar with and content to accept emblems of locality placed on and about their stages to identify the scene of action. Reference to the inventory of theatrical possessions held by the Lord Admiral's company at the Rose in 1598 shows that this company at least—and Edward Alleyn is the link between the company and Christopher Marlowe—possessed emblems of locality of this kind. And that, I think, is as far as we may safely go along the route of architectural reconstruction. It suffices, however, to establish:

i. A raised (but removable) stage platform.
ii. A dressing-room immediately behind the stage (*not* under it).
iii. A wooden or canvas partition between stage and dressing-room with two doors in it and a terrace above.
iv. A number of scenic emblems used as and when specified by the play-maker on the stage itself.
v. No throne with winch mechanism for ascents or descents as yet.

---

[1] See G. Wickham, *Early English Stages*, ii(1), pp. 158–72. [2] *Ibid.*, pp. 196–205.

vi. Probably no permanent 'heavens' or supporting pillars, with the possible exception of the Rose.

Let us now set out along the second route, that of the stage directions within the printed texts of the plays as they have come down to us. I must state at once that in my opinion this is the mistiest route of the three since at no point can we be precise about whose stage directions they actually are— author's, prompter's, actor's memory, printer's or editor's.[1] Two examples of such dangers in the context of Marlowe's plays must suffice. First we know that *The Jew of Malta*, although frequently acted in the 1590's and entered in the Stationer's Register in 1594, remained in MS. till 1633, when it was published with prologues and epilogues by Heywood after performances at court and at the Cockpit.[2] We have no justification whatsoever therefore in regarding the stage directions governing the famous cauldron scene of Act V as being those literally applicable in Marlowe's lifetime. Secondly, in the printed text of *Dr. Faustus* a throne is said to ascend and descend in the Quarto edition of 1616, but no such stage directions exist in the Quarto of 1604. The scene in which Benvolio appears at an upstairs window (III, iv of the 1616 ed.) is again not present in the 1604 edition. Bearing in mind the fact therefore that *Tamburlaine* alone of Marlowe's plays was published in his lifetime, we must move with especial care when seeking to establish anything about the physical appearance of public theatres from the stage directions.

With these caveats before us, however, it is still possible to compare the information obtainable from the stage directions with those elements of knowledge derived from architectural reconstruction. A reasonable starting point is the generalized kind of stage direction: 'Enter', 'Exit', 'From within', or 'Enter at one door . . ., from another . . .' Directions of this sort, because of their frequency and unparticularized nature, postulate little more than a screen dividing the acting area from the changing-room area. 'Within' serves however to enlarge and

---

[1] See G. F. Reynolds, *The Staging of Elizabethan Plays at the Red Bull Theater, 1605–1625*, pp. 33–51.
[2] See Essay 9, pp. 151–62 below.

define the changing-room area since it provides us with an image of a person or persons concealed from the sight of both actors on the stage and spectators, and thus 'screened' from the general view. Similarly, the direction 'Enter from one door . . . from another . . .' adds definition to this screen since it supplies a mental image of at least two practicable doors set in door frames within the screen. The generalized direction 'Enter' or 'Exit' then takes on the guise of a norm or constant, entry to the stage from the dressing-room or departure to the dressing-room from the stage through one or other of the doors in the screen. The implication of this simple conclusion is that the playmaker must (and will) specify either within the dialogue or in a stage direction any entry or exit that is to be made in a different or *abnormal* manner. Marlowe's plays provide us with several examples of these abnormalities; the discovery, the chariot, the ascending and descending throne and, last but not least, the strange direction in *Dido, Queen of Carthage*, 'Exeunt into the cave.' One such abnormality, however, which one might anticipate but does not find, is any reference to entrance or exit through a trap in the stage floor. Even those most cherished of illusions, the rising of Mephistophilis from out of the centre of the circle prescribed by the conjuring Faustus and the descent of Faustus to Hell through that same hole in the floor have no foundation whatsoever in the stage directions of either the 1604 Quarto or that of 1616. In both editions, Mephistophilis is said simply to 'enter'; and, at the close, both editions carry the direction, 'Exeunt Devils with Faustus.'

This fact is to me so startling that I feel it needs closer investigation. There is in fact one word within the dialogue which does *suggest* the existence of a trap; it is the Latin *surgat* which occurs twice in Faustus' invocation to Mephistophilis: it is present in both Quartos. For all that, however, Faustus, in addressing his first line to Mephistophilis after he has 'entered', charges him to 'return' and change his shape: 'descend' would scan but is not used. Instead we get the direction 'Exit Mephistophilis', followed eight lines later (1604), five lines later (1616), with the direction, 'Re-enter Mephistophilis like a Franciscan friar.'

Turning now to the close of the play, Faustus after stating that he has 'but one bare hour to live' cries out,

'O, I'll leap up to my God!—Who pulls me down?'

This phrase, like the word *surgat* in the context of the summoning of Mephistophilis, might suggest the existence of a trap in the floor; in other words, that Faustus is sinking through the floor at that moment: yet not only has he got fifty lines to speak before his 'exit', but he himself succinctly gives the lie to any such idea. 'Earth gape!' he cries; but this precisely is what it will not do.

Whatever one's reactions to this analysis, the fact must be faced that in none of Marlowe's plays do any stage-directions exist authorizing us to assume the existence of a stage-trap at floor level: the two Quartos of Faustus merely conform with the printed texts of all his other plays in this respect. Granted this premise, so calculated an avoidance of floor-trap scenes would seem to argue a conscious awareness on Marlowe's part that such scenes were to be avoided. We cannot know what occasioned this inhibition in the play-maker; but acknowledging its existence goes some way to confirming the impression which we derived from architectural reconstruction that the early play-houses were equipped with removable trestle-stages. Such stages would of themselves make floor-trap scenes an undesirable element within a play.

If Marlowe's plays lack floor-trap scenes, they do contain evidence in text and stage-directions of upper-level scenes. These are to be found in 2 *Tamburlaine*, *The Jew of Malta*, *Dr. Faustus* (1616 Quarto only) and *The Massacre at Paris*. As I have already stated, the text of *The Jew* was printed after performance at the Cockpit and under Heywood's aegis in 1633 and cannot therefore be used as evidence for stage conditions in the late 1580's or early 1590's.[1] The same applies to the 'window' scene and the descending throne in the 1616 edition of *Dr. Faustus* (III, iv). This leaves us with two scenes: 2 *Tamburlaine* (V, i) and *The Massacre* (I, v and vii). These two scenes are not directly comparable. The former deals with the siege of a city;

---

[1] See *Plates VI* and *IX*.

PLATE XI

15   Hell-castle as represented in the Doom, formerly in fresco on the church arch in the Chapel of the Holy Cross, Stratford-on-Avon.

PLATE XII

16 CORIOLANUS
Roman Baths, Bath Assembly, 1952. Cominius (James Grout)
attempts to calm the Roman mob (Act III, scene 1).
Production: Glynne Wickham   Photo: Roger Gilmour

the latter with a murder in an upstairs bedroom: 2 *Tamburlaine* (V, i) starts in Babylon 'upon the walls'; at line 25 'Enter, above, a Citizen . . .'; at line 37, 'Enter, above, a Second Citizen'; Tamburlaine's soldiers simply 'enter' (i.e. at stage level) and then, at line 62, 'they scale the walls'. Tamburlaine then enters himself in his chariot and watches the siege. The soldiers then 're-enter' with the Governor of Babylon as their prisoner. Sixty lines later they 'exeunt' together and thirty lines after that, 'The Governor of Babylon appears hanging in chains on the walls.' He is then and there used as an archery butt. To add to the fun, a bonfire is kindled on the stage.

This scene could be played as it stands in the text in terms of the terrace or gallery that formed the ceiling above the changing-room: alternatively, it could be played on that scenic property known as the 'battlement' which is illustrated for us in the Florentine *Naumachia* of 1589,[1] described for us in detail in the English *Wagner Book*,[2] and which figures so frequently in the Revels Office Accounts of the 1580's.[3] (See *Plate IV*.)

The scenes in *The Massacre* (I, v and vii) take place inside and in front of a house. King Charles visits the Admiral who is 'discovered in bed'. Charles leaves and 'The scene closes'. Immediately the Dukes of Guise and Anjou and their retinue 'enter'. The setting is localized in the dialogue as a street. As presented in the existing corrupt text the detail of the action which follows is confused, but the gist of it is that a group of Anjou's retinue led by Gonzago enter the Admiral's house, murder him in his bed and throw his body down to Anjou and Guise below.

This scene, like 2 *Tamburlaine* (V, i), could be played either above and before the changing-room or in terms of a scenic emblem representing a house instead of a city or 'battlement'. It is significant, however, that within less than ten lines of the end of this scene we are faced with the stage direction, 'Enter Mountsorrell, and knocks at Seroune's door.' Four lines later Seroune enters 'from the house' and is stabbed. Mountsorrell exits and there follows the stage-direction, 'Enter Ramus, in

---

[1] See *Early English Stages*, ii(1), pp. 265.   [2] *Ibid.*, pp. 314–15.
[3] *Ibid.*, pp. 286–9.

his study.'[1] Warned to flee by Talaeus, Ramus cries, 'I'll leap out at the window,' but does not do so. Mountsorrell enters again with Guise, Anjou and others. Anjou kills Ramus and then proceeds within the space of ten lines to 'knock at the door' of the King of Navarre's house where further murders are despatched. Thus four separate houses are presented to the audience within a hundred lines of dialogue, two at least of which involve interior scenes. Such speed and complexity of stage-action is almost impossible to conceive in terms of *one* house, i.e. the dressing-room with its two doors and terrace: for even though it allows the initial 'discovery', the requisite upper-level and two independent entrances, the strain placed upon the credulity of spectators who are asked to accept this one locality as the four separate houses in question is absurd. The case for emblematic 'houses' used in conjunction with the dressing-room area is here a strong one. It is worth adding that if either the Admiral's house or Ramus's house were an independent scenic unit, so too could Barabas' house have been in *The Jew of Malta*, for he, like the Admiral, is 'discovered': the Admiral is 'in bed', Barabas 'in his counting-house, with heaps of gold before him'.

From the evidence of the stage-directions discussed thus far, therefore, it is clear that upper-level scenes did not figure largely in Marlowe's mind. This inclines me to believe that such scenes must have been accompanied with severe disadvantages of a practical or financial kind so to outweigh their obvious theatrical attractiveness. The most likely explanation is that the tiring-house of the early play-houses was structurally unsuited to such scenes while practicable two-storey scenic emblems were expensive, cumbersome and difficult to transport on tour. Both methods were possible, but neither was popular with the company managers. The evidence of the stage-directions is slightly stronger in support of emblematic devices: for while there is no other indication that the roof of the dressing-room was pressed into service by actors or play-makers, other emblems are positively called for in nearly all of Marlowe's plays. The simplest of them is Bazajet's cage in I *Tamburlaine*,

[1] Faustus is also presented 'in his study'.

IV, ii and iv, and V, i: 2 *Tamburlaine*, IV, i requires a tent: 'Amyras and Celebinus issue from the tent where Calyphas sits asleep.' They talk, Amyras instructing Celebinus to 'call forth our lazy brother from the tent'. The tent is needed throughout the scene, but there is no suggestion that it is either put up as the scene begins or struck as it closes: the inference is that it is in position on the stage throughout the play and used when required.

Dido, Queen of Carthage starts, like *The Jew*, with a discovery. 'Here the curtains draw: there is discovered Jupiter, . . .' etc. The scene is not localized either in the directions or the dialogue. The presumption is that the action is so self-evidently set in heaven as to make description of the sort provided in *The Jew* superfluous. Jupiter, Hermes and Ganymede exit leaving Venus on the stage alone. When Aeneas enters she says to the audience, 'Here in this bush disguised will I stand.' Thirty lines later Aeneas speaks of 'these woods'. Another reference, if less direct, is made to the woods at the start of the hunting scene in Act III (line 282). That the bush-cum-woods of Act I and the woods of Act III are the same, however, is made clear in the text by Achates who informs Aeneas (line 330) that it was 'here we met fair Venus'.

In *The Massacre* the bush is raised to the dignity of a tree. There it is used to string up the headless corpse of the Admiral, the stage direction being confirmed by the dialogue. As in *Dido*, the tree is swiftly converted into 'woods' (II, ii, 22) where, in the subsequent scene, a group of Huguenots are ambushed and massacred.

Dido, in addition to 'woods', presupposes both the walls of Carthage (II, 63) and the cave, to which reference has already been made in which, during the storm, Dido and Aeneas declare their love for each other.

Edward II is the most economical of Marlowe's plays in its scenic directions and difficult on that very account to visualize. London, Tynemouth, Scarborough, Killingworth and Berkeley come and go like places glimpsed in a mist, briefly referred to in the dialogue but seldom reinforced with any hint of three-dimensional objects on the stage. A bed, table and brazier are required for the King's murder and a throne in I, iv. This throne however is not said to descend from above the stage like that in the *Faustus* Quarto of 1616: but then *Edward II* was written, played and probably printed before Henslowe installed a throne in the 'heavens' of the Rose.

How far then have we got in terms of architectural reconstruction coupled with a survey of stage directions? Far enough at least to recognize that Marlowe's public playhouses were still related to those of the religious drama and the banquet chamber and not yet as malleable to the playmaker's or actor's will as Jacobean theatres were destined to be. Broadly speaking, not more than one 'spectacular' scene could be carried by the resources of the company in any one play. Most of these scenes demand of the company something more by way of devices to identify place than the stage itself together with the changing-room could provide. All such supplementary devices—tent, trees, cave, throne, battlement, house or study—were traditional items in the recently suppressed religious plays and still in current manufacture in the Revels Office for entertainments at Court: stage machinery, however, although familiar enough in both those contexts, is conspicuously absent in Marlowe's plays even in what I have described as 'spectacular' scenes. For this there must be some reason: and my suggestion is that at least up to the time of his death in 1593 the public playhouses were not well enough equipped to permit its installation. With the building of the Rose and the Swan this situation began to change in the actors' and the playmakers' interest: but that takes us outside the period allowed to us.

There remains the approach that opens itself to us if we choose to put any of Marlowe's plays into rehearsal and production. And this approach at once highlights a point hitherto neglected: it is the extraordinary pace at which the action moves in every play. Events are telescoped with frenzied haste. In consequence the reader of these plays gains the impression that they are poorly constructed, oscillating unevenly between rhetorical scenes of sustained poetic brilliance combined with perceptive character delineation on the one hand and sketchy linking devices on the other. Literary criticism knows no way round this difficulty. I venture to suggest that the opera critic would know better; for few indeed are the operatic librettos which follow any other pattern: and what, in the libretto, looks like a lazy linking device takes on an altogether different air in the theatre when filled out with its full orchestral accompaniment. So too, where Marlowe is concerned, I think we must make greater allowance than is usually admitted for the ritualistic quality of the theatre in which he worked. The coming and goings of his princes, lords and captains which in the text *read* bleakly enough, take on a very different character *on the stage* when seen in their full context of costume, colour and movement. Absorbed as we are in this spectacle, shifting and changing solemnly or kaleidoscopically before our eyes, we have not time to notice, let alone to ponder, the abruptness of a change of locale or the short-circuiting of time itself. All this provides the orchestration which underlies the verbal linking of one great aria to the next. And Marlowe, as I believe, was writing con-sciously for voices, in a way that few other English dramatists have dared to. His lines were 'mighty' on the tongue and in the ears of his contemporaries, not on the printed page. Speed of delivery and action coupled with a firm grasp of rhythm are essential pre-requisites for any realization of the effects aimed at. These go hand in hand with an emblematic stage that is simple enough to allow swift-moving action while still being supplied with scenic devices sufficient to identify each shift of locality within the action for the spectator. Carried at this pace by the actors, an audience can well be swept with Tamburlaine through Asia, with the Duc de Guise through the streets and suburbs of Paris as murders multiply into a massacre, with Edward II through the nightmare of the torture chamber, or even with Faustus through the sky itself to heaven and hell. If Marlowe in his life and imagination was passion's slave, as is generally admitted, then his theatre was perhaps more nearly passion's servant than is generally allowed.

8

Shakespeare's Stage

LIKE many other parents, my wife and I have on several occasions been entertained by our children to something which they called a play. A few years ago when the children were aged respectively eight, five and three, they summoned us one evening to watch an epic, historical drama in three acts entitled 'People through the Ages'. Act I was called 'Early People'. A wing chair with a rug thrown over it represented, we were told, a cave in which an Early Man and an Early Woman were then living. The man went off hunting leaving the woman alone. Immediately there appeared a diminutive Indian brave, armed with bow and arrow, who shot at the woman. The arrow went wide of its mark, but the woman shrieked and gesticulated in a manner which left us in no doubt that she had been wounded. The man returned and shot the Indian with his gun, saying he knew that guns weren't invented yet: he ought to be throwing stones, but he thought that would be dangerous.

Then followed 'The Middle People'. In this Act it was explained that a wicked man had imprisoned a beautiful girl in a castle. The chair which had represented the cave in Act I was now stripped of its rug and represented a castle: the girl stood on the seat. When the wicked man went out to get food for his prisoner, there entered a man in armour as diminutive, it must be said, as the erstwhile Indian brave. He charged the castle with his pogo-stick lance and released the fair prisoner. We were then taken into the future to meet 'Space People'. The girl, standing on another chair, blew bubbles from a bubble-stick: these, we were told, represented the galaxy. Into this cloud of soapy stars there entered two spacemen on their rockets. The very small spaceman, on seeing the galaxy, decided that this was a greater enemy than his rival spaceman and started to belabour it. The other spaceman followed suit; so the drama ended with a splendid crash which toppled the bubble-blower off her chair and got rid of both spacemen and the galaxy at once.

I have called this infantile drama 'a play'. A better name for it might seem to be 'a game'—until of course we realize that both words, play and game, are English translations of the Anglo-Saxon word *plèga* or, indeed, of the Latin word *ludus*. In Tudor England both words—game and play—could still be used virtually as synonymous. The precise nature of the game or play had then normally to be specified by the prefix or suffix attached to it—May-Game, King-Game and so on; sword-play, mummers' play, stage-play, etc. In the same way the Anglo-Saxon *plèg-stòw* or *plèg-hùs* became in Tudor England game-place or play-place, or, as we might say, the recreation-ground: *plèg-hùs* became game-house or play-house. And as a playhouse came to be regarded more or less exclusively as a place for the performance of stage-plays, so the word play-house gradually gave way to the word Theatre—a word which in the 1570's was only being used as a self-conscious latinism to describe one particular playhouse which actors had helped to finance and build. As late however as 1613, the year in which the Globe Playhouse was rebuilt after the fire of 1612, the impresario Philip Henslowe in contracting with the builder Gilbert Katherens to construct the Hope, refers to the building throughout the contract as 'this Gamehouse or Playhouse' and never as 'this Theatre'.[1]

It is in a context therefore much nearer to game or recreation that we must regard the Elizabethan stage-play and the

See *Early English Stages*, ii(1).

playhouse that contained it than to the context which the word drama prescribes for us today with its extensions into opera, ballet, films and television. All these dramatic genres of modern times evoke images that are essentially pictorial. Drama for the Elizabethan Englishman was still the stage-play and, as such, much more firmly rooted in the imaginative context of children's games and the poetic context of the actor's and play-maker's art than the pictorial world of the architect, painter, stage machinist and the electronic engineer. Perhaps I can illustrate this point by reference once again to the children's game which I described. In each of the three tableaux presented, the children found it necessary to identify the place of their make-believe action. In the first, a chair and rug served to present a cave; in the second this same chair, stripped of its rug and with the seat called into use, served to present an upper room in a castle; in the third a stream of soap bubbles represented a galaxy of stars. All this is childish in the extreme, absurd by strictly rational standards. Nevertheless, as devices they succeeded in doing exactly what they were intended to do and with a minimum of fuss: identifying the scene of the action. Each of the three devices used was strictly emblematic: and there is a world of difference between employing an emblematic convention to identify place and abstaining from using any scenic convention at all.

Now it is often said that the Elizabethan dramatist dispensed with scenery, relying exclusively upon the imagery of his verse to keep his audience 'in the picture' as it were. Shakespeare's imagery was both precise and sustained. But this does not mean that he and his actors were enabled on that account to eliminate all other means of identifying the locality of the stage action for their audiences. The notion that an empty stage served their turn is one which I would wish to contest vigorously since it stems from an approach to dramatic literature which is blind to the essential nexus linking game and art in drama. In short, it fails to distinguish between poetry and dramatic poetry. If William Shakespeare was a poet he was also an actor—an actor moreover in a company which in its structure and relationships resembled a large family. His poetic imagination therefore was inextricably linked to the dramatic imagination of the company he served and who owned the copyright in every play he wrote. What I have here called the company's dramatic imagination embraced tradition, the physical conditions of the playhouses in which it worked, the particular vocal and mimetic accomplishments of the individual members of the company and, last but not least, a close working knowledge of audience behaviour. If therefore we are to understand Shakespeare's dramatic technique we must take account of these facts and try to get to grips with a Shakespeare play in the conditions in which it was written and performed; for these conditions unquestionably informed the creative art of writing—more precisely of 'making'—his plays as intimately as the sort of tools and machines an engineer uses affect the final shape and efficiency of the product he invents and constructs. It is this factor which separates an Isambard Brunel from a maker of pre-fabricated houses, or, as *dramatic* poets, Shakespeare from Shelley or Browning: they inhabit different worlds.

In seeking therefore to put ourselves in touch with Shakespeare the play-maker—the complete dramatic artist and not simply the poet—the safest starting point is Johannes de Witt's sketch of the Swan Theatre. This was only discovered in the Library of the University of Utrecht as recently as 1888 (see Fig. 4, p. 213). No other picture is known to survive representing the interior of any playhouse built in London during Shakespeare's lifetime.

The Swan Theatre, erected as a business speculation, opened its doors to the public in 1596. De Witt visited London that year: the sketch at Utrecht, however, is not the original but a copy made for or by a friend, Arnold van Buchel, in what we might call a commonplace book or diary. While therefore this picture does not have the authority it would possess had it been drawn by, say, Richard Burbage or Ben Jonson, there is no reason to doubt the accuracy of the principal features it depicts: and, in the absence of any other picture, it must in any case be regarded as the most reliable evidence we possess. Moreover, particular features of the sketch are corroborated by other Elizabethan and Jacobean documents. The most important of these are the builders' contract for the Fortune Theatre (1600) and for the Hope Theatre (1613), maps and views of London which include theatres, and the vivid verbal description of conditions in the auditorium of a public theatre which Thomas Dekker provides in *The Gull's Hornbook* (1609). This is addressed to the young man about town and necessarily includes a visit to a playhouse. If a gallant wishes to be taken for a man of consequence then let him, says Dekker, 'presently advance himself up to the throne of the stage . . . on the very rushes where the comedy is to dance. . . . By sitting on the stage', he argues, 'you may . . . ask whose play it is; and, . . . if you know not the author, you may rail against him; and peradventure so behave yourself, that you may enforce the author to know you.'[1] Always arrive late, says Dekker. 'Present not yourself on the stage, especially at a new play, until the quaking Prologue hath by rubbing got colour into his cheeks, and is ready to give the trumpets their cue that he's upon point to enter. . . . It shall crown you with rich commendation to laugh aloud in the midst of the most serious and saddest scene of the terriblest tragedy.' Such behaviour will ensure that 'all eyes in the galleries will leave walking after the players, and only follow you'. It is in conditions of such general noise, movement and frequent rudeness that Shakespeare and his fellow actors had to strive for a hearing. We would have to try to present a play at a Greyhound Stadium in between races or in the cabaret spot at a rugger club dance to encounter an equivalent atmosphere today; though Italian opera in the open air in Italy can sometimes provide similar sensations.

Since Shakespeare wrote most of his plays for a company which, after 1598, had a proprietary interest in the Globe Playhouse more attention has been focused upon this building than any other. It is unfortunate therefore that so many of the scholars who have attempted to reconstruct it, either in the form of models or in speculative essays, should have chosen to give far greater weight to their own wishes and hypotheses than to de Witt's testimony. Nowhere has this wilful distortion of the evidence had more serious consequences than in the resulting

[1] Ed. R. B. McKerrow, n.d., pp. 49–55.

mental image of the structure and function of the tiring-house or dressing-room area at the back of the stage.

We see it as an integral part of the circular (or polygonal) galleries of the auditorium and equipped at stage level with a curtained recess for which we have even invented a name—an 'inner' stage. De Witt, by contrast, shows us a tiring-house (*mimorum aedes*) that stands out from the galleries behind it and that is equipped with two doors and a gallery, but no alcove, recess or 'inner stage'. The gallery above the tiring-house is quite independent of the galleries that make up the frame. There can be no shirking these facts: either we accept them as facts, or we join the large brotherhood of inventors and fabricate a theatre of our own imagining. If we choose to adopt the latter course there is no point in any further discussion: if, on the other hand, we choose to face up to the facts of the de Witt drawing, two important consequences follow. First, we must regard the stage and tiring house as a unit in itself, and independent in design, construction and use from the architectural frame of the auditorium. Secondly, we must think of such normal dramatic features of Elizabethan and Jacobean plays as 'dumb shows' and 'discoveries' in some context other than that of the non-existent 'inner stage'.[1]

Before we attempt to do this, however, we must take account of another fact which is just as important in its implications. We have been thinking so far of what are generally known as Public Theatres. Our knowledge that Shakespeare's company had a proprietary interest in one of these theatres, the Globe, and that Shakespeare himself derived a part of his income in the form of box office receipts (a return for his own capital investment in this building) can easily blind us to the fact that this same company performed its stock repertory of plays on other stages. The company bought the Blackfriars Theatre in 1596 and used it regularly in the winter months from 1608 onwards; it was called upon to perform its plays in the banqueting halls of a variety of royal palaces; and at those times when acting in London was forbidden on account of plague, the

[1] See Essay 9, p. 156–61 below: also D. Mehl, *The Elizabethan Dumb Show*, 1965.

137

company was obliged to tour the provinces. Actors who have to earn a living in these conditions must adopt a flexible attitude to the physical conditions in which performances are given, or starve. It is absurd therefore for us to reconstruct in our mind's eye a Globe Theatre, or any other metropolitan public play-house, which is so rigid in its architectural design as to forbid the plays written for performance in it to be satisfactorily presented in any other conditions. To do so carries with it a disregard for factual evidence which is just as mischievous as distorting the de Witt sketch to suit our own ends. The starting point of any intelligent discussion of Shakespeare's stage there-fore must be the actors for whom he wrote his plays, who interpreted them originally to people as far apart geographically as London from Chester, or York from Bristol and socially as widely separated in rank and personal income as the sovereign and the meanest commoner.[1]

Elizabeth I and James I commanded these actors to attend before them at Whitehall, Greenwich or at Hampton Court: the City apprentice and the farm labourer paid his penny and took time off (often as an absentee) to stand in the yard of the Globe or on the floor of the local guildhall to see the same play. The actors were professionals. From the sovereign they received hospitality and a gratuity for the entertainment provided. In any provincial town they could expect the same treatment from the Mayor and Aldermen at the first performance: sub-sequently they charged gate money as they did in their Lon-don houses. The ticket money was of secondary importance to the financial prospects for the future which a reputation, enhanced by this honour, was likely to secure. Public per-formances were strictly geared to the box-office returns.

Taking account of Shakespeare's commercial interest in his theatre as actor, playmaker and property owner in no way diminishes the artistic or literary value of his work: it serves only to place his plays as works imagined and written down for actors to perform and for audiences to hear and to view in the context in which he was himself employed by the Burbage family. This is a safer context in which today to discuss the first

[1] See Essay 3, pp. 42-3 above.

productions of his plays by James Burbage and his sons, Richard and Cuthbert, than any modern context embracing, as it must, orchestra pits, proscenium arches, scenery and the other devices of stage naturalism, which combine to substitute an image of a style of theatre that is the antithesis of the multi-purpose game-house of Shakespeare's day.

One of the first advantages of viewing Shakespeare's stage within the professional context of which he was himself a part, instead of restricting our vision to an architectural or a literary context alone, is that it allows us to look at the Globe not only as simply one among many stages and auditoriums available to actors in his lifetime, but as an integral part of a natural process of theatrical development from a style of performance that we label for convenience 'mediaeval' towards another which we describe as 'Restoration'. Both of these styles of theatrical presentation are familiar enough in a variety of pictures. Of the two examples I have chosen to include here (Fig. 3, p. 118), the first represents a typical religious play, the plot of which narrates the life and martyrdom of St. Lawrence: it is dated 1581. Its form is that of a chronicle play, just as the Miracle Cycles are abbreviated chronicles of the history of the world, and bears comparison with those chronicles of more modern history represented by Marlowe's *Edward II* or Shake-speare's 'histories'. The other picture (*Plate XV*) shows the proscenium arch and one of the landscape scenes designed by Inigo Jones for *The Mask of Florimène* (1636); but it could just as well serve to illustrate one of those quasi-operatic plays adapted by D'Avenant and Dryden from Shakespeare and set to music by Purcell such as *The Tempest* (1670) or *Macbeth* (1673).

If we now compare these two illustrations, it will at once be seen that while the two styles, 'mediaeval' and 'Restoration', which they exemplify are noticeably different, neither is notably more or less spectacular than the other. Both provide the spectator with much to look at. In the Jones design we have something which we can at once recognize as stage scenery: sky, trees, fields and cottages are there and so set out in relation to one another as to provide us with a representation of a rural landscape. Only the fore-stage with its steps into the auditorium and the proscenium arch tells us that it is a landscape artificially constructed in canvas, wood and paint and not a real one. The setting for the St. Lawrence play is not so familiar to us in style, nor can we recognize so easily what it represents. True, there is plenty to look at—two trees, two thrones, an obelisk, an altar, a number of doors in a wall and so on: but perhaps our first reaction is to ask why so many curious objects should be assembled together on the stage. Yet the boards, and the barrels which support them, tell us just as plainly as does Inigo Jones' proscenium arch in the *Florimène* design that this is a stage prepared for a play. Both pictures therefore have three factors in common: neither is an actual scene, both being manufactured by artifice: both provide the playgoer with plenty to look at: both set out to identify the locality of the play's action, one in a landscape-artist's terms of reference, the other in terms of a collection of objects with particular associations. The latter can be fairly described as symbols or, perhaps better, as emblems. Yet Jones' woodland scene, being constructed and not real, is also an emblem; a picture appropriate to the scene, not the scene itself.

Here lies the crux of the matter. Nothing about a play is real; it is all make-believe, pretence. The characters are not real persons, but actors temporarily personifying them; the dialogue is not real speech, but words attributed to the characters by the author; the scene is never the setting proper to the events, only a suitable approximation. This is as true of Elizabethan or Jacobean plays as it is of plays of the mediaeval or Restoration periods. If therefore we assume that Elizabethan and Jacobean plays were presented to audiences of that time devoid of scenic background we shall be breaking the natural law of the theatre; rather should we assume, unless we have strong evidence to the contrary, that the conditions known to have existed both before and after the Elizabethan and Jacobean era existed also in the period between. In other words, our proper course of action is to proceed from a premise which accepts a manufactured setting of some sort approximating, in terms of the conventions of the period, to the scene or scenes prescribed by the stage action, and then attempt to define what these conventions were. Where Tudor England is concerned, much more information survives concerning these scenic conditions than has generally been admitted. Several religious plays have come down to us, like the German St. Lawrence play, which tell us in their stage directions what scenic equipment was needed in performance and how it was arranged on the stage. Of these the Passion and St. Anne plays from Lincoln (better known as the *Ludus Coventriae*) and the plays of Mary Magdalene and St. Paul in the Digby Manuscript are the fullest. We possess the list of equipment, if not the text, of a play of Tobias and the Angel, also from Lincoln. This list includes three separate 'cities', a tomb or monument, two 'palaces', two 'houses', heaven, hell and a prison. The list is dated 1584—a mere three years later than the St. Lawrence play. These were all large three-dimensional objects which at that time were being stored in case they should be needed again.

Now if we turn to the Accounts kept by the Master of the Revels between 1558 and 1603 we find not only that all these same scenic items—palaces, cities, tombs and so on—are listed there together with many others—rocks, arbours, castles, battlements, senate houses and the like—but that these were constructed to equip plays which were performed before the Queen by the leading acting companies of the time, including Shakespeare's. (See *Early English Stages*, ii(1), pp. 206–44.)

If it is argued that what was required for religious plays on the one hand and for performances in royal banqueting halls on the other does not reflect the tastes of popular audiences in the public theatres, then we can produce the even fuller records of the London Livery Companies concerning the scenic properties made to equip the annual Lord Mayor's Shows. Again it is a story of mountains, tombs, arbours and the other familiar emblems of both the religious stage and the Revels Office. If we add to this the fact that many of these same emblems figure in a list of equipment belonging to Edward Alleyn's company of actors which has survived among Henslowe's Papers and is dated 1598, the picture is virtually complete.

In short, Elizabethans expected *all* dramatic performances to be accompanied with *some* scenic equipment. The purpose of this equipment was twofold: to identify the place of the stage-action and to delight the eye. It was not thought necessary to co-ordinate these several emblems into a picture of a real landscape or to arrange for place to be represented in terms of a sequence of landscapes, one following upon another. Not until Inigo Jones started to work on the Court Masks in 1604 was any attempt made to do either of these things. It then took him thirty years to evolve a system of changeable scenery of the kind that is depicted in his design for *Florimène*. Shakespeare witnessed the early attempts in this direction in the last ten years of his life, but neither he nor any of his fellow actors attempted to copy it. When the Globe was burnt down in 1613 it was immediately rebuilt, but as a virtual replica of its former self and not in imitation of the proscenium-arched stage of the Whitehall Masks. The reasons are clear enough. Scenery of the kind illustrated in the design for *Florimène* (*Plate XV*) had to have a theatre specially built to contain it and this would at once deprive the actors of the opportunity to perform their plays in any place other than this one theatre. If obliged to work under a restriction of this kind, no Elizabethan or Jacobean acting company could hope to remain solvent for long, depending as these actors did for the greatest part of their income on ease of movement from one playing-place to another both in London and the provinces. It is to be noted therefore that when after 1660 theatres were built at Covent Garden and Drury Lane incorporating changeable scenery, provincial touring was not resumed.

The traditional emblematic method of stage-decoration, however, was ideally suited to the working conditions of such a company as Shakespeare's. Granted the basic stock of emblems any repertory of plays could be played anywhere. A tomb, for example, is a basic requirement for Christ's Resurrection, or the Raising of Lazarus, whether these plays be performed on a Pageant-wagon or in a *plèg-stòw* or round (as in Cornwall) or on a single fixed stage as at Lincoln. It also meets the needs of the stage directions of *Romeo and Juliet* or *Antony and Cleopatra*. The opening stage direction of Robert Greene's *King James the Fourth* (c. 1591) tells us moreover that a tomb is to be placed *on* the stage. At this point in the play it is used by a character called Bohun and his two sons: later in the play, with a different inscription hung upon it, the same tomb serves as grave and monument for King Cyrus. Dido's tomb and Guido's tomb both figure in the Henslowe/Alleyn property list of 1598 In other plays this emblem can serve just as well to represent a cave: as such it meets the requirements of a play like *Macbeth* (when it accommodates the witches) or *Cymbeline* (where it accommodates Belarius and his two sons). Such a tomb-cave can even do double duty in extremity for a rock, hill or mountain. All that is required to effect this change is some kind of painted door or curtain to cover (and thus shut) the normal cave opening. This technique forms the basis of all discovery scenes. The scenic emblem, whether 'palace', 'house', 'castle', 'arbour' or 'rock', was constructed like a three-sided hut with a door at the back and a 'traverse' or curtain across the front. A stage direction from the *Ludus Coventriae* illustrates the technique admirably.

Here Christ enteryth into the house with his disciples and eats the paschal lamb; and, in the meantime, the council house beforesaid shall suddenly unclose shewing the bishops, priests and jews sitting in their orders of Estate like as it were a convocation.

Whether it is Shakespeare's King Richard III dreaming in his tent on the night before the Battle of Bosworth Field or Webster's Duchess of Malfi shocked by the sight of the corpses of her husband and children in her prison cell, this is the scenic convention that we have to visualize.

All the emblems required for a particular play were normally set out on the stage in the manner depicted in the St. Lawrence play before the performance started. The stage itself (what we would call the acting area) then assumed the identity of the particular scenic emblem which the actors were using or talking about at that time: it changed its identity as soon as the actors ceased using that emblem and they, or other actors, started to use another. To illustrate from Fig. 3 (p. 118), if the Emperor Augustus was seated on his throne the stage would represent his throne-room; but as soon as he and his courtiers had made their exit and Jupiter's High Priest had entered and had begun some action in the area of the altar or monument, the stage would assume the identity of the Temple of Jupiter.

As a theatrical device, this scenic convention has the great advantage for the dramatic poet of allowing him freedom to move virtually wherever he wants to within his narrative. In other words he need not be seriously circumscribed in his treatment of his poetic theme by any practical necessity to subscribe to theories of unity of place or time. This system was first evolved in the abbeys and cathedral churches of Europe to meet the simple requirements of the Easter sepulchre play and the Christmas crib. Developed experimentally over the centuries it was bequeathed to Shakespeare and his contemporaries intact. In England it had no rival until Inigo Jones' experiments with the landscape scene of Italian origin were incorporated in the two London theatres built in the first decade of Charles II's reign. In these experiments Jones was not a pioneer in the strictest sense of the word since he had at least a hundred years of Italian innovation to draw upon when he started work himself. There, scholars and artists had started to enquire whether any means existed for identifying place on the stage which might be preferable to those familiar conventions inherited from the Church and from heraldry. Serlio had answered this question for them as early as 1547 with a firm 'yes' in his *De Archittetura*: by amalgamating the pre-Christian precedents of the Roman stage with the modern skills of the architects and landscape painters of his own day, he had pointed the way to a new formula—the replacement of the symbol with an illusion of the actual. This new formula did not preclude the use of the old symbols. Use of them however was to be conditional upon two factors, both of them new, and both of them owing their authority to Vitruvius. The first was appropriateness; the second, subordination to the optical rules of receding perspective. In other words, the old emblems could continue to be used, but the number of possible combinations was drastically reduced and each of those in fact admitted must be so co-ordinated with its fellows in position, size and colouring as to conform with the pictorial image which the artist aimed to provide. (See Essay 6, pp. 107–10 above.)

The Serlian objective of a theatrical scene that both con-
formed with the strict differentiation of dramatic genre prescribed by academicians, and at the same time provided
trompe d'œil illusion of town or country, carried within itself a
threat to the traditional balance of power among theatrical
practitioners: for, once accepted, it not only obliged the 'inventor' or 'deviser' or author of a play to subordinate his narrative
to the exigencies of the architect-painter in respect of the locality
of the stage action, but it also restricted the actor in his freedom
of movement upon the stage lest, like Gulliver in Brobdignag,
he should make the scene look absurd by dwarfing it. This
shift in emphasis lies not only at the heart of the quarrel
between Inigo Jones and Ben Jonson about responsibility for
'inventing' or 'devising' Masks which Jones won (see Essay 6),
but also behind Jones' design for the Cockpit-in-Court (1630)
where Shakespeare's company of actors succeeded in preserving
the essential features of The Globe and The Blackfriars playhouses notwithstanding apparent concessions in visual appearance to Italian innovations (see Essay 9).

We cannot therefore say that there was no knowledge in the
English theatre of the sixteenth century of Italian precept either
in respect of the supposed 'unities' of time and place or the
pioneer methods of giving these ideas practical expression on
the stage; but we can safely say that there was little interest in
either. Whether we turn to the expense accounts of the civic
guilds concerned with the production of religious plays or to the
bursarial account books of Schools and University Colleges or
to those of the Revels Office, we find throughout the second
half of the sixteenth century ample evidence of ornate and
costly 'houses' and 'devices' constructed and painted for use in
dramatic entertainments, but no evidence whatsoever of 'scenes'
arranged in receding perspective. 'Cloths', 'great cloths' and
'painted cloths' abound in the Revels Office Accounts, but
in my opinion these items should not be regarded as component
parts of Serlian perspective scenes; for, so long as the Queen
herself and other notable spectators sat on the stage itself,
there could be no point in even attempting to provide pictorial illusion of this kind.

There is a much simpler explanation of these cloths. Most of them were provided, not for the stage at all, but to decorate the walls and roof of the halls in which the entertainments were given. Some were designed for use as hangings round the stage; others for attachment to wooden 'frames' used in the construction of 'houses' and 'devices'. Occasionally painted cloths (quite probably painted in perspective) were used in conjunction with a particular device as a background to provide a particular device with a particular identity.[1] In this context, however, their use marks only an extension of a traditional emblematic device to incorporate a more sophisticated and aesthetically pleasing embellishment of the device than a simple label or 'scripture' of the normal sort which Sidney deplored when 'coming to a Play, and seeing *Thebes* written in great letters upon an olde doore'.

Given these separate and independent units, the 'frame' or auditorium on the one hand and the stage and tiring-house on the other, the question that we must ask ourselves is: 'Where did they both come from?' If this question is once put, the answers are surprisingly easy to find. Circular auditoriums of this kind had been commonplace in England for generations. Chaucer in his *Knight's Tale* describes one constructed for a tournament: Agas map of London c. 1560 shows two on the South Bank, one used for bear-baiting the other for bull-baiting. This sort of auditorium has the great advantage of allowing the maximum number of spectators the best possible view of the entertainment provided. In the fifteenth and early sixteenth century, as far as we know, these entertainments consisted of sword-play, wrestling, fencing, cock-fighting and the baiting of bulls and bears: but when in 1574 Elizabeth I gave the Earl of Leicester's company of actors a Patent to perform plays regularly on weekdays in London, actors at once acquired as close an interest in such auditoriums as any other showmen. Their obvious interest in the potential box-office receipts of a large arena-style auditorium was further increased by the pressure put on them by the City Council to quit the eating and drinking houses in which they had

[1] See *Early English Stages*, ii(1), pp. 282 *et seq.*, and *Plates III* and *IV*.

habitually given their performances. So much for the auditorium.

Now for the stage. For the arenas to be suitable for plays, the actors had to insist on the installation of a raised stage together with a room for changing and storing their properties and scenic emblems. The owners of the arenas, on the other hand, had to safeguard their interest in other traditional forms of entertainment and could not allow the players to put the 'Game' or 'Play' house permanently out of action as places for the promotion of sports and games. The compromise reached was a stage and tiring-house that could be quickly set up and as quickly dismantled within the confines of the arena itself. In 1574 the actors had not sufficient capital to build a theatre exclusive to their own needs: they were thus obliged to think in terms of a compromise of this sort, at least in the first instance.[1] As their hold on the public improved and stage plays came to take precedence over other forms of entertainment so the actors began to improve their bargaining position with their business partners—Langley at the Swan, Henslowe at the Rose and the Fortune, Holland at the Red Bull. Shakespeare's company even attained complete independence of commercial speculators. As this happened, so, inevitably, the strictly theatrical features of the building became more important and architecturally more permanent: but the need to take plays on tour did not change, and we should not forget that as late as 1613 Henslowe, in building the Hope, still regarded the multi-purpose auditorium as a sound financial investment.

The feature of the stage and tiring-house, as depicted by de Witt, which most seriously interferes with mobility is the roof over the stage—the 'shadow' or 'heavens'—supported on large posts. It is impossible to conceive of this being dismantled every time the arena was needed as itself or set up again whenever the actors wanted to use the theatre for plays. In 1613, Henslowe and his builder, Gilbert Katherens, solved this problem at the Hope by cantilevering the 'heavens' so that the projecting roof remained a permanency but the awkward posts supporting the outer edge could be dispensed with. Before

[1] See Essay 7, pp. 122–6 above.

that time we lack adequate evidence to do more than assume that 'heavens' supported on posts were normal in playhouses built between 1590 and 1610, but had probably not become an integral part of theatres built between 1576 and 1590. These 'heavens' were of course a scenic emblem in themselves, being no more than a ceiling painted over with the signs of the Zodiac on a blue background. After 1595, a trap-door in the middle gave access to the loft above, and from that loft it was usual to let down another popular emblem, the throne: it also enabled supernatural beings to descend to earth or return to heaven. From the loft the trumpeter could step out to announce the start of the play and call for silence. From there too the actor's flag could be hoisted to advertise the fact that a performance was being given that day. Last, but not least, the 'heavens' served to protect such emblems as were normally set out at the back of the stage (and thus close to the tiring-house doors) from the harmful effects of rain and sun. These emblems—tombs, tents, trees and so on—were expensive capital items which, if they were worth putting on an inventory were also worth protecting from the rigours of the English climate. To this extent the roof or shadow was a necessity in an open-air playhouse: in an indoor playhouse (whether it was the banqueting hall of a palace, the guildhall of a provincial city or one of the 'Private Theatres'), the problem of representing 'heaven' could be solved both differently and more simply. For the Lincoln play of Tobias, one of the emblems listed in 1584 was 'a firmament, with a fiery cloud and a double cloud'. A heaven of this kind is depicted, sitting on the floor of the hall along with an arbour, a wood, and a fountain, in the French *Ballet Comique de la Reine* of 1582 (*Plate III*). It is to be noted however that when the Cockpit-in-Court came to be remodelled for the King's Men by Inigo Jones in 1630 the public-playhouse style of 'heavens' was ingeniously incorporated into the new building by means of canvas blinds (see Essay 9, p. 156 below). Before this convention is dismissed therefore as crude and absurd it is worth remembering how long and varied a life it enjoyed in the English theatre and reflecting on the calibre of the dramatists and actors that it served.

One might think that performances at Court were quieter and better ordered than those in the public playhouses or in the provinces. If so, this is an opinion which, along with others, needs to be corrected. Performances at the Universities and at the Inns of Court, even in the presence of the sovereign, were often rowdy affairs. Professor Coghill has argued that the Prologue and Epilogue to *Troilus and Cressida* were specially written to 'protect' the play from its audience when it was transferred from the Globe to the Inns of Court.[1] I have already instanced a Mask called *Solomon and the Queen of Sheba* prepared for James I and Christian IV of Denmark which degenerated into a drunken rout.[2] This was presented in 1606, a year after Shakespeare completed *Othello* and a year before the first performance of *King Lear*. A fiasco of this sort, one hopes, was the exception rather than the rule. Yet the very possibility of such an occurrence on such an occasion serves as a good corrective to the more extreme, romantic notions we may entertain that the text of a Shakespeare play was sacrosanct either to actors or spectators in his own lifetime. Lines were cut, scenes were transposed, actors 'ad-libbed', authors even formed syndicates to provide an act each within a single play: and I have given examples enough to show that audiences in general conducted themselves no better. That Shakespeare was a poet of genius is a fact of paramount importance; but a fact of no less importance is the professional mastery of dramatic art that he acquired in his working life. As a stage poet he wrote trippingly for the tongue and so lucidly in his imagery as to provide that close-knit family of actors that was his company with precise directions for the formulation of a character. As a sharer in the Globe/Blackfriars syndicate he had cause never to undervalue popular support at less than its commerical worth, and as a household servant, first of the Lord Chamberlain and then of King James I he knew how to balance the common denominator of the company's livelihood against the whims of Court taste and academic fashion. As a travelling player, however much London had to offer when free of plague, he never lost touch with provincial life or the English countryside in all

[1] *Shakespeare's Professional Skills*, 1964, pp. 78–97.   [2] See Essay 6, pp. 114–15 above.

seasons of the year. Last but not least, all these facts compounded to give him and his company a healthy respect for
scenic conventions that were emblematic rather than pictorial.
Artificial they undoubtedly were, but no more so than the
artifice of verse as a form of speech. Indeed such artifice, as we
are slowly rediscovering for ourselves today, is much more
closely in harmony with the game of make-believe that is a play
(that is the theatre as opposed to films and television) than that
pictorial realism which inhibits imaginative energy by placing
arbitrary controls of place and time upon the poet's and the
actor's freedom of movement within their make-believe action.

Slowly we are coming to realize that Shakespeare's stage
was not a single, rigid theatre such as we have become acclima-
tized to in various reconstructions of 'The Globe', but a frame
with a stage in it that was as adaptable as was necessary to meet
the needs of a travelling company of professional actors.
These actors took over all the long-established stage-conven-
tions (including scenic conventions) of their ancestors, modify-
ing them and adding to them as new needs arose. The most
important change in Shakespeare's lifetime was the acquisition
of permanent homes in London. Initially these had to be
shared with other entertainers; but as the popularity of stage-
plays increased and the actors themselves grew richer, so the
acting companies acquired both the power and the capital to
insist that their own needs in those theatres should take precedence over those of anyone else. Even so, the particular pressures
of the period made it impossible for any professional company
to think in terms of its open-air playhouse alone. In the last
decade of Shakespeare's lifetime, his company was forced by
weather to quit the Globe in the winter months for the Blackfriars, was obliged also to give command performances at
Court and was driven by frequent outbreaks of plague to leave
London altogether for long visits to a wide variety of provincial
town halls. These differences in the physical conditions of
performance of Shakespeare's plays in his own lifetime must
each and all play as large a part in any concept of how they
were first staged as any deductions that can be made about the
physical appearance of the great Globe itself.

9

Notes on Inigo Jones' design for the Cockpit-in-Court[1]

WHEN I last saw the late Professor F. P. Wilson at his home near Oxford in 1961 he presented me as I was leaving with a bundle of typescript notes and a large photographic print. The typescript was a copy of his own transcript of the Accounts of the Office of Works for the years 1578–1642 annotated with his own MS. comments; the print, measuring 19″ × 15″, had been given to F. P. Wilson by Sir Edmund Chambers. At the time I did not spot any link between these two gifts, and I suppose I shall never know whether F. P. Wilson had himself done so. What I am now sure of is that the one explains the other, the Works Accounts providing the vital descriptive evidence needed to identify the plan and elevation of the theatre depicted in the photograph. I duly recorded my thanks for the gift of the transcript under 'acknowledgements' in vol. II (pt. 1) of *Early English Stages*, but saw no reason to do so for the print since it was at once recognizable as that used by Chambers to form the frontispiece to vol. IV of *The Elizabethan Stage*. It was only when I began to work in earnest on the reasoning behind

[1] Reprinted from the *New Theatre Magazine*, vol. 7 (1967), no. 2, pp. 26-35.

the design and construction of Elizabethan and Jacobean theatres when preparing part 2 of vol. II of *Early English Stages* that I began to realize that the descriptive entries in the Works Accounts relating to building activities within the Cockpit playhouse in Whitehall between 1629 and 1632 bore some resemblance to pictorial details represented in the large photographic print which had accompanied F. P. Wilson's gift of his transcript of the Works Accounts. Inspection of the print showed these resemblances to be strikingly close.

II

The print is a photograph of an original drawing in the library or Worcester College, Oxford, which Chambers entitled 'Design by Inigo Jones for the Cockpit Theatre in Whitehall' (*Plate VI*). Chambers based what little he had to say about it in the text of his *Elizabethan Stage* (i, pp. 216, 234) on an article by Hamilton Bell in *Architectural Record* (N.Y., xxxiii, 1913, pp. 262–7). The first person to have drawn public attention to the Worcester College sketches was Professor Lethaby in an article in *The Architectural Review* (xxxi, 1901, pp. 189–90). Bell developed this discussion independently and concluded that the designs depicted the new theatre built in Whitehall and referred to by Thomas Heywood in a Prologue printed in 1637, in which viewpoint he was supported by J. Q. Adams in his *Shakespearean Playhouses* (N.Y., 1917, pp. 391–400). Chambers followed Adams in thinking that this playhouse opened 'about 1632' (*Elizabethan Stage*, i, 234).

Two years after the publication of *The Elizabethan Stage* William Keith challenged this verdict in an article in *The Architectural Review* (1925, lvii, no. 2, pp. 49–55). He argued that the drawings more nearly resembled the style of Jones' pupil John Webb than that of Jones himself, and that they must therefore represent a theatre built for Charles II rather than one built before the Civil War. In this view he had the independent support of L. B. Campbell in *Scenes and Machines on the English Stage* (1923, pp. 202–6). Eleanor Boswell in *The Restoration Court Stage* (1932) accepted Keith's attribution of the draw-

152

ings to Webb but not his post-Restoration dating. Allardyce Nicoll in *Stuart Masques* (1938) appears to follow this lead, and there the matter has rested without further definition or question. It is only fair to add that all scholars who have tried to decide whether the sketches should be attributed to Inigo Jones, c. 1632, or to John Webb, c. 1660, have had their task distorted and confused by the existence of two other drawings relating to theatres which are clearly identifiable as the work of Inigo Jones. One of these is a plan and elevation for a theatre found by Mr. Keith in Jones' annotated copy of Palladio at Worcester College: the other is a hastily executed drawing in the Chatsworth Collection labelled in Jones' hand, 'for ye Cockpitt for my lo Cha(m)berlin 1639' (see *Plates VII* and *VIII*). A glance at these drawings in conjunction with *Plate VI* will quickly show how easily confusion can arise. With the aid however of the Works Accounts together with a suggestion made by Professor G. E. Bentley in vol. I of his *The Jacobean and Caroline Stage* (1940) it is now possible to be much more precise about the design, purpose and nature of this theatre. Moreover, since it was restored for use in November 1660, but quickly abandoned as new theatres became available despite the money spent on repairs, all the information we have about it relates much more directly to Caroline, Jacobean and even Elizabethan theatre practice than to that of the Restoration period.

III

Where the Works Accounts are concerned, two points arrest attention above all others. First, in the accounting years 1st October to 30th September 1629–30 and 1630–1 large sums of money were spent and much attention was given to 'sundry Extraordenary workes about the Cockpitt and Playhouse there' involving carpenters, carvers, painters and labourers. Secondly, descriptive details of the work that these men were required to do bear a marked resemblance to features of the Jones-Webb sketches.

We learn that before 1st October 1630 an elaborate façade was erected within the playhouse containing 'twoe stories of

Collomnes'; that there were 'X^{en} Collomnes uppon eu^{r}y Story Corinthia and Composita finishing the heads w(i)th Architrave, freeze and Cornishe uppon each Story'; that this façade contained 'five doores in the first Story and in the second story one open dore and iiij^{er} neeches in the same upper Storye'.[1] A glance at the sketch reveals that all these items are there too—the two storeys, the ten columns with their Corinthian capitals on each storey, the five doors in the lower storey and the single opening in the upper storey flanked by two niches on either side. Correspondence at every point and in such detail can only be taken as proof that Inigo Jones, in his capacity as Master Surveyor of the King's Works, was commissioned to remodel the Cockpit, that work began in 1629 and that the Worcester College sketches provide us with the ground plan, dimensions and elevation of that theatre.[2]

When then was it finished? This is more difficult to determine precisely. According to the Works Accounts, construction and painting work were still in progress between 1st October 1630 and 30th September 1632. Chambers took the date of completion to be c. 1632 and has been followed in this by Harbage, *Annals of the English Drama, 975–1700*, in the revised 1964 edition. Two features of the Works Accounts however suggest an earlier date. In the first place, the final entry for the year 1629–30 (i.e. near 30th September 1630) reads,

to divers Artificers and labourers for expedicon in theire woorke uppon extraordinary hast and for bread and drinke amongst them woorkinge very late in the nighte vij^s (P.R.O. E 351/3263).

---

[1] P.R.O. E 351/3263. Particular sums of money were paid out at this same time to 'Zachary Tyler Carver . . . ffor Cuttinge and Carvinge x^{en} Corynthian Capitalls for Collomes at xiij^s iiij^d the peece' and also 'ffor Cuttinge and Carvinge ij^{oo} Corinth pillauster Capitalls at xiij^s iij^d the peece', and to 'John Hooke Turno^d . . . for turninge x^{en} great Pillars for the Cockepitt at viij^s the pece and iiij^{ll} for turninge x^{en} smaller Pillars for the same place at vj^s the peece, lxi^s.' *Ibid.*

[2] Whether the Worcester College sketches are Jones' own work or a copy made by Webb must remain a matter for Art historians to determine. It is quite possible that Webb made a copy of his master's cartoon: what is inconceivable is that Charles I would have entrusted as important a project as this to anyone other than his own surveyor. The Works Accounts for 1630/31 make it explicit in any case that the carpenters followed 'the Designes and Draughtes given by the Surveyor . . .' P.R.O. E 351/3264.

Anyone familiar with the everyday conditions of a working theatre will recognize this intelligence as having about it the all too familiar ring of last minute preparations for a first night which has been publicly advertised and cannot be postponed.

The second curious feature of the Works Accounts is that one of the entries for the year 1st October 1631–30th September 1632 contains the phrases 'ffor new painting the freez in the Cockpitt over the Stage' and 'ffor repayring & mending twoe great peeces of paynted woorke . . . wch were much defaced'. These activities suggest maintenance work; the timely refurbishing of decorations soiled by use.[1]

The inference to be drawn from these two striking features in the Accounts when taken in conjunction is that the Cockpit-in-Court as remodelled by Inigo Jones for Charles I opened around October 1630 and was used frequently enough to require minor repairs and redecoration before September 1632. In other words, the theatre did not open in 1632 as Chambers, Harbage and some others have thought, but in 1630 as Professor Bentley suggested in vol. I of *The Jacobean and Caroline Stage* (pp. 27–9). In his chapter devoted to the fortunes of the King's Men, Bentley published a bill of plays for 'this present year of o^r Lord God. 1630' which he discovered in the Folger Shakespeare Library (MS. 2068.8). This states that four plays were performed by the company at Hampton Court between 30th September and 24th October and that sixteen plays were presented 'At the (Co)ck-pitt' between 5th November 1630 and 21st February, 1631. The programme for 5th November was 'An Induction for the Howse, And The Madd Louer'. Bentley concludes a lengthy footnote to this entry by saying,

I can see no reason for not accepting the implication of this bill that the new theatre was opened with *An Induction for the Howse* performed by the King's Men in November 1630 (*op. cit.*, i, 29).

The evidence now available from the Works Accounts vindicates Bentley's earlier surmise completely.

---

[1] P.R.O. E 351/3256. John de Creet and Matthew Gordericke, painters, were also paid 20s. the following year 'for mending the Statues in the Cockpitt altering the inscriptions and clenzing other woorke . . .' P.R.O. E 351/3267.

The importance of this information to all future discussions of late Tudor and early Stuart stage conventions can scarcely be exaggerated: for not only are we now equipped with a plan and elevation of a theatre that can be directly compared with De Witt's drawing of the Swan Theatre and the surviving builders' contracts for the first Fortune and the Hope, but we know that Shakespeare's company was the first to use the new theatre in 1630 and that the repertoire on that occasion included such old favourites as *Everyman in His Humour, Volpone, The Duchess of Malfi* and *Philaster. A Midsummer Night's Dream* was revived this season, but played at Hampton Court, not at the Cockpit.

IV

The Office of Works Accounts do considerably more than establish Jones' ground plan and elevation as those of a theatre actually used by the King's Men: they amplify the drawings with information about areas of the theatre not depicted in the drawings and enable us to reconstruct it as it was when used as a theatre for plays in performance.

Taking the stage area first, the problem of providing 'heavens' containing a trap for lowering the throne and winged actors to match this normal facility of a public playhouse was resolved most ingeniously by Inigo Jones in terms of a ceiling which opened and closed as required.

Cutting, fitting and soweing of Callicoe to cover all the roome over head w(i)thin the Cockpitt C^s
Cutting a great number of Starres of Assidue [silver foil] and setting them one the Blew Callicoe to garnish the Cloath there.
Setting one a great number of Copp(e)rings to drawe the cloth to and fro . . . (P.R.O. E 351/3265).

The purpose of splitting the cloth ceiling painted to resemble the sky in this way is made explicit by the preceding entry in the Accounts:

John Walker Property maker vizt: for hanging the Throne and Chaire in the Cockpit w(i)th cloth bound about w(i)th whalebone, packthred and wyer for the better foulding of the same to come downe from the Clouds to the Stage (*ibid.*).

The acting area was lit by candelabra, 'tenn smaller and twoe greater then thother about and before the stage'. The post-Restoration Accounts confirm the existence of 'a rayle and ballisters' round the edge of the stage, as depicted in Jones' ground plan. This would seem to eliminate the possibility of footlights. The stage itself was covered with 'Greene Manchester Bayes [cloth] lyned w(i)th Canvas' and the floor of the room under it was covered with matting: both these items figure in the renovations undertaken in November 1660.[1] A curious omission is any reference to a stage trap: no provision for it is shown in the designs nor is any reference made to one in either the building or the renovation Accounts.

Turning our attention now from the stage to the Palladian *frons scenae* which backed it, the only aspect of the sketch of the elevation amplified by the Accounts is that the façade, like the much earlier Swan playhouse, was painted and the Corinthian capitals gilded. The Accounts, however, are much more informative about the area behind this façade, the tiring-house. This was divided into two rooms one above the other, the upper room usually being referred to as 'the gallery over the stage'. Here, Jones' sketch serves as a useful check on the interpretation to be placed on the word 'gallery': clearly it was not a balcony external to the façade, but a gallery in the more normal sixteenth- and seventeenth-century use of the word—a long, open room. Its floor corresponded with the architrave above the five doors, and its single large window as depicted in the sketch (or 'one open dore' as it is described in the Accounts) looked out over the stage. The lower room, besides its five doors opening onto the stage, had two windows in the opposite, outer wall and a fireplace in the 'stage-right' corner. When the theatre opened, the lower room with its fire was the dressing-room and the upper room the wardrobe and musicians' gallery; after the Restoration the employment of actresses to play women's roles made it necessary to adjust the fittings and uses of these rooms. 'Two peeces of hangings and great curtaine rodds' were supplied in December 1662, 'to make partitions between the Men and Weomen'. At the same time the walls of

---

[1] See Boswell, *Restoration Court Stage*, pp. 15 and 16.

'the upper tyring roome' were hung with green cloth, and the dressing-rooms refurnished with three tables, twenty chairs and stools, a large dressing mirror for the ladies 'such a glass (being) too big to bee brought every night from their howse'.[1] Two additional fireplaces were added, possibly in the upper room.

Two points relating to the auditorium and its furnishings require attention: the first relates to the King's throne and the second to the galleries overlooking the pit and linking the King's box to the stage and the Palladian *frons scenæ*. The ground plan shows the throne directly opposite the large central door in the façade: designed by Jones this arrangement could only have one objective—to provide the sovereign with the best view of the perspective of any piece of painted scenery placed in or behind the arch, as was normal in the Banqueting Hall for Masks. As W. G. Keith recognized in his study of the plan and elevation in 1925, this large arch provides a frame which at least corresponds with that in the unidentified scenic designs at Chatsworth: on the other hand just as much weight must be given to the item in the post-Restoration Wardrobe Accounts relating to the provision of a large four-poster bed, since this indicates that the actors at least continued to employ this familiar emblematic scenic device.[2] The other point about the auditorium which should be remarked is that seats in the galleries (as opposed to the pit) were provided on two levels. The upper galleries were supported at the front by six pillars clearly discernible in the ground-plan and referred to in general terms in the Accounts both before and after the Restoration. The decoration of the walls and galleries included, according to the Works Accounts, paintings by Palma and 'greate Emperours' Heads' by Titian.[3] When these seating arrange-

[1] This information is given in a Lord Chamberlain's Warrant to the Master of the Great Wardrobe, 10 xii. 1662, quoted by Boswell, *op. cit.*, p. 18.

[2] 'One property Bedd w(i)th a redd Taffeta Coverlet and taffata Curtaynes & quilt & one Couch.' Lord Chamberlain's Warrant, Dec. 1662, *cit.* Boswell, p. 18.

[3] P.R.O. E 351/3265. Were these 'Heads' the famous set of twelve imaginative portraits painted by Titian for the Duke of Mantua and bought by Charles I? They seem to have been paintings and not sculptures, since 70/- was paid to painters 'ffor repayring mending and new varnishing vij[en] of the greate Emperours' Heades that were done by Titian being likewise much defaced'. Only seven were repaired.

PLATE XIII

17   A MIDSUMMER NIGHT'S DREAM
Prior Park House, Bath Assembly, 1951. Puck's Epilogue.
Production: Glynne Wickham   Photo: Roger Gilmour

PLATE XIV

18 EFFIGY OF JOHN COOKIN

19 EFFIGY OF DAME MARY BAYNTON

Both of these painted statues may be seen in the Lord Mayor's Chapel, Bristol, where they were installed *c.* 1670. The memorial to eleven-year-old John Cookin might as easily be one to Mamillius in Leontes' Chapel, while that to Dame Mary Baynton, complete with statue, 'Lords' and curtains, provides just as vivid an image of Hermione's 'tomb' in Paulina's Chapel in the final scene of *The Winter's Tale*.

Photos by Eric de Maré

ments are considered in conjunction with the openings in the *frons scenæ* and in terms of sight-lines it becomes evident that any possibility of the existence of an inner stage in this theatre built for the King's Men is precluded absolutely (see Fig. 1, p. 64).

V

If the King's Men were expected to present such established plays from their repertoire as *Volpone* and *The Duchess of Malfi* in this theatre without an inner stage, the question at once arises whether they ever possessed or needed one. If no such facility existed at the Swan in 1596—and De Witt's sketch makes it clear that it did not (see Fig. 4)—and if it did not exist at the Cockpit-in-Court in 1630, the case for its existence at the Globe, the Fortune, the Hope, Red Bull, Phoenix and Blackfriars during the interim period becomes very difficult to sustain. (It should be remembered that there is no mention of an inner stage or anything like it in the builder's contract for either the Fortune or the Hope.) *Volpone* and *Malfi* moreover are both examples *par excellence* of the sort of Jacobean play which promoters of the 'inner stage' theory insist can only be fully realized in performance with the aid of this amenity. Yet, where *Volpone* is concerned, the four-poster bed of the post-Restoration Wardrobe Accounts can be thrust out of the lower tiring-room through the central doorway to a centre-stage position where the actor has the best command over his audience, whether counting his gold with Mosca or attempting to rape Celia. The dumb-show in *The Duchess of Malfi* (III, iv) and the sequence of horrific 'discoveries' in Act IV are all equally easy for the actors to handle on the stage of the Cockpit with its five doors.

What then was Inigo Jones trying to do in providing the King's Men with this theatre? One thing is certain: he was not giving them a single-arched proscenium-stage with changeable scenery of the kind constructed by Aleoti at Parma in 1618 and

---

but the phrasing suggests that there were more. The other paintings restored at this time were 'the Story of David and Golia(t)h, thother of Saule's Conversion', both by Palma (*ibid.*).

evolved independently by Jones himself in England for the Court Masks presented in the Banqueting House. There are, I think, three answers or three parts to the single answer. The first is to be found in the structure of the Cockpit before alteration. It was built as an octagon within a square, with seats or standing room around the arena in which the cock-fighting took place. To provide a stage and tiring-house within this building, Jones had to remove three of eight galleries of the original building but preserve the four pillars in the angles of these sections which supported the conical roof (see Fig. 2, p. 64). The straight dotted lines on the ground plan reveal where these galleries used to run (*Plate VI*), and it will be seen that Jones has cunningly incorporated the original pillars within the fabric of his new *frons scenæ*. By setting the latter on a gentle arc he succeeds in concealing this artifice by deflecting attention from the old shape on to a completely new one which is echoed nowhere else in the building. If it is asked why he should have troubled to cover up his tracks in this way, it should be remembered that an artist as wholeheartedly committed to Vitruvian and Palladian principles of stage architecture as Inigo Jones, who had already challenged and outfaced Ben Jonson on the subject, could not conceivably offer so fastidious a sovereign as Charles I anything so vulgar and plebeian as a recognizable rehash of a gothic game-house.

It remains to ask why Jones should have stopped short of the fully developed proscenium-arched landscape scene of which he was capable by that time when executing a Court commission of this importance. My own answer is that Jones encountered an obstacle here at least as formidable as the roof supports of the original building—the objections of Hemings, Lowin, Taylor and the other members of the King's company of players. Eager as they were for new plays and novelty, their artistic and financial strength rested in their existing repertoire and their commitments to audiences at the Globe, the Black-friars and provincial halls, factors which argued forcibly for the retention of all basic features of their traditional stagecraft. Jones had accordingly to provide them with a large railed stage projecting into the auditorium, a room below it, 'heavens' complete with trap mechanism above it, substantial dressing-room and storage space behind, and openings at stage and first-floor levels in the wall dividing the stage from the tiring-house. It is hard to see how they could have dispensed with a trap in the stage-floor, but even if the ground-plan and building accounts make no mention of it, the provision of a room below the stage argues for its existence. The 'inner-stage' is another matter. Certainly it did not exist at the Cockpit: if the actors had wanted it, the structure of the original building would have allowed Jones to incorporate it into the new one without difficulty. The fact that he did not do so therefore implies that the actors did not ask for it: and why indeed should they ask for it at the Cockpit if they were content without it at the Globe and the Blackfriars?

As an architect, then, Jones' freedom of artistic expression in the Cockpit brief of 1629/30 was restricted by three external factors—the structure of the original building, the taste of his sovereign, and the functional requirements of the actors. The building was to be adapted and refurnished, not demolished and rebuilt; the King, like Jones himself, wanted a modern theatre in the fashionable Italian neo-classical manner; the actors wanted a theatre that met the requirements of plays normally presented in playhouses of traditional, English design. Compromise between three such conflicting viewpoints might seem impossible of attainment. It is a tribute to Jones' imagination and craftsmanship that he met the problem so successfully. The source of inspiration for this solution was the Teatro Olimpico at Vicenza. The conflict between the octagonal shape of the old Cockpit and the rectangular form of Palladio's proscenium at Vicenza, between the game- or play-house of English tradition and the neo-classical theatre that was his own and his sovereign's ideal, was resolved in terms of the gently curving *frons scenæ* that at once resembled the Olympic Theatre and masked the four pillars in the stage area support-ing the roof of the Cockpit. The conflict between the style of theatre he was himself championing in the Banquet House for Masks and that demanded by the more conservative actors of the King's company was resolved by amalgamating the proscenium and orchestra of the Teatro Olimpico (*Plate V*, no. 8) into a single stage and forestage of ample dimensions, with access to it from five doors instead of two or three (but stripped of the streets of houses in receding perspective that are so distinctive a feature of the Teatro Olimpico), and with a ceiling incorporating a trap mechanism over this stage. This solution unites the gothic tradition (adapted game-house, apron-stage, and emblematic scenic conventions) with neo-classical innovation (Palladian *frons scenæ* and ornament, an elliptical auditorium within a square or rectangle centred on the royal box aligned with the vanishing point of the landscape-artist's horizon) in an astonishing harmony of design and function. The Cockpit-in-Court, thanks to the happy survival of Jones' designs, the late F. P. Wilson's researches in the Public Record Office which provided the transcription of the Works Accounts, and Professor Bentley's discovery in the Folger Library of the King's Men's playbill for November 1630, can now be fully reconstructed and live again as the triumphant apotheosis of mediaeval and renaissance dramatic art that it was in its own time.

Section Four

Studies in Shakespeare

IO

Shakespeare's 'King Richard II' and Marlowe's 'King Edward II'

'The reluctant pangs of abdicating Royalty in Edward furnished hints which Shakespeare scarcely improved in his *Richard II*; and the death-scene of Marlowe's King moves pity and terror beyond any scene, ancient or modern, with which I am acquainted.'— Charles Lamb.

THE title page of the First Quarto of *Richard II* (1597) describes the play as 'The Tragedie of King Richard the Second'. The First Quarto of *Edward II* describes that play on its title page as 'The troublesome raigne and lamentable death of Edward the second, King of England: with the tragicall fall of proud Mortimer'. These titles suggest that Shakespeare's play is a true tragedy while Marlowe's is really a Chronicle play with tragic undertones. Certainly the stage-history of the two plays appears to confirm this assumption, if only because *Richard II* has remained in the vanguard of the professional repertory while Malowe's play, if frequently discussed in books of criticism, is rarely produced and then normally by adventurous amateurs. I want in this essay to question this assumption and to suggest that of the two plays *Edward II*, despite its shortcomings, is the true tragedy in the classical sense of the word and that *Richard II* is really the Chronicle play with tragic consequences.

That Shakespeare was in debt to Marlowe for the dramatic treatment of the deposition and downfall of a king is not in doubt: nor is there much question that a simple repetition of Edward's fate in terms of Richard's reign would have held little appeal either to the Lord Chamberlain's company of actors or to their patrons. Thus if *Richard II* does represent a borrowing there is good reason to suppose that the difference of treatment is as notable as the original borrowing.

Any sensitive director will notice this, I think, immediately he comes to consider casting the two plays: for where the King and Bolingbroke of *Richard II* are matched in *Edward II* by the King and Young Mortimer, Marlowe's play demands actors to play Gaveston and Young Spencer and an actress to play Queen Isabella whose artistry transcends talent in a way that the supporting cast of Shakespeare's play does not. I am not saying that the gardener in *Richard II*, Gaunt, York, the Bishop of Carlisle, Northumberland and the Queen can be played by anybody: only that with these parts in the hands of competent actors the director can still hope to provide his audiences with a presentable production of the play. He could not have the same confidence however (or should not) when tackling *Edward II* in these circumstances. The reason for this is that Gaveston, Spencer and the Queen in one way or another collectively bring both Edward and Mortimer to their ruin where Richard is the victim of circumstance and his own folly. Some directors might well argue that the part of Lightborn in *Edward II* also requires exceptional care in casting.

The casting problem, once it has been remarked, points the way to differences in the narrative line of the two plays which are no less significant from the standpoint of stage-production, The first of these is the contrast in the fate of the respective antagonists: Mortimer is led off to execution and his severed head is added to the funeral furniture on Edward's hearse in the closing scene, while Bolingbroke, anxious and disillusioned as he may be, wears Richard's crown as King Henry IV at the play's close. This difference in the fate of the antagonist could be said to be simply one of the facts of history to which the dramatists were tied by their sources, the Chronicles; but it may also indicate a difference of moral and artistic purpose since both dramatists felt free to alter the ordering of historical event if it suited them and their actors to do so. The second difference in narrative line relates to the initial cause of conflict. Richard, by banishing Bolingbroke, makes him into his antagonist and, by depriving him of his titles and estates, provokes in Bolingbroke a degree of personal animosity that serves as a rallying point for general discontent. Edward's troubles start for the opposite reason, the revocation of the banishment served on Gaveston in the previous reign, an action which in creating general discontent serves to create a need for a leader in the ranks of the opposition. The question of consequence to the dramatic development of *Edward II* is 'who will fill this role?' and the answer is Young Mortimer. This is never a question of consequence in *Richard II* since it is obvious from the outset that Bolingbroke is the offended adversary: the question there is whether he can find sufficient support to claim compensation or revenge. The one point that both plays have in common is the personal contribution made by Edward and Richard respectively towards answering these questions in a manner that invites their own destruction. Thus these differences in the narrative line of the two plays reinforce the difference which the casting problem exposes: taken together they suggest strongly that Marlowe and Shakespeare were working to very different ends.

Alerted to such a possibility, we can escape from the usual critical preoccupation with parallelism grounded in Charles Lamb's famous aphorism quoted at the head of this Essay and examine the plot structure of both plays more objectively.

In *Richard II* Shakespeare allows us to see two kings fulfilling the same primary function of their calling and thereby allows us to judge them as men in terms of their actions. Each is given one scene, a test case, the circumstances of which are very similar. The subject is a charge of sedition. In Act I, scene i, Mowbray is accused by Bolingbroke of plotting against Richard. The King suspects a private vendetta and questions Gaunt to this effect; but Gaunt confirms to the King that the quarrel springs from

> . . . some apparent danger seen in him [Mowbray]
> Aim'd at your highness, no inveterate malice.

Richard, however, having accepted this and having allowed the formal Trial by Combat to take place vacillates at the last minute and in Act I, scene iii—'The Lists at Coventry'—when the full heraldic ritual of the law has reached its climax, forbids the Combat to go further and pronounces banishment on both the contestants. A more inappropriate moment to reach such a decision and a more inappropriate solution to the problem could scarcely be imagined. The sentence of banishment (I, iii, 118–53) delivered, according to Richard, to avoid 'the dire aspect/Of civil wounds plough'd up with neighbours' swords', invites this very sequel, since two wrongs cannot make a right. To this injustice, as foolish as it is arbitrary, Richard immediately adds another by cutting the ten-year sentence on Bolingbroke to six for no better reason than that he is moved by Gaunt's 'sad aspect', even though he has just silenced a far more eloquent Mowbray with

> It boots thee not to be compassionate:
> After our sentence plaining comes too late.

Richard is thus presented to us as a weak-minded, self-indulgent man whose personal failings preclude him from discharging two of the most important functions of kingship efficiently: the administration of justice between individuals and the preservation of civil order. In Act V, scene iii, Bolingbroke is presented to us as King confronted with a situation similar to that of Act I, scene i, the Oxford plot against the King's life. With Aumerle in his hands, his father York speaking as his accuser and his mother pleading for his pardon, what is the King to do? He listens carefully to both sides (Shakespeare lavishes a hundred lines on plea and counter-plea) and then as the Lord's Annointed should, mingles mercy with his justice. He pardons the sinner who has confessed and repented, but orders the immediate arrest and execution of those who have not. His conduct is exemplary. Where Richard was impetuous, arbitrary and self-contradictory, Bolingbroke is patient, self-possessed and consistent. Where Richard acted on whim, Bolingbroke acts on principle. Similarly, where in other scenes Richard encourages extravagance and effeminacy in Court circles, Bolingbroke in this scene condemns his own son's conduct as 'unthrifty', 'wanton' and 'dissolute'. Judged as men, therefore, there can be no question but that Bolingbroke is much better fitted to wear the crown than Richard; and Shakespeare plans both the structure of his play and his dialogue to ensure that we should recognize this important fact. Yet where an opportunist might regard this verdict as the end of the matter and sufficient to account for Richard being dead by the end of the play while Bolingbroke is alive and King, Shakespeare regards it as only the beginning. Bad King Richard may be, but for all that he is God's choice, he is the Lord's Annointed. And who are mortal men to judge an issue of this magnitude?

This question is put to the audience simply and straightforwardly in the second scene of the play (a scene, alas, more often cut in production than left in place). The Duke of Gloucester's widow asks John of Gaunt to revenge his brother's murder. Gaunt's reply is categoric.

> God's is the quarrel; for God's substitute [i.e. King Richard],
> His deputy annointed in His sight,
> Hath caused his death: the which if wrongfully,
> Let heaven revenge; for I may never lift
> An angry arm against His minister.

True to this principle, Gaunt never takes arms against Richard nor incites others to do so even on his son's behalf. On his death-bed he upbraids the King to his face and prophesies both personal and national disaster as the price to be paid for his abuse of his vocation and privilege. Gaunt's son however, like Lucifer and Adam before him, is tempted to take the law into his own hands. In the Parliament scene of Act IV, scene i, Bolingbroke is first warned by the Bishop of Carlisle of the consequences of plucking this forbidden fruit.

> . . . let me prophesy;
> The blood of English shall manure the ground,
> And future ages groan for this foul act;

Gaunt's famous vision of 'this blessed plot, this earth, this realm, this England' will be translated into,

> The field of Golgotha and dead men's skulls.
> O, if you raise this house against this house,
> It will the woefullest division prove
> That ever fell upon this cursed earth.
> Prevent it, resist it, let it not be so,
> Lest child, child's children, cry against you 'woe'!

Thirty lines later it is Richard himself who plays the role of Eden's serpent.

> Here, cousin, seize the crown;
> Here cousin;
> On this side my hand, and on that side yours.

Emotionally, for protagonist and antagonist on the stage and for every spectator in the audience, this is the climactic moment of the play. Richard's metaphor of the well with its two buckets is ironically apt: for as Richard abdicates so Bolingbroke falls. Divine providence deserts Richard the moment Bolingbroke yields to temptation and takes the crown. The blasphemy implicit in Bolingbroke's

> 'In God's name, I'll ascend the regal throne'.

is now confirmed and the 'many years of sunshine days' wished him by Richard are swiftly transformed into the threats, anxieties and storms that are to deprive him of any pleasure in the sceptre he wields and to deny him the repose and comfort of sleep.[1] Nor does God's wrath end there. Rebellions breed like boils; battle follows battle; Cain kills his brother Abel; Sodom and Gomorrah are exterminated, and a second Flood overwhelms England in the Wars of the Roses.

Thus *Richard II*, when its structure is examined, is seen to be not so much a tragedy in the classical sense as a political

---

[1] See *Henry IV*, Pt. 2, III, i, 4–31.

morality in the mediaeval sense. Expulsion from the Garden of Eden will follow disobedience to the Coronation oath as surely as it followed Adam's disobedience in respect of the Tree of Knowledge. King Richard is a tragic figure who moves us more by pathos than by horror in his fall; but he is merely the first victim of Bolingbroke's crime against the nation, contributor though he may be to his own downfall. As anyone who saw the complete Cycle of these history plays presented by the Royal Shakespeare Company in 1964 and 1965 will know, *Richard II* is a prelude to a catastrophe and not a self-contained tragedy despite its title; for it is the English nation that is to be crucified and England itself that is to become 'the field of Golgotha and dead men's skulls' in the seven plays that follow and together span the course of English history in the fifteenth century.

Marlowe's *Edward II*, by contrast, is not a prelude; it is not an historical morality; it is an entity; it is a tragedy. Like Richard, Edward is young, impetuous and extravagant: both of them are self-indulgent, but there is a marked difference in the form this self-indulgence takes. Likewise with Young Mortimer who, in his grasp of political reality and his firmness of purpose resembles Bolingbroke and thus provides an antagonist for Edward as sharply contrasted as Bolingbroke appears when measured against Richard. Yet again there is a difference. These differences reside in the emphasis which Marlowe and Shakespeare place respectively upon psychology of characterization and political morality when compressing their source material into dramatic form. Edward is presented as a thorough-going homosexual and masochist: this aspect of Richard's character, if present, is quite peripheral to the main action: he is certainly narcissistic, but that is not necessarily the same thing. Mortimer is presented as a heterosexual adventurer with marked sadistic tendencies: Bolingbroke is not a sadist but does labour under a sense of personal injustice. Once this is recognized it will be seen why Gaveston, Young Spencer and the Queen (as I remarked earlier) present such difficulties in the casting of *Edward II*: they are lynch-pins within the structure of this play, where Mowbray, Aumerle and Queen Anne are only useful types in *Richard II*. Divine providence figures in both plays, but again this is used very differently.

If *Edward II* is exposed to an examination of the narrative line of the kind we have just applied to *Richard II*, it will quickly become apparent how the two plots diverge. The seeming resemblance which the subject of banishment gives to the opening scenes is superficial: for where Richard uses banishment to inflict an injury on two families, Edward by revoking it repairs one to a friend. Richard's conduct is reprehensible by any standards: the worst that can be said of Edward's is that it is unwise. Gaveston's role however is crucial; for not only does he alienate Edward's spiritual and temporal advisers by his flamboyant behaviour, but he drives a wedge of distrust between Edward and the Queen. If active homosexuality in a young King can be excused by the nobility (and Marlowe gives Old Mortimer ten lines in Act I, scene iv, to plead for tolerance on this score) the Queen cannot brook it in her husband. A lonely young Frenchwoman in an alien country, she first becomes subject to depression.

Young Mortimer: Madam, whither walks your Majesty so fast?
Isabella: Unto the forest gentle Mortimer,
   To live in grief and baleful discontent;
   For now, my lord, the King regards me not,
   But doats upon the love of Gaveston. (I, ii, 46–50)

This is not a general complaint but one based on detailed observation.

   He claps his cheeks, and hangs about his neck,
   Smiles in his face, and whispers in his ears;
   And when I come he frowns, as who should say,
   'Go whither thou wilt, seeing I have Gaveston.'

It is the mixture of 'grief and baleful discontent' in the Queen that is to undo Edward: for the more Gaveston provokes Edward to slight her womanhood, the easier victim does she become to any young man who is prompted by lust or self-interest or both to flatter her femininity. Such a man is Young Mortimer—

'gentle Mortimer', 'sweet Mortimer'. These physical relationships—Gaveston's with Edward and Mortimer's with the Queen—develop visually and verbally as the play proceeds. At first they are tentative and subtle; but, as commitment increases, they become less discreet. The point of no return is reached in Act I, scene iv, where the Queen surprises her husband in Gaveston's company. Edward is screwing himself up to part with Gaveston following the second banishment which he has signed. It is an intensely sado-masochistic parting, with Edward enjoying an ecstasy of grief as he is verbally flayed by Gaveston for his treachery. The climax comes at line 137.

Edward: The time is little that thou hast to stay,
And, therefore, give me leave (*note the order of those words: Gaveston is to give Edward leave*) to look my fill:
But come, sweet friend, I'll bear thee on thy way.
Gaveston: The peers will frown.
Edward: I pass not for their anger—
(*at this point the line is broken; there is a pause; something happens; then it continues*)
Come let us go
O, that we might as well return as go.
Enter Queen Isabella.

This curt stage direction marks the final breach between Edward and Isabella. In production Isabella must be seen to enter one and a half lines earlier following Edward's 'I pass not for their anger—' that is, at the point where the line is broken and Edward embraces Gaveston. This is what occupies the pause. Caught thus in the act, Edward, who has already thrown discretion to the winds in dismissing the anger of his nobles, dismisses her's as rashly.

'Fawn not on me, French strumpet! get thee gone!'

From this point forward the scene gets steadily more intemperate and hysterical and reaches its climax at lines 165–70.

Isabella: Witness this heart, that, sighing for thee, breaks,
How dear my lord is to poor Isabel.

173

Edward: And witness Heaven how dear thou art to me:
  There weep: for till my Gaveston be repealed,
  Assure thyself thou com'st not in my sight.
            Exeunt Edward and Gaveston.

The Queen then breaks down completely in the following soliloquy. The structure, pace and emotion of the scene demands that what Edward calls Heaven (and Isabella) to witness in line 167 is his physical relationship with Gaveston. What he should do at this point therefore is to walk slowly and deliberately to Gaveston and kiss him on the mouth, leaving the Queen to recoil in horror at the truth now wholly revealed. For the next fifteen lines Isabella has the stage to herself. The next person to enter, in company with other lords, is Mortimer. Edward has sealed his own doom.

Isabella: Ah Mortimer! now breaks the King's hate forth,
  And he confesseth that he loves me not.

The divorce, in nature at least, is complete, and Mortimer wastes no time in seizing his opportunity.

Mortimer: Cry quittance, madam, then; and love not him.

Inflection, eye and gesture suffice to suggest the next step: and once Young Mortimer's ambition has been supplied with this double objective of possessing both Isabella and the crown, the wheel of Fortune starts to raise him up and to carry Edward down. The repeal of Gaveston's banishment transpires to be only the prelude to his death: the flight of Mortimer from England only the prelude to his return under Isabella's banner and as custodian of the heir-apparent. Edward withstands these blows to his pride and confidence with remarkable resilience and fortitude. There is no talk from him of sitting on the ground and telling sad stories of the death of kings while battles rage round him: only a high courage in the field, a self-righteous blaze of indignation and an obstinate adherence to his own nature. Young Spencer (who where stage make-up is concerned should clearly bear a strong physical resemblance to Gaveston) simply refills the gap in his life left by the departed Gaveston, a second pirate succeeding to the duties of the first. Edward

PLATE XV

20   THE MASK OF FLORIMÈNE
Design for a pastoral stage-setting by Inigo Jones, 1635. Reproduced
by permission of the Trustees of the Chatsworth Settlement.

PLATE XVI

21   RUBENS' PAINTING OF BRITANNIA
Perfecting the Union of England and Scotland under James I: Whitehall
Engraving by Simon Gribelin, 1720, of a panel in the ceiling of
Inigo Jones' Banqueting House commissioned from Rubens by
Charles I. The panel is one of the two rectangular paintings flanking
the Apotheosis of James I and depicts the Union as an infant
identifiable by means of the armorial shield in the top left-hand
corner in which the Arms of the King of Scotland are crossed with
those of the King of England. Britannia is depicted in the act of
crowning the child in the presence of King James.

Reproduced by permission of
the British Museum

cannot control or escape his own nature and this leads him to the act of political folly that is destined to cost him his life. With all his enemies captured and in his power, he singles out Young Mortimer for imprisonment instead of execution with the other rebels. Thus given a second chance Mortimer escapes and returns with Isabella to subject Edward to a crushing military defeat. Neither Edward's courage nor his generosity can save him now. Betrayed at Neath Abbey, stripped of his regalia and friends at Kenilworth and crucified in the cesspits of Berkeley Castle, Edward's fall arouses pity and terror in the spectator of truly tragic proportions. Meantime we see Mortimer possessed of Isabella and aspiring, under the guise of Lord Protector to Prince Edward, to rule as a dictator in the land.

> The prince I rule, the queen I do command,
> And with a lowly congé to the ground,
> The proudest lords salute me as I pass;
> I seal, I cancel, I do what I will. (IV, iv, 48–51)

This is another Faustus, another Tamburlaine, another Hitler or a Stalin. Yet beyond position lies the opportunity that such power provides to indulge the nature that craved it. Mortimer wants power in order to be feared.

> Feared am I more than loved;—let me be feared,
> And when I frown, make all the court look pale.[1]

The young puritan of Act I, scene iv, who condones Edward's 'wanton humour' but cannot abide gaudy apparel and luxury, reveals himself to be a sadist devoid of compassion and seeking to inflict pain on his victims. It is in this spirit that he commissions Gurney, Matravis and Lightborn to undertake their heartless and despicable errands, having first won round Isabella to connive at Edward's murder. Both Isabella and Mortimer are betrayed by the circumstancial evidence of the return of Mortimer's letter to Gurney into the hands of the young Prince Edward and are executed for their crimes.

---

[1] Dramatic precedent for these sentiments is provided by the bombastic tyrant Herod of the Towneley Cycle following the massacre of the Innocents.

Thus both Edward and Mortimer, protagonist and anta-gonist of this drama, die violently as victims of their own natures: but Edward, the masochist homosexual playboy, and Mortimer, the sadistic heterosexual puritan, are deliberately contrasted as rulers in the course of the play's action and both found wanting. Marlowe achieves this with an 'alienation effect' worthy of Brecht. The most interesting feature of it, at least in rehearsal and production, is the impact which it has upon the emotions of the audience. For most people, Edward's conduct in respect of Gaveston and more particularly in respect of the Queen, evokes a kind of horrified fascination together with a rapid withdrawal of respect: the beneficiary is Mortimer whose solid virtues and championship of the Queen win the sympathy and admiration that is draining away from Edward. In the central section of the play Mortimer acquires an ascend-ancy over Edward in the esteem of the audience by presenting himself as the fearless champion of the oppressed and the rooter-out of corruption in high places. This ascendancy is main-tained so long as it is on the Queen's, Prince Edward's and the country's behalf that his courageous and at times desperate actions are undertaken. Immediately it becomes clear however that this seeming generosity is merely a cloak for his own ambitions, Mortimer, like King Edward before him, begins to lose the audience's respect. The character whom Marlowe uses to effect this *volte-face* is Edmund, Earl of Kent, who first deserts Edward in Act III, scene iii (banished for speaking his mind), only to regret in Act IV, scene v, the folly of his decision to join Mortimer. On the battlefield near Bristol a dim realiza-tion of Mortimer's real intentions dawns upon him which leads him to speak his mind in soliloquy.

> Edward, this Mortimer aims at thy life!
> O fly him, then! But, Edmund, calm this rage,
> Dissemble, or thou diest; for Mortimer
> And Isabel do kiss, while they conspire:
> And yet she bears a face of love forsooth.
> Fie on that love that hatcheth death and hate!

Kent's suspicions are immediately confirmed in the latter part of the scene by Mortimer's ambivalent attitude to Prince

Edward and by his brutal treatment of his elderly prisoner, Old
Spencer. As this happens so King Edward begins to rise again
in the esteem of the audience. Dignified in defeat, loyal to his
friends, generous to his enemies, he grows in stature as suffering,
first spiritual, then physical, descends upon him.

> O Gaveston, 'tis for thee that I am wronged,
> For me, both thou and both the Spencers died!
> And for your sakes a thousand wrongs I'll take.
> The Spencers' ghosts, wherever they remain,
> Wish well to mine; then tush, for them I'll die.
>
> (V, iii, 41-5)

His resignation to grotesque indignities and his fortitude under
torture release a nobility of spirit which serve in the auditorium
to engender an anger against the perpetrator of this cruelty and
which the strict, poetic justice of the manner of Edward's
murder only serves to increase. Better an Edward with all his
faults (they are at least hot-blooded and warm-hearted) than a
Mortimer with his, reared as they are on envy, pride and the
pleasure derived from inflicting pain. It is these astonishing
reversals of sympathy which create the remarkable alienating
effect. Our emotions may well be engaged subjectively with the
fortunes of the principal characters, indeed Marlowe takes
great pains to ensure that they are: but at the play's close we
cannot escape viewing both protagonist and antagonist objectively. The cathartic draining of pity and fear leaves the mind
free to distinguish tints of virtue from shades of vice and to
assess Princes in terms of the effect of power upon their characters. We may apply our conclusions to English Princes, but the
historical source material of the play itself is strictly subordinate
to moral and psychological issues of universal application which
this historical source material serves to illustrate.

Thus, if I am anywhere near correct in this analysis of the
narrative line of Edward II, it would seem that Marlowe was
here attempting to write a tragedy in the full classical sense of
the word. English history of the fourteenth century is used in the
true Aristotelian sense of 'myths', the hero is a Prince and
'harmartia', 'peripeteia' and 'discovery' are all used schematic-
ally to effect a catharsis. Edward is the hero and his 'harmartia'

is his inability to observe that discretion in his relations with Gaveston urged upon him by his peers. As a willing accomplice to Gaveston's outrage upon the Bishop of Coventry in Act I scene i (lines 175–207) he brings down a curse upon his head.

Gaveston: He shall to prison, and there die in bolts.
King Edward: Ay, to the Tower, the Fleet, or where thou wilt.
Bishop: For this offence, be thou accursed of God!

This folly reaches its climax in Act I scene iv when Edward's treatment of the Queen translates her love to hate and provides Mortimer with his opportunity to focus opposition to Gaveston on his own leadership. The 'peripety' or reversal follows Edward's military victory over his opponents and is contained in his decision to order their immediate execution but to reserve Mortimer for judgement and punishment at a later date (III, iii). The following scene (IV, i) contains Mortimer's escape and thus the start of Edward's overthrow. The discovery begins at the end of Act IV when Edward becomes Mortimer's prisoner, and extends through Act V to reveal both the other half of Edward's nature and the true colours of both Mortimer and Isabella. These revelations are so juxtaposed as to produce a cathartic effect in terms of both pity and terror.

The case therefore for regarding Marlowe's *Edward II* as a successful attempt at tragedy in the Aristotelian manner is a strong one. If accepted it certainly provides the producer in the theatre with a much stronger directive for casting and rehearsal than Marlowe's own cumbersome title. The latter invites episodic treatment of historical narrative for its own sake which, if followed, dilutes the concentrated attention upon character which makes this play the remarkably close-knit entity that it really is. By the same token, a literal interpretation of Shakespeare's title for *Richard II* invites the cutting of all material that is not strictly relevant to Richard's fall, a treatment which, if followed, inevitably destroys the wide-ranging political morality invested in the fortunes of Henry Bolingbroke for which Richard's tragic fall is only the launching platform.

It is my contention therefore that Marlowe's play may fairly be described as neo-classical in intention and execution, the sort of product, in short, that might be expected from a Cambridge graduate in 1590. Shakespeare's play, just as self-evidently, is not: rather does the relationship of its form to its content spring naturally from the native, English dramatic tradition, grounded on biblical narrative treated typologically. The key to the interpretation of the parable lies in Act III scene iv, which appropriately enough is set in a garden. It is there that Queen Anne hears the rumour that her husband is to be deposed.

Gardener: Depress'd he is already, and deposed
          'Tis doubt he will be: . . .
Queen: Thou, old Adam's likeness, set to dress this garden,
          How dares thy harsh rude tongue sound this unpleasing
             news?
          What Eve, what serpent, hath suggested thee
          To make a second fall of cursed man?
          Why dost thou say King Richard is deposed?
          Darest thou, thou little better thing than earth,
          Divine his downfall?

This is not just a casual, rhetorical response to shock and distress: it is a deliberate forecasting of the events of the next scene couched in prefigurative language designed to equip the audience to interpret the parable that the play represents as it approaches its point of crisis, Bolingbroke's 'disobedience' and the consequences that this will have for everyone in England for generations. This is indeed tragedy, but Christian in spirit and cast in a form not dreamed of by Aristotle or the ancient Greeks.

I I

'A Midsummer Night's Dream':
The Setting and the Text

So often has it been said that Elizabethan public playhouses were devoid of scenery of any sort that critics of Elizabethan plays have come to regard the actual settings prescribed by Shakespeare and his contemporaries as of little or no direct relevance to either the form or content of their plays. The purpose of this essay is to question this assumption in the light of what I have said about the use of scenic emblems in the mediaeval and Elizabethan theatre in Essay 8. In discussing *A Midsummer Night's Dream* therefore my object is to examine the particular relationship of setting to text within this play rather than to attempt a critical analysis of fable and story for its own sake: for I believe that mediaeval and Elizabethan playwrights were just as vividly aware of the visual aspects of drama as any of their successors and took as much care to assist the spectator to an understanding of their plays through setting and costume as through verbal imagery: but they were careful, like the Greeks before them and unlike the Romans or contemporary Italians, to keep spectacle in a subordinate relationship to character and action.

In the theatre *A Midsummer Night's Dream* shares with *Twelfth Night* the reputation of attracting more patrons than any other Shakespeare comedy. Its popularity rests largely on the romantic appeal of the fairies combined with the broad humour of the mechanicals. Both these aspects of the play have been strongly reinforced by factors external to the text, notably Mendelssohn's music and the open air productions of Max Rheinhardt and Robert Atkins. (See *Plate XIII*, no. 17.) Tyrone Guthrie created a critical stir in 1952 with his production of the play for the Old Vic by revealing to audiences that, given the right actors and the right direction, the lovers could be at least as entertaining if not more so to today's audience than either the fairies or the mechanicals. This possibility, once recognized, raises the question of where artistic unity is to be found in a play compounded of such diverse elements or, indeed, if any exists: for in addition to the three strands of narrative already mentioned there is a fourth, the story of Duke Theseus and Hippolyta. It is normal to couple the Duke and his bride with the lovers in critical discussions, but this assumption is not born out by the actual shape of the plot since their story provides a distinct frame within which the other three threads of the plot are set, rather than a third pair of lovers to make the confusion between the other two couples the worse confounded. If therefore there are four narrative elements within the play these are not matched by a direct correspondence of settings. The action passes either at the Athenian Court (where all is clarity) or in the wood near Athens (where all is confusion): reason dominates the one, emotion the other.

A strikingly similar relationship of settings to plot may be discerned in Milton's *Comus,* and also the much less familiar but no less important Pastoral, *The Faithful Shepherdess* by John Fletcher. Fletcher's scene is Thessaly, not Athens, and the contrast in the double setting is between open pasture and forest. Milton presents his Maskers first in 'a wild wood' and then before Ludlow town and the President's castle. In each instance the setting is used by the dramatist for a purpose beyond that of simply identifying the locality of the stage-action, for it is picked up figuratively within the imagery of the dialogue and is thus made indicative of the relationship between theme and fable. In other words, these woods are both themselves in a literal sense and also a symbol of the state of being in which at least some of the principal characters are presented and discussed. Nor can there be much doubt that on the literal and symbolic levels Fletcher borrowed as much in his Pastoral tragi-comedy from Shakespeare's Comedy as Milton did from both in devising his Mask.

I do not wish here to discuss the degree of this borrowing in any detail: suffice it to say that Puck, the Satyr and the Attendant Spirit resemble one another in what they do and say at many points (and notwithstanding major differences of character and function), that Fletcher's Amoret and Amarillis resemble Hermia and Helena in the vicissitudes of their love affairs as closely as Milton's Sabrina mirrors Fletcher's God of the River, and that in all three entertainments the forest serves to confuse love with lust and temperance with infatuation. In *Comus*, moreover, the real-life figures of the Earl and Countess of Bridgwater to whom the Maskers are presented provide a frame for the story of the Lady and her brothers (in reality the Earl's own children) of a kind that has marked affinities to the function of the Theseus and Hippolyta story in *A Midsummer Night's Dream*. What therefore seems to be quite plain is that central to all three entertainments is a discussion of adolescent attitudes to sex and that this idea is emblematically presented in terms of a forest that is at once hospitable and frightening; hospitable to wild beasts and outlaws, frightening to travellers whose way leads through its dark and narrow paths. Yet whether the wood is regarded as friendly or hostile it is something through which all of us must pass.

For Milton it is 'this ominous wood' which Comus chooses for his home and it is 'in thick shelter of black shades imbower'd' that Comus lays his snares for 'every weary traveller'. One such is the Lady whose distress makes her uncertain whether to describe her environment as 'the kind hospitable woods' or 'the blind mazes of this tangled wood'. Hermia, having first welcomed the protection offered by the wood for her elopement, comes to regard it very differently.

182

Never so weary, never so in woe;
Bedabbled with the dew, and torn with briers;
I can no further crawl, no further go.

Milton's Brothers directly echo this same sentiment in debating
where their sister may 'betake her / From the chill dew, among
rude burs and thistles'. For Fletcher as for Milton the forest is
'ominous' (*F.S.*, IV, iii, i); while for eager lovers it offers
prospects of delight, each of them comes to learn that bushes
shelter beasts. Both Fletcher and Milton make the dangerous
and ominous aspect of their woods explicit in the characterization of its principal occupant, the Sullen Shepherd and Comus.
Both of these characters represent the sensuous part of human
nature which will control us unless we learn to control it.
Comus, it is to be noted, is not killed or taken prisoner; he
lives as an enduring threat.

Shakespeare, in his treatment of the subject is more subtle.
Lust is not characterized as it is by Fletcher in the savage
actions of the Sullen Shepherd or by Milton in the brutish rout
who make up Comus' entourage. Throughout *A Midsummer
Night's Dream* the perils of sex for adolescents, even its tragic
potentialities, are treated comically.

All three dramatists thus present sex as a wood through
which in adolescence everyone is obliged to pass. On the far
side of the wood is marriage and survival in the blessing of
children. Within the wood itself lie the pitfalls of physical
infatuation which may or may not be matched by the ties of
reason: if not so matched, the infatuation will resolve itself
farcically or tragically at the lovers' expense. Once the significance of the forest setting for the major part of the dramatic
action in *A Midsummer Night's Dream* has been grasped, the
structural pattern of the play emerges clearly enough.

Theseus and Hippolyta represent mature love, a state in
which reason and desire are in perfect equilibrium. For
Theseus this is no first affair, as we learn from Oberon and
Titania in Act II scene i; and Hippolyta who was his enemy is
now his friend. This mutual regard in which they hold one
another is no cold affair of the head alone, for in the opening
lines of the play they are eagerly contemplating the physical

consummation of their betrothal: yet they are sufficiently in command of their natures to observe protocol and wait upon the lunar omens.[1] This contrast between hot passion and cool reason is the foundation of the play and is appropriately spelt out at length by Theseus in Act V scene i, lines 2–22, in his famous speech about the lunatic, the lover and the poet. He and Hippolyta also enter the wood but when they do, it is with their hounds: it holds no terrors for them. Oberon and Titania have made up their quarrel and the fairies have vanished with the morning lark.

Against the self-disciplined love of Theseus for Hippolyta is set the impetuous ardour of Lysander, Demetrius, Hermia and Helena, youngsters whose discovery of love as a force in their lives makes them heedless of either parental advice or the law of the land. Quite unable to appreciate in this first heady rapture that parents may have been through this situation before them, the strength of their emotion makes them deaf to reason. Elopement to the wood in the face of both parental and magisterial opposition thus figures for the audience the headstrong determination of young lovers to learn by their own experience rather than by that of their elders.

Once in the wood the force of the arguments urged upon them by their elders begins to become apparent. What exactly do they love? The physical image of the loved one? The talk and companionship of the lover? Perhaps both? Perhaps neither? The longer they stay in the wood the swifter do their feelings seem to change and the more perplexed and exhausted do they become with each *volte-face* in their feelings towards each other. The controlling agent in these changes is presented figuratively to the audience in the persons of Oberon and Titania and their fairy trains whom of course the lovers never see. They stand as emblems for nature, depicted here in the guise of lunar control over sex and fertility. The moon is thus not only 'the governess of floods' (II, i, 104) but the presiding genius over the wood of sex. The present turmoil in the ordering of nature,

---

[1] It is for the same reason that Milton's Lady escapes from Comus, not because she has killed or rejected her sensual nature, but because she has learnt to control it.

or the distemper that is adolescence—we may take it either way —is presented to us in terms of the quarrel between Oberon and Titania that has 'disturb'd their sports since middle summer's spring'. While they are at odds with each other—be the cause a disputed Indian boy or anything else as trivial—climate, seasons, courtship and procreation will be subject to alteration and miscarriage. In the play, this quarrel is resolved by the close of Act IV and so is the story of the lovers. By then Jack does love Jill, parents (Egeus) come to accept the inevitable and the law (Theseus) is satisfied: the play is over. Why then did Shakespeare find it necessary to spin it out for a further thirty minutes with a fifth Act, and why did he bother to complicate a straightforward stage action by adding the story of the mechanicals?

My own answer is that both steps were necessary if the farcical and tragic potentialities of Hermia's elopement as well as the simple mutability of first love were to be illustrated to the audience within the framework of a comedy. These serious possibilities are made apparent through Titania's absurd courtship of an ass and Thisbe's luckless wooing of Pyramus: Titania almost marries a beast, Thisbe is killed by one. The play of 'Pyramus and Thisbe' with its 'tragical mirth' both provides the excuse for adding the story of the mechanicals to the narrative skein of the plot and allows the tragic consequences of infatuation, essential to the full thematic development of the play, to be treated in a manner befitting a comedy: for not only can it be used to parody the earlier part of the Hermia/ Lysander story but, even more daringly, to parody an already familiar tragedy devoted to this very subject, *Romeo and Juliet*. Capulet's orchard walls 'are high and hard to climb' and seemingly as effective a barrier to Romeo's approach to Juliet as 'the Wall' 'presented' by Snout the Joiner is to contact between Pyramus and Thisbe. Yet 'passion lends them power' and, just as Romeo finds his way to Juliet's balcony, so Pyramus finds a cranny 'right and sinister / Through which the fearful lovers are to whisper'. The moon presides over both encounters. Juliet, waiting for Romeo addresses a passionate invocation to the night sky:

Come night, come Romeo, come, thou day in night;
For thou wilt lie upon the wings of night
Whiter than new snow on a raven's back.
Come, gentle night, come, loving, black-brow'd night,
Give me my Romeo. (III, ii, 17–21)

Pyramus, in a similar plight, opines:

O grim-look'd night, O night, with hue so black,
O night, which ever art, when day is not:
O night, O night, alack, alack, alack,
I fear my Thisbe's promise is forgot. (V, i, 168–71)

Similarly acute and hilarious parody of Capulet's monument is presented at Ninus' tomb. First, Romeo:

Eyes, look your last!
Arms, take your last embrace! and, lips, O you
The doors of breath, seal with a righteous kiss
A dateless bargain to engrossing death!
Come, bitter conduct, come, unsavoury guide!
Thou desperate pilot, now at once run on
The dashing rocks thy sea-sick weary bark.
(V, iii, 112–18)

Then, Pyramus:

Eyes do you see!
How can it be!
O dainty duck! O dear!
Thy mantle good,
What, stain'd with blood!
Approach, ye Furies fell!
. . . .
Come, tears, confound
Out, sword, and wound
The pap of Pyramus; . . . (V, i, 269–87)

The use which Shakespeare makes, however, of the mechanicals' play is not confined to turning his own *Tragedy of Romeo and Juliet* inside out for its comic potentialities; it serves also to remind the audience of everything they have just witnessed in the wood near Athens following Hermia's elopement. Again, however, the essential thematic images of wood and lunar dominance over love and fertility are turned to comic effect.

Quince: This man, with lantern, dog, and bush of thorn,
　　Presenteth Moonshine; for, if you will know,
　By moonshine did these lovers think no scorn
　　To meet at Ninus' tomb, there, there to woo.

(V, i, 134-7)

Presumably the bush of thorn had to do double duty for the
'mulberry shade' in which Thisbe, according to Quince's Prologue, was tarrying when Pyramus found her blood-stained
shawl.

Having used the mechanicals in this way to meet the difficult
problem of presenting the tragic possibilities latent in sexual
infatuation between young lovers without distorting either the
pattern or mood of a light-hearted comedy, it was a relatively
easy matter to employ them to deal with the farcical aspect of
the subject, an infatuation which, once spent, leaves in its
wake amazement and disgust. Shakespeare simply interpolates
this into the heart of his principal stage action, thus linking the
kaleidoscope fantasies of the lovers with both the rehearsal of
the mechanicals' play and the discord between the fairies. For
this purpose two characters are required, a delicate and
sophisticated lady with a mind of her own and a sufficiently
privileged position in society to use it, and a good looking young
workman whose tastes and conversation are as brutish and
banal as his physique is striking. The first of these requirements is to hand in Titania who is both a Queen and ethereal:
the other is available in Bottom—Bully Bottom the Weaver—
who, once he has been crowned with a donkey's head, becomes
as well defined a symbol as the Fairy Queen herself: he is,
indeed, 'translated'. To the audience he is an emblem of all
brainless bullies, but to Titania he is an 'Angel'.

　Mine ear is much enamour'd of thy note;
　So is mine eye enthralled to thy shape. (III, i, 133-4)

For her it is love at first sight. Bottom is honest enough to
express surprise: 'and yet, to say truth, reason and love keep
little company together'. Like all women, Titania thinks that
she can change Bottom by 'purging his mortal grossness'.
Bottom, however, remains obstinately gross using his fairy
'servants' to no better purpose than to assist him in scratching

187

and in providing crude music and coarse food. As Titania awakes from her thraldom so she is consumed with shame and disgust at the folly of her conduct.

O, how mine eyes do loathe his visage now. (IV, i, 79)

The destruction of sensuality is thus achieved in this instance by sensuality itself.

In point of structure therefore this play takes the form of a narrative contained within four acts, together with a recapitulation and cadenza added in a fifth Act. The frame for the narrative is provided in Theseus, presented as lover, Duke and judge: the discord between parent and child which is brought to him for arbitration in I, i is resolved by him in IV, i. The exposition is necessarily slow since the audience has to be carefully introduced to the seemingly disparate components of this complex parable. Lovers, mechanicals and fairies are thus each given a scene to themselves in which to communicate their thoughts and purposes in relation to the moonlit wood and their presence in it. Once this is clear the spirit of laughter that is to inform the comedy can begin to spread its wings: it is directed first at the spectacle of young lovers who have no sooner sworn eternal devotion with their lips than their eyes begin to betray them. This basic situation is milked of all its possible permutations by the exaggeration of poetic licence and is then synthesized in the farcical spectacle of Titania's infatuation for the ass-headed Bottom. With this completed the moon can enter a new phase, Oberon can reach a new accord with Titania, Theseus and Hippolyta can effect a reconcilement between the lovers that accords with both their own hard-won knowledge of themselves and the law and prepare to consummate their own marriage.

The fifth Act provides the room to show how 'the story of the night told over . . . grows to something of great constancy'. This important task is entrusted to Theseus and Hippolyta in the first thirty lines. It only remains thereafter to comment on an aspect of the woodland adventure which might have transpired but happily did not, the untimely death of one or more of the lovers. This fitly forms the subject of the evening's

Revels. Demetrius and Lysander may laugh in a sophisticated manner at the amateurish presentation of the 'tedious brief scene of young Pyramus / and his love Thisby'; but the laughter which this brilliantly compressed parody of *Romeo and Juliet* provokes in the auditorium is directed as much against them and their recently observed cavortings with Hermia and Helena in the wood near Athens as at the ham actors who meet violent ends in the moonlit mulberry shade and thorn thicket beside old Ninus' tomb. With every aspect of the midsummer madness that is young love thus gracefully explored, Shakespeare proceeds to his Epithalamium. Theseus and Hippolyta can now receive the blessing of nature on their marriage from Oberon.

> To the best bride-bed will we;
> Which by us shall blessed be;
> And the issue, there create,
> Ever shall be fortunate.
> So shall all the couples three
> Ever true in loving be.

If moral were wanted for this gossamer vision of adolescent love, its trials, heart-aches and rewards, it is to be found in the final song in *Comus* which Milton uses to reunite the Lady and her Brother with their mother and father.

> Noble Lord, and Lady bright,
> I have brought ye new delight,
> Here behold so goodly grown
> Three fair branches of your own;
> Heav'n hath timely tried their youth,
> Their faith, their patience, and their truth,
> And sent them here through hard assays
> With a crown of deathless praise,
> To triumph in victorious dance
> O'er sensual folly, and intemperance.

The actual scenic requirements of the play comprise three or possibly four simple and commonly used emblems: the throne (Theseus' palace), three or four trees (the wood), a mossy bank and possibly an arbour (for Titania). As all these scenic items formed part of the normal Revels Office stock, Court performance was readily provided for.[1] In a public playhouse the throne would have been pre-set centre stage for Act I scene i, taken up into the 'heavens' (where the moon kept company with the sun and stars) at the end of that scene and not be lowered again until the start of Act V. The centre-stage area would thus have been free for the main action of the play (I, ii–IV) within the wood. Each of the two stage doors would in my opinion have been flanked and to some extent masked by a pair of trees: the alternating actions in different parts of the wood could then be easily represented by alternating use of the centre-stage/stage-left and centre-stage/stage-right areas. The locality of a highly mobile stage-action is thus constantly and easily identifiable for the spectator. The whole fore-stage is free at all times for action both before Theseus in the Palace and for the fairies, mechanicals and lovers in the wood. The economy of means is itself remarkable and possesses the added advantage of making it possible for the acting company that owned the copyright in the text to transport the play complete with its settings to any hall in town or country where an audience could assemble to see it.

[1] See G. Wickham, *Early English Stages*, ii(1), Appendix G, pp. 339–40.

12

Hamlet

(i) *Notes for an actor in the role of Hamlet*[1]

APPROACHING this part nearly four hundred years after Richard Burbage created it, the actor of today is likely to have heard more about the academic debate which has been waged over Hamlet's delay in killing Claudius than about the practical problems which the title role presents to its interpeter.

In killing Claudius . . .

Why should Hamlet kill Claudius, his uncle, his mother's second husband, and King of Denmark? It is this question rather than any question relating to 'delay' which the actor should ask himself in the first instance. He must next establish for himself the approximate age of the Prince who has to answer the first question. For the actor, the most important pointer to Hamlet's age is to be found in the age of Richard Burbage when he created the part. Burbage was thirty-five or thereabouts. That settled, the actor is at liberty to reduce Hamlet's age by as many years as best suits his own person within the limits set by recent university studies at Wittenburg at one end of the scale and Burbage's own age at the other.

Possessed of this knowledge the actor should then ask himself

[1] This section is reprinted from *To Nevill Coghill from Friends*, edited by John Lawlor and W. H. Auden, Faber & Faber Ltd., 1966, pp. 66–81.

what cause he has, if any, deliberately to murder his uncle beyond a commission to that end received from a Ghost. Examination of the text will show that there is none. When the play opens Hamlet does not consciously suspect that his father was assassinated, let alone by his uncle, Claudius. He is in a state of shock following the sudden death of his father, a common case in such circumstances. In this instance, however, the natural shock of bereavement is aggravated by two other blows to personal security and self-confidence. First, although his father's only son and heir, Hamlet has not succeeded to his father's throne: this has passed to his uncle. Secondly, his mother, far from being as shocked as Hamlet by her husband's death, has actually reinforced his uncle's claim to the throne in opposition to his own by marrying Claudius 'within a month' of becoming a widow. It is the unnaturalness of these events which make Hamlet so prickly in his dealings with his uncle-step-father and mother-aunt in Act I, scene ii, and which provoke his first soliloquy at the close of that scene.

The shock of bereavement, wounded self-esteem in being cheated of his hopes of the throne, disgust at an incestuous relationship close enough to contaminate him personally and the anger born of frustration in being powerless even to discuss these issues, complete the range of emotions that the actor may legitimately represent on giving his audience its first acquaintanceship with the character. Only when the Ghost appears *and speaks* is Hamlet given the excuse to focus this collection of hostile emotions upon the person of Claudius and in the direction of a personal revenge.

Ghost: If thou didst ever thy dear father love—
Hamlet: O God!
Ghost: Revenge his foul and most unnatural murder.
Hamlet: Murder!
Ghost: Murder most foul, as in the best it is,
But this most foul, strange and unnatural. (I, v, 23–8)[1]

---

[1] This and all other quotations and references from the text are taken from The Temple Shakespeare, not because it is necessarily the best edition, but because it is the edition which actors find it most convenient to carry in a pocket.

To events which have hitherto been regarded by Hamlet as no
more than 'strange and unnatural' is here added the suspicion
of murder: and to this possibility the next dangerous thought is
swiftly added.

Ghost: The serpent that did sting thy father's life
          Now wears his crown.
Hamlet: O my prophetic soul!
          My uncle!   (I, v, 39–41)

With father's and uncle's places now sharply etched within
this mirky mental picture, what of mother's? To incest, add
adultery.

Ghost: . . . that incestuous, that adulterate beast,
         . . . won to his shameful lust.
         The will of my most seeming-virtuous queen.   (I, v, 42–5)

These then are the true colours of the mother who derided her
son with the unnecessary 'seeming' of his mourning clothes (I, ii,
68–78)! The Hamlet who leaves the stage at the end of Act I,
scene v, is thus in a very different state of mind from that of the
young man who left it three scenes earlier. Gone is the bewilder-
ment of shock, grief and irritation; in its place stand sharply
defined suspicions that his 'noble' father did not die, but was
murdered, that the ever-smiling uncle is a 'damnéd villain', a
murderer, and that the 'seeming-virtuous' queen and much
loved mother is a pernicious woman, a lewd adulteress and
perhaps an accomplice in her husband's murder. The focus of
these new definitions is at first so clear to Hamlet that he nearly
confides them to his friend Horatio and to the officers of the
watch.

The question the actor must now ask, and answer for himself,
is this: what stops him? Why, when he is on the point of blurt-
ing out the whole story upon mention of the word 'Offence'
(I, v, 135–40) does he break off so abruptly and take refuge in
platitudes? To argue that if he did confide in Horatio and the
officers the play would be over by the end of Act I is to evade
the question. Hamlet knows that he is now possessed of an
explanation for a seemingly inexplicable sequence of events: he

knows just as clearly that as an explanation, whether arrived at by intuitive processes or by ghostly revelation, it is one that lacks the smallest particle of proof. What reaction will the story produce in the rational and fair-minded Horatio? Incredulity; perhaps a charge of slander; certainly no action. Shakespeare, it should be noted, has given the ambivalence of Hamlet's situation theatrical (i.e. visible and audible) form by the physical placement of the Ghost in this scene. The Ghost is recognized in silhouette against the sky, both seen and heard on *terra firma*, and heard under the earth. Such ubiquity may be a characteristic of God and his spiritual servants: Elizabethans also recognized it as a characteristic of the Devil.

Proof. That is the next step for Hamlet, to find proof: proof of murder, proof of adultery, and proof that the Ghost is a 'truepenny', not Satan in disguise. But where? No shred of evidence beyond the word of this ghost (and that's equivocable) exists to substantiate either murder or adultery. No one saw anything untoward in the orchard. A month has passed and not a murmur has been heard in any part of the court. Even the charge of incest appears to have lacked backers in this court where churchmen are only noticeable by their absence. What happened? An unfortunate chance encounter with a viper and sudden death: so much for father. In the meantime a robust, hard-drinking uncle, duly elected, crowned, impregnable among unsuspecting courtiers who have pledged their honour to defend him and who regard the nephew as a prickly young-ster nursing wounded pride, is swiftly consolidating his authority by dealing firmly with Norwegian enemies. A mother who might naturally be counted his best ally has become estranged from him by marriage to the enemy. In such a situation can the intuitive image of the truth ever be matched by the factual evidence which alone can give it substance? For the actor, as for the Prince, there can only be one answer—not without some extraordinary stroke of luck. As day follows day, this predica-ment becomes more acute. One by one young Hamlet's friends, like his mother before them, are deliberately estranged from him. The initial corruption of the murderer appears the more obvious to Hamlet in the evident contagion which spreads from contact with his uncle's mind and person. Rosencrantz and Guildenstern, the honest companions of university days, are translated into spies. Even Ophelia, once the chief object of his affections, is blighted. Yet, paradoxically and infuriatingly, as conviction grows in proportion with the contagion, so the chances of securing factual evidence of guilt grow ever more remote. Claudius smiles, Polonius smiles, Gertrude smiles. Denmark for anyone trapped between these smiles and his own suspicions is indeed 'a prison' (II, ii, 245–70). Hamlet is prompted by his intuition (commanded by the Ghost) to kill Claudius. Yet, lacking the proof that Claudius murdered King Hamlet, where does young Hamlet stand should he kill his uncle and find that in doing so he has himself murdered an innocent man?

It is this dilemma which underlies his thinking in his next two soliloquies. 'O what a rogue and peasant slave am I!' and 'To be or not to be . . .' The first is triggered off by the ease with which a company of actors can deal out death and destruction on the stage in the certainty that all their victims will get up again in time to join their killers for supper and with no crime on their conscience to spoil their appetite. If actors in a mere 'dream of passion' can be so active and resolute, what sort of a figure does Hamlet, 'the son of a dear father murdered', cut with the world? Here the intuitive image has become equated with fact. Murdered. The evidence for this surmise is no whit firmer at this point in the play (unless the estrangements of former friends be taken as evidence) than it was yesterday or on any day since his father died. Yet the mere effort of translating surmise into supposed fact allows the actor-Prince to work himself into a passion which eclipses in rhetorical bombast the dream-passion of the First Player and permits him, in the release of emotion which it brings, to devise a plan that will force the missing evidence to declare itself. With 'false fire'—a re-enactment of his father's 'Murder' performed as a tragedy to entertain the King and Queen—the Prince will 'tent' his uncle 'to the quick'. The plan is imaginative: it is also pathetic. What can it achieve? The King may dislike the play; he may even take offence at it; but what can this *prove*? Nothing, and Hamlet knows it. 'To be, or not to be . . . '

It is in the context of this famous soliloquy that we meet him next, a mere fifty lines later, the energy and elation of the previous scene drained away; in its place a thoughtfulness as frustrated, despairing and suicidal as that of Act I, scene ii. Compare the opening lines of the two speeches:

Hamlet: O, that this too too solid flesh would melt,
Thaw, and resolve itself into a dew!
Or that the Everlasting had not fix'd
His canon 'gainst self-slaughter! (I, ii, 129–32)

Hamlet: To be, or not to be—that is the question;
Whether 'tis nobler in the mind to suffer
The slings and arrows of outrageous fortune,
Or to take arms against a sea of troubles,
And by opposing end them? (III, i, 56–60)

The point for the actor to grasp in the second of these two soliloquies is that the 'outrageous fortune' to which Hamlet refers is not a general exclamation against the human condition, but a particular summary of his personal predicament, grave suspicions of gross private wrongs without a shred of evidence acceptable in a court of law with which to seek redress. Even the supposed test of the forthcoming 'Tragedy of Gonzago' is an illusion: his own surmises may be strengthened still further, but no one else will be one whit the wiser or less likely to greet an open accusation with derision.[1] The exception is Horatio. Hamlet has taken him into his confidence (III, ii, 80), but he admits that the best they can do after testing the King with the play is to join judgements 'in censure of his seeming' (line 92). Suicide appears to offer an escape from this impasse as it did from his earlier malaise before his encounter with the Ghost: but as in the former instance (I, ii) this path was blocked, at least to him, by 'the Everlasting's canon' or Divine law, so now (III, i) it is conscience which forbids recourse to this solution —*his* conscience, Hamlet's, the actor's. It is conscience which provokes the famous question, 'To be, or not to be . . .'; his conscience in anguished conflict with his predicament. If con-

[1] For members of Burbage's audience, derision is too mild a word: such an accusation then could well supply the basis for a charge of high treason.

science wins, it is because Hamlet's conscience is his own, an orthodox, Elizabethan, Christian conscience, and because he has already despaired of finding the legal evidence that will release him from his predicament.

Since he is left so clearly a slave to his conscience at the end of this soliloquy, it is important that the actor should know precisely what this conscience tells him; for it is this which will inform all his subsequent actions. It prohibits suicide: that much is explicit, repeated twice and the reason given. Quite as important, it prohibits murder. That is implicit in the nature of his own predicament: he would not be consulting his conscience at the present time unless he recognized murder as a crime and one that must be punished. The clarity of this thinking however is 'sicklied o'er' as the loneliness and complexity of his actual situation bears in upon him. Is this a case of murder? Supposing that it is, whose is the responsibility for avenging it? His own as anger, disgust and honour dictate? Or that of the same Everlasting Being whose divine law forbids murder and suicide? The Ghost confirmed his own instinct.

> *Ghost:* If thou didst ever thy dear father love
> Revenge his foul and most unnatural murder.

Claudius' case in Hamlet's eyes is no better than Cain's, a fact which Claudius will later admit to himself and to the audience.

> *Claudius:* O, my offence is rank, it smells to heaven;
> It hath the primal eldest curse upon't. (III, iii, 36-7)

But Hamlet does not know this. And what sort of a Ghost is it that urges him to commit a murder without giving him and his friends the *prima facie* evidence of guilt?

It is difficult for us with our intimate knowledge of the text as literature ever to forget the chapel scene in which Claudius admits his guilt and to view the situation confronting Hamlet with Hamlet's eyes: yet in the theatre knowledge of Claudius' guilt is deliberately withheld from us until Act III, scene iii.[1]

---

[1] This full confession is prefigured by Shakespeare in a powerful hint dropped for us two scenes earlier. 'How smart a lash that speech doth give my conscience', etc. (III, i, 49-54).

We must make the effort therefore required to remember the ambivalence of the Ghost's command to Hamlet. If we do so, we will not fall into the trap of criticizing the Prince for his 'delay' in executing it instead of commending him for the nicety of his scruples. Alas, our very sophistication in respect of this play more often makes us guilty of jumping to the same rash conclusions as Hamlet almost does himself, equating surmise with fact without evidence. By blaming both Claudius for his cynical hypocrisy and Hamlet for his delay in despatching him we distort the form of the play—the shape that Shakespeare actually gave to it—and thus the play's meaning.

Whatever fashionable or personal fetishes a director may care to release on his actors in the name of this play, the actor in the title role must cling to the one certain fact about the part: Hamlet himself never at any time throughout the play obtains the proof he needs that Claudius murdered his father or committed adultery with his mother. Where Claudius and Gertrude are concerned, the worst charge that Hamlet can prove against them before the final Act is one of incest. In that last Act a strict pattern of justice is meted out to all guilty parties. Laertes kills Hamlet in revenge for the murder of Polonius. Hamlet revenges himself upon Laertes. Claudius murders the Queen (inadvertently by poison) and meets his own death at Hamlet's hands for this act. Claudius' own admissions at the *prie-dieux* in III, iii, prove for the audience that the Ghost was indeed a 'truepenny'; but Hamlet dies as he had lived without the proof of guilt that he had sought. Order is restored and Denmark cleansed by the wholesale destruction of both families, leaving a fresh start to be made by Fortinbras. The actor who knows this is more than halfway to the shaping of a firm and consistent portrait of the Prince.

Most of what remains for him to do in drafting the outline of the character that he is going to present derives from a knowledge of how to handle the 'antic disposition'. If Hamlet himself is to be believed, this is something 'put on', a disguise for his true feelings and intentions, an act. In no play is Shakespeare's creative imagination more richly coloured by his personal knowledge of the actor's profession than it is in *Hamlet*.

The constant harping upon the seemingness of outward appearances, the company of players and their play, the 'fantasy and trick of fame' that masks the horrors of war (IV, iv, 61), the hollow ring of rhetoric in a graveyard and the antic disposition assumed by Hamlet are all threads from the same skein: they are woven into the fabric of the play as recurrent reminders or reflections of Hamlet's own predicament. The actor, therefore, should try to approach them not as separate aspects of the character or of the plot but rather as a pianist would tackle variations upon a theme within the movements of a Sonata.

When the audience first meets Hamlet in I, ii, he believes himself to be, like Troilus, 'as true as truth's simplicity'.

Hamlet: Seems, madam! Nay, it is: I know not seems. (I, ii, 76)

Yet a mere two scenes later (I, v, 169–79) it is this same young man who is resolving to employ that same 'ambiguous giving out' as he objects to so violently in the conduct of his uncle and his mother. This should be recognized by the actor for what it is, the start of that contamination of Hamlet's mind which contact with the murderer induces; for, without noticing what he is doing, he allows the harsh facts of life to corrupt him into adopting an expedient—the 'seemingness' of the antic disposition—which he recognized in others as the factor which distorts truth's simplicity into pretence and duplicity. Pretence in the actor is something Hamlet can admire: successful assumption of passions which he does not feel is not only the basis of his vocation but the yardstick of his skill in it. Offstage, however, pretence is duplicity and a disguise for cowardice, hypocrisy and guilt.

Once Hamlet has decided to make use of the 'antic disposition' his character begins to disintegrate, to split up into three related but independent selfs, one normal and two abnormal. Of these abnormal personalities one is deliberately put on and taken off as occasion demands, the wayward, clowning, lovesick and sometimes vicious antic disposition of the actor: this is quite self-conscious, external to himself and used to baffle and torment those people about him with whom he is not deeply involved emotionally. Polonius, Rosencrantz and Guildenstern bear the brunt of it. Over this disposition or 'conceit' (II, ii, 579) Hamlet the man is always himself the master. The other abnormal personality or disposition, however, is more serious and sinister since it is unselfconscious and takes possession of him in ways which he only becomes aware of after the passion has spent itself. This is no 'conceit': it is an enslaving madness which, in Hamlet, is provoked into active life by contact with those people with whom he is (or becomes) closely involved emotionally—Claudius, Ophelia, Laertes, the 1st Player and, above all, his mother. It manifests itself in a variety of destructive rages from which spring the brutal *volte-face* in his treatment of Ophelia within Act III, scene i,[1] the ineffectual mousetrap of the-play-within-the-play, the murder of Polonius and the first fight with Laertes in Ophelia's grave, the actions which collectively bring Claudius and Laertes together into the fatal conspiracy that is destined to cost Hamlet his life.

There is a further point about these variations on a theme of rage which deserves attention from the actor: those which stem from contact with or reflection upon Claudius are noticeably forced and rhetorical. Hamlet recognizes this himself in the middle of his 'O, what a rogue and peasant slave am I!' soliloquy.

Hamlet: Why, what an ass am I! This is most brave,
That I, the son of a dear father murder'd,
Prompted to my revenge by heaven and hell,
Must, like a whore, unpack my heart with words,
And fall a-cursing, like a very drab,
A scullion! Fie upon't! foh! (II, ii, 611–15)

The really dangerous emotional fuse is Gertrude. Hamlet's emotional relationships with others, however close, are not tainted by considerations of heredity as they are with her.

Queen: Have you forgot me?
Hamlet: No, by the rood, not so:
You are the queen, your husband's brother's wife;
And would it were not so! You are my mother.
(III, iv, 15–17)

---

[1] No one has written more feelingly about the acting of this scene than Nevill Coghill himself: see *Shakespeare's Professional Skills* (1964), pp. 16–24.

It is Gertrude then, more precisely, thoughts of her conduct
in terms of her relationship to him, who generates the passion
which transforms him into its slave notwithstanding all the dic-
tates of his conscience and rational self. This too may be gathered
from the text, if only by inference, from the Ghost's warning.

Ghost: . . . let (not) thy soul contrive
      Against thy mother aught; leave her to heaven,
      And to those thorns that in her bosom lodge
      To prick and sting her. (I, v, 85–7)

And just as Hamlet can, on occasion, recognize the hollowness
of his own rhetorical or 'dream' passion, so he can acknowledge the fatal ease with which the more dangerous passion of
genuine anger can rob his mind of control over his actions.
Apologizing to Horatio for fighting with Laertes in Ophelia's
grave he says,

Hamlet: . . . the bravery of his grief did put me
      Into a towering passion. (V, ii, 78–9)

For the actor, therefore, these sorties into richly varied forms
and styles of passion present major technical problems of
control and modulation, mental, sensory, physical and vocal.
If he is to tackle them successfully, he must establish for himself
a behavioural norm which can serve as a departure point for
the varied forms of abnormality demanded by the role: these
can then be sharply contrasted against and securely superimposed upon the norm. Perhaps the safest starting point for this
is Ophelia's vision of her suitor,

The courtier's, soldier's, scholar's, eye, tongue, sword. (III, i, 159)

Essex could not have shone more brightly in Elizabeth's eyes
than Hamlet in Ophelia's: yet Hamlet tells her that he is 'very
proud, revengeful, ambitious' (III, i, 126). So too was Essex,
as Elizabeth discovered to her cost. Shakespeare allows us to see
Hamlet as Ophelia describes him when he is relaxed and talking
in prose with the players in II, ii, with the grave-diggers in
V, i, and with Horatio in V, ii. We are introduced to his darker

nature, the irritation born of wounded pride and thwarted ambition, in our first encounter with him in I, ii.

On to the light and shade of this basic disposition, it is a comparatively easy matter for the actor to graft the antic disposition of the stage-player; for whether it is an extension of his relaxed self cracking jokes at Polonius' or Osric's expense or an extension of his darker nature throwing out veiled threats in puns and epigrams in the direction of Guildenstern or Claudius, the effect is to provoke laughter in the auditorium. One might well say that an intelligent understanding of the lines, a clear articulation and an accurate sense of timing suffice to meet these problems.

The antics of passion's slave, however, call for skills of a much more exacting kind; for here the heart rather than the head must appear to govern the actor's conduct. Not only does this impose a strain upon both voice and physique, but empty rhetoric and the true Promethean fire must be distinct and distinguishable from each other in the auditorium. How is this to be achieved? This is a question to which no advice, written or verbal, will provide an answer; only rehearsal. When the words have been understood, confided to memory and become second nature to the actor, when they have been thrown about the stage, first this way then that, answers will begin to emerge.

As these answers emerge, often as alternatives and invariably as exciting discoveries, so the actor will feel a growing need to co-ordinate them, selecting and rejecting possibilities by relating one speech to another and one scene to the next. And here an external regulator can, I feel sure, assist him to attain that control over the character as a whole that he is seeking. This regulator is Hamlet's conscience. It works on the simple premise that while both murder and suicide are criminal acts, honour not only permits but impels a son to revenge the murder of a father or a mother upon the murderer. In taking care that Hamlet should lack proof that Claudius murdered his father, Shakespeare provides this conscience with a trip-wire at which it gibs or stumbles. Scrupulous to refrain from killing Claudius without proof of guilt, Hamlet murders Polonius by mistake when in the grip of passion: he murders Claudius when he has proof that Claudius murdered his mother. Only in this moment, when Hamlet is already dying, does Shakespeare allow the passion generated by contact with his corrupt mother to fuse with the rational clarity of vision that has seen enough of life to recognize 'special providence in the fall of a sparrow': these two facets of his nature at last combine into a single source of energy and thus enable him 'with perfect conscience' to determine without doubts or delay precisely what he has to do.

Hamlet: (to Claudius): Here, thou incestuous, murd'rous, damned
Dane,
Drink off this potion. Is thy union here?
Follow my mother. (V, ii, 334–5)

His tragedy is to have murdered Polonius. For this there was no just cause and can be no forgiveness: it has served moreover to vitiate all the scruples of conscience he has entertained towards his uncle and has invited his own death at Laertes' hand. Wise after the event, Hamlet acknowledges that Laertes is fully justified in seeking vengeance for Polonius' and Ophelia's deaths. To Horatio he says,

. . . by the image of my cause I see
The portraiture of his. (V, ii, 76–7)

No apology could be more ironic. Laertes' cause does *not* mirror Hamlet's. Had it done so, Claudius would not still have been alive when Hamlet draws this analogy, and Hamlet himself would not have been so close to death. Laertes' cause is firmly rooted in the proven fact that Hamlet killed his father: Hamlet's cause is grounded only on surmise. Between fact and surmise lies conscience. What Hamlet has to cope with is a constant conflict between a scrupulous conscience which recognizes hypothesis for what it is and the passion awakened by a sense of contamination from an incestuous and possibly adulterous mother which translates hypotheses into facts. It is this conflict within his own person that provides the actor in the role of Hamlet with the essential dynamic for a performance that is consistent with itself in every mood and in every situation with which the character is faced.

(ii) *Uncle-father and Aunt-mother*

One of the more unusual features of the cast-list of *Hamlet* is
that the antagonist of the conflict represented within the play is
equipped, like Janus, with two heads. Claudius and Gertrude
appear before the audience as King and Queen together in
nine scenes out of a total of twelve and only in three as individuals. Claudius has two scenes without Gertrude, Gertrude one
scene without Claudius: otherwise, although on three occasions
they may enter or exit separately, they are always seen and
heard in each other's company.[1] As a dramatic device for con-
fusing the protagonist this is a masterly stroke of technical
skill; as a result, Hamlet himself, when confronted with his
adversary, is rarely sure of his emotional response and can
seldom communicate directly with either of them because the
other's presence inhibits him in speaking his mind. The processes therefore of sorting out his own reactions to his own situation both before and after his encounter with his father's Ghost
are necessarily made slower than they need otherwise have
been. Laertes has no mother to worry about, only a father and
a sister. Much of Hamlet's delay therefore in coming to a
reckoning with his adversary derives from his uncertainty as to
who this adversary really is—the uncle suspected of popping in
between the election and his own hopes of the crown and (later)
of murdering his father, or the mother who has offended him
personally by a second marriage which has translated her into
his aunt. It is therefore worth making a closer study of this
simple if unusual device, since examination of its workings
comments directly on the structure of the play.

The first point to notice is that each encounter between
Hamlet and his adversary from the start of the play to the end of
Act III, scene ii, is one with Claudius and Gertrude together
and that each of these encounters provokes a major soliloquy
from Hamlet by way of response. It would seem therefore as
though Shakespeare were making provision for the inhibitions
induced in Hamlet by the King and Queen in company to be

[1] Appearances together: I, ii, II, 5, III, ii, III, ii, IV, v, IV, ii, IV, vii, V, i and V, ii.
Appearances singly: Claudius—III, iii, IV, iii; Gertrude—III, iv.

released when he is alone, and that each soliloquy is thus a reflection upon the previous encounter. This pattern of confrontation is repeated throughout the latter part of the play, i.e. following Hamlet's return from England (IV, v–V, ii), but without the soliloquies. Only in the middle, Act III, scene iii, to Act IV, scene iii, is Hamlet allowed to encounter Claudius and Gertrude singly.

Closer inspection of this tripartite pattern reveals a progression from one section to the next each of which is clearly distinguishable from the others in terms of stage-action and can be labelled. The first group of encounters are all in the nature of probes or tests: the second group are direct confrontations: the third comprise the reckoning.

This information, when corroborated by detailed reference to the text, becomes of signal importance to the director in rehearsal, since it controls both the shape and pace of the production as a whole.

Part 1: The Testing—I, i to III, ii

This section is itself possessed of a clear structural pattern. Act I, scene i, is occupied with a simple question. Why should the ghost of the late King of Denmark be walking the battlements of Elsinore? This is followed in scene ii with the simultaneous presentation of the protagonist and antagonist(s) of the drama. Hamlet is reprimanded by both Claudius and Gertrude in open Court for his sullen silence and his irritatingly flamboyant mourning apparel: Claudius and Gertrude are then reprimanded by Hamlet in private soliloquy for mixing 'mirth in funeral' and 'dirge in marriage' in a manner so unbefitting to their stations. Thus the audience, while introduced to both protagonist and antagonist, is deliberately invited to question which is which. As this question is put to the test, therefore, in the succeeding scenes, so the audience is inevitably involved in the testing. To match the authority bestowed on Claudius and Gertrude by their crowns, Hamlet, following his own encounter with the Ghost, assumes an 'antic disposition'. Thus every step that Hamlet takes to test the veracity of the Ghost's story

about Claudius and Gertrude of Act I, scene v, can be matched
by their steps to reveal the truth behind the smoke-screen of the
antic disposition. Claudius and Gertrude attack first by placing spies at Hamlet's side, Rosencrantz and Guildenstern.
Hamlet parries this thrust by neutralizing their efficacy as agents
and plans an attack of his own through the visiting actors.
Before he can deliver his thrust, however, Claudius and Gertrude
attack again, this time through Ophelia: an attack which
Hamlet only just succeeds in parrying. Then it is his turn and
both Claudius and Gertrude are attacked in the play of
Gonzago's murder. It is indeed 'miching mallecho' and 'means
mischief' for this is the play-test and his answer to their spy-test
and their love-test. There is a progression in this sequence of
testing, a crescendo of viciousness in forethought and danger in
aftermath, which must be matched in the pace and tension of
the playing. If Hamlet is alerted to the danger of his own situation by the discovery that Rosencrantz and Guildenstern are
his adversary's agents—that he is thus literally a prisoner in
Denmark—Claudius is just as quick to recognize the danger to
himself that threatens in Hamlet's reaction to the love-test: 'he
shall with speed to England'! By the time that Claudius and
Gertrude desert the players' play, dismissing it derisively rather
than running away from it impetuously, protagonist, antagonist
and audience alike have had enough of 'testing'—the pace is now
too hot—and Shakespeare hurries into the second part of play.

Part 2: The Confrontation—III, iii to IV, iv

In Act III, scene iii, when Claudius is at his prayers alone,
Hamlet is given the chance to kill him: he elects to pass it by.
This scene is to be exactly matched in Act IV, secne iii, when,
following Hamlet's murder of Polonius, Claudius has the chance
to kill Hamlet by execution in the name of justice—Macbeth's
way with Duncan's grooms—but he too shrinks from it, prefer-
ring to postpone the reckoning. These two confrontations, the
latter an inverted version of the former and a point that can be
made visually in production by a repetition of grouping and
movement patterns, are punctuated by Hamlet's confronta-

tion with Gertrude. By coupling the fatal sword-thrust at
Polonius with the question, 'Is it the King?', Hamlet reveals to
Gertrude what his supposed madness concealed: by the same
deed and the impertinent 'Farewell, dear mother' addressed to
his uncle's face, Hamlet reveals to Claudius what had lain
behind the mourning suit and antic disposition. From this time
forward relations between them can never be the same again.
The 'testings' of Part 1 have led directly to the 'revelations' of
Part 2. There only remains

Part 3: The Reckoning—IV, v to V, ii

Part 1, as we have seen, moves relentlessly and at increasing
speed into Part 2 with dramatic tension reaching its climax in
the killing of Polonius. By contrast there is a sharp time-
break between Hamlet's departure for England at the end of
Part 2 and Part 3 which brings Laertes back from France and
Hamlet from England. Part 3 starts at a greatly slackened pace
with the long lyrical sequence of Ophelia's madness and
Claudius' tortuous corruption of Laertes. This is matched by
an equally pronounced change in what we are allowed to see
and hear of the protagonist and antagonists in this section of the
play. Claudius deteriorates steadily scene by scene from the
credible to the despicable. This deterioration should, I think, be
marked visually in production by an increasing addiction to
drink, the authority for it being taken from Act I, scene iv,
lines 8–38. Gertrude by contrast appears to have done as
Hamlet instructed her, thrown away 'the worser part' of her
nature and 'lived the purer' with the other half. At least she is
never seen again as a party to Claudius' machinations. Hamlet
too after his baptism by sea voyage, like Jonah before him, is a
new person. All vestiges of the 'antic disposition' have been
discarded; nor, with the exception of his reaction to Laertes'
grief at Ophelia's grave, is passion much in evidence. The
neurotic fear of death of the earlier scenes has given way to a
philosophical acceptance of it with wry jokes at Yorick's and
'my lady's' expense replacing the ghosts and sickly dreams
of Acts I to III. Even Horatio can be dispensed with. This

remarkable regeneration prepares the way for the swift and decisive actions which are required of Hamlet in the final scene: Laertes' death for his own, Claudius' death for his mother's and last but not least the prevention of Horatio's attempted suicide. These are the practical implications of recognizing a special providence in the fall of a sparrow.

It may seem crude and insensitive to strip down a masterpiece notable for the richness of its texture to the level of a simple scenario; but as the principal difficulty which any director aspiring to produce this play has to face is the rich confusion of poetic and psychological detail with which the text confronts him together with the ornate superstructure of critical appraisals that have grown up around it, his first task must be to obtain a firm grasp of the basic theatrical conflict that underpins the story. The play's form holds the key to its meaning. If this form is to be made apparent to audiences, then somehow the actors must be equipped with the stamina to follow the testing with the confrontation without break; somehow they must be persuaded to play the early exposition slowly enough to admit of acceleration as the testing proceeds, and somehow they must realize in terms that are theatrically valid that both the protagonist and antagonists have undergone a sea-change, spiritually as well as literally, before they approach the final reckoning.

(iii) *The Lord Chamberlain*

It is one of the more astonishing quirks of actors and producers, professional and amateur alike, that they usually insist upon approaching Polonius in the terms which King Lear uses to describe himself, 'a very foolish, fond old man'. Some justification for this image can be culled from the text provided that the phrases which give rise to it are taken at their face value and divorced from any serious consideration of the cumulative effect of Polonius' conduct towards Hamlet's family and his own.

Hamlet in moments of irritation describes Polonius as 'that great baby' and as 'a tedious old fool', while his jokes at Polonius' expense provide an outlet for his pent-up feelings.

Most of these jokes, however, are outward manifestations of the 'antic disposition'. What is significant is the fact that Hamlet senses the need to use it whenever he is confronted with Polonius for this derives from a fundamental distrust of him.

Polonius: Do you know me, my lord?
Hamlet: Excellent well: you are a fishmonger.
Polonius: Not I, my lord.
Hamlet: Then I would you were so honest a man. (II, ii, 173–6)

Polonius smiles just as Claudius smiles; but just as the King's unctuous smile is a mask, so is Polonius' benign smile. Behind it lies the mind of the Lord Chamberlain and the Chief of the Intelligence Service.

The great temptation for the actor and director is to mistake the mask for the man. It is a temptation if only because a long sequence of previous performances of this role has proved how easy it is to win laughs and a warm response from audiences by sentimentalizing the part. This is generally achieved by two specific means, one of which is caricature of the foibles of an octogenarian in posture and facial gesture and the other an exaggeration of paternal affection and anxiety. Something of these qualities must be present in any characterization of Polonius since these are the elements of the mask, the benign smile: but they must not be plastered all over the part in so self-indulgent a manner as to prevent the audience from recognizing how formidable an opponent Hamlet has to cope with in Ophelia's father and Claudius' most intimate personal adviser.

A useful historical fact in this context is the authority vested in the Lord Chamberlain's Office in Shakespeare's lifetime over the Revels Office and thus over the theatre itself. The censorship and suppression of plays, the licensing of acting companies and theatres, the imprisonment of actors and dramatists were all matters on which he had the last word, short of the sovereign's own. Within the Royal Household he stood between the sovereign and her subjects, largely determining how and when audience should be given. As a member of Queen Elizabeth's own Lord Chamberlain's personal company of players no-one could have had closer experience of the *authority* vested in the office than Shakespeare himself when creating the role of Polonius. If this is remembered, the director may not yield quite as readily to the temptation to cut the scene between Polonius and the spy, Reynaldo (II, i, 1–73), as is usually the case: nor will the actor be quite as easily disposed to sentimentalize Polonius' relations with his children on the one hand and to play the buffon *toute simple* for the laughs that he can get on the other. The audience may then have a chance to recognize the man himself for what he is (a devil as rotten in his own way as is the King in his) notwithstanding the image of himself that he has created for public consumption. When Gertrude impatiently derides Polonius for his euphuistic use of language—

More matter, with less art (II, ii, 95)

—it is not that she doubts whether he has anything important to say, but because she regards circumlocution as inappropriate to the matter in hand. Claudius likewise trusts his judgement. To the direct question 'What do you think of me?' he replies, 'As of a man faithful and honourable.' Even after Polonius' death Gertrude still speaks of him to Claudius as 'the unseen good old man'.

To them, of course he is 'faithful', 'honourable', 'good', even if no longer young; but this is not how Shakespeare presents him to the audience. It is as an eavesdropper and peeping-Tom that we see him; it is as father whose trust of his own children consists in setting spies upon them that we are asked to assess his affection for them; and it is as a spy in the Queen's bedroom that he meets his death. Hamlet, on discovering who he has killed describes him as a 'wretched, rash, intruding fool'. Before taking this verdict as a complete portrait of Polonius, however, the actor and director should notice that just as Claudius who has killed by poison dies by poison, so Polonius who has lived by 'going round to work', dies by a surfeit of it. In short, the cold-hearted devil that is the inner man requires as much care in rehearsal portraiture as the gait, make-up and other external trappings of the benign old fool that the outer man gives himself out to be.

This despicable dichotomy within the character of Polonius is depicted at its subtlest by Shakespeare in the famous advice to Laertes which begins,

> . . . these few precepts in thy memory
> Look thou character . . .

and ends,

> This above all: to thine own self be true,
> And it must follow, as the night the day,
> Thou canst not then be false to any man. (I, iii, 55–80)

What those who regard this advice as thoroughly commendable fail to notice is that the young man who receives it and acts upon it, is going to play Hamlet doubly false at Claudius' bidding with an unbaited and poisoned rapier. Christ's rules for human conduct place a premium upon conscience: love God and love thy neighbour as thyself. Polonius' precepts are satanic: distrust your neighbour and love yourself. This advice denies any share in original sin and thus amounts to a positive mandate to replace all striving to do God's will with full indulgence of personal whims and passions which, by orthodox Elizabethan Christian standards is an open invitation to damnation and accounts for Laertes being so easily led by Claudius into the paths of dishonour. Confronted with his father's murder and his sister's suicide he is angry: his anger prompts revenge and allows the end to justify the means without reflection on the ethics of such conduct. Unlike Hamlet, Laertes is not troubled by scruples of conscience: by being 'true to himself' he has let his conscience die. Only knowledge of the imminence of his own death rekindles it: confession then paves the way to a repentance made explicit in his plea for forgiveness.

> Exchange forgiveness with me, noble Hamlet;
> Mine and my father's death come not upon thee,
> Nor thine on me! (*Dies*) (V, ii, 340–3)

Polonius' counsel to Ophelia is no better than his advice to his son. Having led Laertes directly towards dishonour, he fails to recognize honour in Hamlet. Instead, he forbids Ophelia to associate with Hamlet on the grounds that, as a parent, he must safeguard her honour.

> You do not understand yourself so clearly
> As it behoves my daughter and your honour. (I, iii, 96-7)

Yet, just as he reassures the protesting Reynaldo that it is no dishonour to slander his son in conversation because the end justifies the means, so he is prepared to gamble with his daughter's most private feelings and known distress in order to improve his own standing in the opinion of the King and Queen.

Polonius: You know, sometimes he walks for hours together
          Here in the lobby.
Queen: So he does, indeed.
Polonius: At such a time I'll loose my daughter to him;
          Be you and I behind the arras then. (II, ii, 160-1)

Polonius' dealings with his own children give the clearest possible indication of the opportunist shifts, deceit and distorted ingenuity of which his political wisdom consists.

> And this do we of wisdom and of reach,
> With windlasses and with assays of bias,
> By indirections find directions out. (II, i. 64-6)

It is this sort of wisdom as much as anything else which is 'rotten' and 'amiss' at Elsinore.

For the actor then who plays Polonius the greatest imaginative challenge in the characterization of the role is to define a dichotomy between the man and his mask as distinct as that between Hamlet's own nature and his 'antic disposition'. The difference lies in the fact that where Hamlet is a novice in this sort of subterfuge, Polonius has been steeped in it so long for it to have become a part of him. Hamlet's 'antic disposition' occasions comment from all who encounter it, but Polonius' disguise of the benign, absent-minded old sage is taken so for granted as not to be recognized for what it is by anyone except Hamlet.

I believe myself that if the actor has once recognized the two-faced nature of the character, private man and public image, he will already be well on the way to defining an accurate portrait of this despicable Lord Chamberlain. What is attractive about Polonius belongs to his mask. The character must be built on the man and the mask superimposed upon the man: opportunities must then be found for the mask to be dropped from time to time when the audience is listening and watching so that both man and mask respectively may be recognized for what they are.

13

Macbeth

Two Correspondences in Jacobean and Mediaeval Stage-plays

(i) *Hell castle and its Door-keeper*[1]

FEW scenes in Shakespeare can have provoked more laughter in the theatre and more discomfort in the classroom than *Macbeth*, II, iii. At the centre of this paradox lies the character of the Porter, and in particular the obscenities which punctuate his remarks. These obscenities moreover are inextricably linked to a string of references to hell and the devil. How is this scene to be handled by the actor, and how is it to be handled by the schoolteacher?

The experience of being woken up in the middle of the night out of a deep sleep to deal with some disturbance in the house is as irritating as it is common: it is therefore a situation which if exposed to view in the theatre by a good mimic is certain to provide an amusing spectacle. Macbeth's porter, asleep when he ought to have been awake and on duty, stumbling towards the castle gate still rubbing his bleary eyes and hastily adjusting his costume, arouses a host of personal associations for everyone in the audience and is a sure-fire raiser of laughter in consequence. The fact that in this instance he is suffering from a bad hangover only adds to the fun for adults. Yet it is in this addition that trouble begins; for out of it spring the particular

---

[1] This section is reprinted from *Shakespeare Survey 19*, ed. Kenneth Muir, 1966, pp. 68–74.

obscenities through which the Porter gives expression in his language both to his predicament and to his feelings. Normally speaking the teacher must reckon both this predicament and these feelings to lie outside the experience of schoolchildren; in consequence, no great effort of imagination is required to understand why many teachers (and some editors) should find themselves perplexed if not embarrassed when faced with the task of explaining this scene to their pupils. To take refuge in the old nostrums of a corrupt passage in the text or, more frequent, of 'comic relief', may ease the embarrassment, but shirks the challenge which the scene presents. Are the references to hell, the devil, drink and lechery to be regarded simply as a rag-bag of swear-words habitual to a coarse, unlettered peasant? Or are they pointers to the true significance of the scene and its function within the structure of the play?

I think it may be useful both to the actor and to the teacher to know that anyone familiar with mediaeval religious drama is likely to recognize a correspondence between the vocabulary of this scene and that of a similar playlet within the English Miracle Cycles, 'The Harrowing of Hell'. If this story has become unfamiliar, this is partly because it is an aspect of Christian belief which theologians of the Reformation distorted, and partly because modern Anglican opinion prefers to ignore it. Yet I think it is the story which provided Shakespeare with his model for the particular form in which he chose to cast Act II, scene iii, of *Macbeth*, and possibly for the play as a whole.[1]

[1] John W. Hales in his *Notes and Essays on Shakespeare* (1884) regarded the Porter as a possible borrowing from the English Miracle Cycles (pp. 284–6). He appears only to have been familiar with *Ludus Coventriae*, the one cycle of the four in which Belzebub is not a character of importance in 'The Descent into Hell'; but he also draws attention to the porter of hell gate as depicted by Heywood in *Four P's* and in the much later anonymous Interlude *Nice Wanton*: see also William Hone, *Ancient Mysteries Described* (1823), pp. 120–47.

This suggestion does not appear to have been carried much further until John B. Harcourt raised it again in 'I Pray You, Remember the Porter', *Shakespeare Quarterly*, XII (1961), 393–402. This important article, which was brought to my attention after the completion of this short essay, anticipates several of the points made in it and draws attention to several other significant details in the scene. The fact that the two articles were written independently of each other and in different continents perhaps serves to strengthen the more important conclusions that are common to them both.

On the mediaeval stage hell was represented as a castle, more particularly as a dungeon or cesspit within a castle, one entrance to which was often depicted as a dragon's mouth.[1] Its gate was guarded by a janitor or porter. Christ, after his crucifixion, but before his resurrection, came to this castle of hell to demand of Lucifer the release of the souls of the patriarchs and prophets. The setting for this play was either the interior of the gatehouse or the courtyard of the castle: Christ's arrival was signalled by a tremendous knocking at this gate and a blast of trumpets. The gate eventually collapses allowing the Saviour-avenger, accompanied by the archangel Michael with his flaming sword, to enter and release the souls held prisoner within. It is in circumstances not unlike these that Macduff knocks at the gate of Macbeth's castle and that Malcolm and Donalbain escape from it in the course of Act II, scenes ii and iii. What did hell look like? How did its door-keeper behave? And where did the authors of the Miracle Cycles obtain descriptive information? The starting point may be found in two of the oldest mimetic ceremonies within the Catholic liturgy, the *Ordo Dedicationis Ecclesiae* and the *Tollite portas* procession to the city gates or church door on Palm Sunday, later elaborated and put to different use in the *Officium Elevationis Crucis*. Karl Young thinks that the inspiration of all these ceremonies is to be found in both the twenty-fourth Psalm, verses 7–10, and the second part of the 'Gospel of Nicodemus', the *Descensus Christi ad Inferos*.[2]

The first six and the last four verses of Psalm xxiv are virtually separate. It is the latter section which bears directly upon the liturgical ceremonies.

7. Lift up your heads, O ye gates, and be ye lift up, ye everlasting doors: and the King of glory shall come in.

8. Who is the King of glory: it is the Lord strong and mighty, even the Lord mighty in battle.

9. Lift up your heads, O ye gates, and be ye lift up, ye everlasting doors: and the King of glory shall come in.

---

[1] See *Plate X*, no. 14 (1).

[2] *The Drama of the Medieval Church* (1933), I, 149 ff. See also *The Middle English Harrowing of Hell and Gospel of Nicodemus*, ed. W. H. Hulme for E.E.T.S. (1907), pp. lxii ff.

10. Who is the King of glory: even the Lord of hosts, he is the King of glory.

(Book of Common Prayer)

These words appear in the Latin text of the *Descensus* but as a duologue between Christ and Satan. This dialogue is brought to life in emblematic manner within the *Ordo Dedicationis Ecclesiae*.

A church before consecration was regarded as impure, the dwelling-place of Satan and in need of cleansing. Accordingly the bishop approached the building in procession on Christ's behalf, knocked at the West door with his staff three times and said in Latin.

Tollite portas, principes, vestras, et elevamini, portae aeternales, et introibit rex gloriae.

A cleric replies from within the building,

Quis est iste rex gloriae?

This dialogue is repeated three times after which the bishop declares,

Dominus virtutum, ipse est rex gloriae.

As he enters the church the cleric slips out. The church itself is then cleansed by censing. This ceremony can be traced back to the fourth century in Jerusalem.[1]

A full account of the symbolic representation of the Harrowing of Hell derived from the *Elevatio* survives in England from the monastery of Barking, near London. Katherine of Sutton, abbess of Barking from 1363 to 1376, established a ceremony there incorporating the *Tollite portas* verses and lying immediately between the close of Matins on Easter Day and the normal *Visitatio Sepulchri*. At Barking, members of the convent were imprisoned within the Chapel of St. Mary Magdalen, thus representing the souls of the patriarchs confined in hell. A priest approaches the door with the words *Tollite portas*; the door is opened and the erstwhile prisoners file out into the church carrying palm branches signifiying victory over Satan

<hr>

[1] Young, *op. cit.*, pp. I, 102.

and death, singing *Cum rex gloriae*. This ceremony also survives from Dublin in two forms.[1]

The authors of the vernacular cycles therefore had a long liturgical tradition behind them as well as the Gospel of Nicodemus to assist them when they came to prepare their play-books of the Harrowing of Hell. The story itself was familiar enough to require little development: ample opportunity existed, however, for the addition of descriptive detail. In this the authors were further assisted by artists in stained glass and by painters who, from Fra Angelico to Bellini and Dürer, had persistently represented Christ with the banner of the cross in his hand standing victorious, like St. George above the dragon, before the shattered gates of hell with Satan cringing at his feet. (*Plate X*, no. 14[2].)

In *Macbeth*, Macduff enters Macbeth's castle twice, first in II, iii, when Duncan's murder is discovered and Malcolm and Donalbain escape, and again in V, ix, when, as a victorious general, he arrives from the field of battle and addresses Malcolm:

> Hail, King! for so thou art. Behold, where stands
> Th' usurper's cursed head: the time is free.[2] (V, ix, 20–1)

There is thus no attempt on Shakespeare's part to provide a direct parallel to the Harrowing of Hell within the play of *Macbeth*; but there is ample evidence within the text of the play of a conscious attempt on Shakespeare's part to remind his audience of this ancient and familiar story so that they may discern for themselves the moral meaning of this stage narrative abstracted from the annals of Scottish history. To make this point as forcibly as I think it should be made it is first necessary to reconstruct from the texts and stage directions of the surviving Miracle Cycles the picture of hell and its inhabitants that was familiar to Tudor audiences together with the salient aspects of the story as it was treated on their stages.

Hell itself was represented as a combination of castle, dungeon and cesspit. Of the four surviving English Cycles,

---

[1] Young, *op. cit.*, pp. 168 ff.

[2] This and other quotations from *Macbeth* are from the Arden edition.

Towneley (Play xxv), 'The Deliverance of Souls', follows York (Play 37), 'The Saddlers', almost verbatim at times: both are derived in large measure from the Middle-English poetical 'Gospel of Nicodemus' of the early fourteenth century.[1] It is from these versions of the play that we learn that hell is equipped with walls and gates like a castle.

TOWNELEY
Belzabub: Go, spar the yates, yĺt mot thou the!
    And set the waches on the waĺt. (E.E.T.S., lines 120–1)
YORK
Bellial: We! spere oure ȝates, all ill mot þou spede,
        And sette furthe watches on þe wall.
    (L. Toulmin-Smith, *York Plays* (1885), p. 380, lines 139–40)

This image of Hell-castle is later reinforced in Towneley (lines 146–9) by Belzabub who calls to Satan

Belzabub: Thou must com help to spar
        we are beseged abowte.
Sathanas: Besegyd aboute! whi, who durst be so bold
        for drede to make on us a fray?

In the *Ludus Coventriae* Anima Christi describes hell as 'the logge (*prison*) of helle' (E.E.T.S., p. 305). This is followed by a stage direction which reads: 'The soule goth to helle gatys . . .' which gates Christ further specifies as being a 'derke dore' (*ibid.*, p. 306). This image of a prison is consistently maintained in the plays of 'The Fall of Lucifer' and the 'The Assumption' from the same Cycle and is further particularized by Belial (p. 319) as 'helle gonge', i.e. latrine. In the Towneley 'Deliverance' hell is also described as a 'pryson' (by Jesus, line 236) and as 'that pytt' (by Jesus, line 285) and as 'hell pyt' (by Satan, line 360). Prison, pit and dungeon are the words used variously in the Chester cycle to describe hell. (See *Plate XI*, no. 15).

What we must visualize is an edifice which, viewed from outside, resembles a castle and, viewed from inside, a sequence of dark dungeons and torture chambers pervaded by stench and heat. This picture, built up from details in the texts of English

[1] See W. H. Hulme, *op. cit.*, pp. xviii ff.

cyclic plays set in hell, closely resembles the MS. picture of Hell-castle illustrating the Valenciennes Passion Play of 1547. (See *Plate X*, no. 14 [1].) Further detail, if we want it, can be found in the Account Book of the Mons Passion Play (1501) where the walls of hell are said to have been 'plastered'.[1] A Scottish castle, therefore, through the gates of which a kingly guest has been welcomed by a host who promptly murders him, might be calculated to recall this other, satanic castle with its 'ʒatys of sorwatorie (*torment*)'.[2] Both castles moreover are equipped with a janitor or porter.

The authors of the Cycles found this door-keeper in the poetical 'Gospel of Nicodemus' where, as a character, he already borders on the comic.

Dominus: Wer ys nou þis ʒateward?
me puncheþ [*thinketh*] he is a coward.
Janitor: Ich haue herd wordes stronge,
ne dar y her no lengore stonde;
kepe þe gates whose may,
y lete hem stonde ant renne away.[3]

This idea is elaborated upon by the York and Towneley scribes. In both plays the porter acquires a name; significantly it is Rybald, a word defined by *O.E.D.* as meaning 'Scurrilous, irreverent, profane, indecent' and as derived from the French *ribaut*, a menial. A more succinct and apposite description of Macbeth's porter could scarcely be found. In the Towneley play Rybald receives his orders from Belzabub. In *Macbeth*, the porter's first question is,

Who's there, i' th' name of Belzebub? (line 4)

We should surely expect him to say 'in the name of my master' or possibly 'in the name of Macbeth'; but, since Macbeth has just murdered Duncan, 'in the name of Belzebub' or 'in the devil's name' is just as appropriate. The knocking has at least put the porter in mind of Hell-gate: his comments put it in our

---

[1] See G. Cohen, *Le Livre de Conduite du Régisseur et le Compte des Dépenses pour le Mystère de la Passion joué à Mons en 1501*, Paris, 1925, pp. 498, 528.

[2] *Ludus Coventriae* (E.E.T.S.), p. 306. See also p. 230 below,

[3] Harley MS. Text L, *The Harrowing of Hell*, ed. cit., p. 13, lines 139–44.

minds too. In the Towneley 'Deliverance' it is Rybald who first answers Christ's knocking.

Rybald: . . . what devill is he
    That callys hym kyng over us all?
    hark belzabub, com ne,
    ffor hedusly I hard hym call. (E.E.T.S., lines 116–19)

The 'hideous call' is a fanfare of trumpets followed by the familiar,

Attollite portas, principes, vestras & eleuamini porte eternales, & introibit rex glorie. (Towneley, lines 115–16)

At York and Chester the Latin is followed by a translation, phrase by phrase, into English.

In *Macbeth* the porter receives no answer to his thrice-repeated 'Who's there?' The knocking continues remorselessly, but the questions are answered rhetorically by the porter himself. In his drunken condition he stumbles about the stage like a man waking out of a dream who still regards the environment of his dream as more real than that confronting him on waking. Just, as today, one might be woken by one's own telephone and at the same time fancy oneself called to some other 'phone in another house within the fabric of one's dream, so the porter, dreaming that he is Rybald and in hell, associates the real knocking on Macbeth's castle-gate that has obtruded upon or into his dream with Christ's arrival at hell's 'dark door'. When the porter asks for the first time who is knocking he is still firmly in his dream-world.

Who's there, i' th' name of Belzebub? (line 4)

When he asks for the second time he is already beginning to slip out of his dream, for he can't recall the name of any other companion in this diablerie.

Who's there, i' th' other devil's name? (line 8)

By the time he has repeated this question a third time the chill of dawn is bringing him swiftly back to reality.

—But this place is too cold for Hell.
I'll devil-porter it no further: (lines 18–19)

This gate is not shattered: the porter opens it. Macduff enters. The porter asks for a tip.

> I pray you, remember the porter. (line 22)

This remark is ambivalent, for it can be addressed by the actor both to Macduff and to the audience. As in the porter's dream, it is in two worlds at once; that of Macbeth's castle and that of another scene from another play which has just been recalled for the audience and which the author wants them to remember. If we take the remark in this latter sense, we recollect that it was Jesus who with a loud knocking entered Hell-castle in search of Satan. At this point in *Macbeth* Shakespeare has not yet informed us that Macduff is destined to avenge Duncan's murder, but in his use of the porter he gives us a clear hint of what to expect.

In the next sixteen lines of conversation with Macduff, the porter sobers up and drops every aspect of his earlier hallucination; but in the ribaldry of the language, humour and (where the actor is concerned) gesture, he remains equivocal. When Macduff asks him,

> Is thy master stirring? (line 43)

we are still at liberty to regard him both as Macbeth's servant and as Satan's.

It is then left to Lennox who has entered the castle with Macduff to draw the audience's attention to another strange phenomenon.

Lennox: The night has been unruly: where we lay,
Our chimneys were blown down; and as they say,
Lamentings heard i' th' air; strange screams of death,
And, prophesying with accents terrible.

Of dire combustion, and confus'd events,
New hatch'd to th' woeful time, the obscure bird
Clamour'd the livelong night: some say the earth
Was feverous, and did shake.
Macbeth: 'Twas a rough night.
Lennox: My young remembrance cannot parallel
A fellow to it. (lines 55–63)

An older memory, however, might well recall a parallel. In

the cyclic plays of the Harrowing of Hell it is the strange noises in the air which alert the devils of impending disaster.

TOWNELEY

Rybald: Sen fyrst that hell was mayde / And I was put therin, / Sich sorow neuer ere I had / nor hard I sich a dyn; /

     . . . .

     how, belsabub! bynde thise boys, / sich harow was neuer hard in hell.

Belzabub: Out, rybald! thou rores, / what is betyd? can thou oght tell?

Rybald: Whi, herys thou not this ugly noyse? (lines 89–95)

When Christ arrives at the gates there is more noise including trumpets and knocking.

CHESTER (stage direction)

Tunc veniet Jhesus et fiet Clamor vel sonitus materialis magnus . . . (line 144)

Still more succinct is the stage direction of the Mons Passion;

Lors se doi(b)t faire en En(f) fer une grande tempeste et la terre doit trambler.
  (ed. cit., p. 412)

Lennox might be supplying a literal translation of this last line with his 'some say the earth was feverous and did shake'.[1]

It is Lady Macbeth who completes the picture. It was she who first heard the knocking at the south gate from the direction of England and it is she who, when the bell starts tolling, says,

> What's the business,
> That such a hideous trumpet calls to parley
> The sleepers of the house? (lines 81–3)

It was Rybald in the Towneley 'Deliverance' who cried out to Belzabub on hearing Christ's trumpets at Hell-gate

---

[1] These extraordinary noises are clearly intended to be associated as much with the murder of Duncan as with the arrival of Macduff and are derived as clearly from the noises associated with the actual moment of Christ's death as from noise associated with the arrival of Anima Christi before the gates of hell. The Harley Text of the *Gospel of Nicodemus* describing this moment reads:

> þe stanes in sonder brak,
> þe erth trembled & quaked,
> with noys als man it spak,
> Slyke mane for him it maked.
>   (Hulme, *op. cit.*, for E.E.T.S., p. 68, lines 705–8

   . . . come ne,
ffor hedusly I hard hym call. (lines 118–19) (See *Plates X and XI*)

Thunder, cacophony, screams and groans were the audible emblems of Lucifer and hell on the mediaeval stage. Those same aural emblems colour the whole of II, iii of *Macbeth* and, juxtaposed as they are with thunderous knocking at a gate attended by a porter deluded into regarding himself as a devil, their relevance to the moral meaning of the play could scarcely have escaped the notice of its first audiences.

In the cyclic plays of the Harrowing of Hell, Satan (or Lucifer) is physically overthrown, bound and either cast into hell pit or sinks into it.

CHESTER (stage direction) Iaceant tunc Sathanam de sede sua.
                                         (line 168)

TOWNELEY
Sathan: Alas, for doyll and care!
        I synk into hell pyt. (lines 359–60)

In the York play the rescued souls leave the stage singing *Laus tibi Domino cum gloria.* Towneley ends with the *Te Deum*. In *Macbeth*, when Macduff has successfully brought Macbeth and his 'fiend-like Queen' to justice, it is Malcolm, the new King-elect, who brings the play to its close in joy and thanksgiving.

Malcolm: So thanks to all at once, and to each one,
        Whom we invite to see us crown'd at Scone. *Flourish.*
        Exeunt. (v. ix, 140–1)

Scotland has been purged of a devil who, like Lucifer, aspired to a throne that was not his, committed crime upon crime first to obtain it and then to keep it, and was finally crushed within the refuge of his own castle by a saviour-avenger accompanied by armed archangels. Hell has been harrowed: 'the time is free'.

(ii) *Out-heroding Herod*

When watching a recent performance of the Wakefield Cycle at Bretton Hall[1] it struck me that if the play of the Harrowing of

---

[1] Produced by John Hodgson, designed by and acted by staff and students of the Teachers' Training College (Art, Drama, Music) at Bretton Hall, Yorkshire.

Hell provided Shakespeare with only half of the pattern for the thematic treatment of the story of Macbeth as a dramatic tragedy, the other half was provided by the two plays about Herod the Great—the Visit of the Magi and the Massacre of the Innocents: three wise men, a prophecy of a King in Israel descended from David not Herod, an abortive attempt to frustrate prophecy by murder, the final overthrow and damnation of the butcher-tyrant. This is the story-line of the Herod plays. It also bears a remarkable correspondence to the events depicted in Shakespeare's *Tragedy of Macbeth* from Macbeth's coronation to his execution: three weird sisters, a prophecy of a King in Scotland descended from Banquo not Macbeth, an abortive attempt to frustrate prophecy by murder first of Banquo and Fleance and then of other innocents, the final overthrow of the butcher-tyrant. In the performance at Bretton Hall it was the sharp, emotional impact of the brutal killing of the children and their mothers' despair which brought the image of Lady Macduff, the 'shag-hair'd villain' and the 'young fry of treachery' vividly to mind and thus extended outwards to embrace other features of *Macbeth*.

The authors of the Cycles had enjoyed almost as much liberty of imagination in approaching the story of the Massacre of the Innocents as they had done in constructing the play of the Harrowing of Hell since their source for the former was restricted to a single Gospel account, St. Matthew's.[1] In their treatment of King Herod as a character they had more liberty since he himself, his soldiers and his advisers were all mortal men. The portrait of this irascible, black-bearded tyrant that emerged on the religious stages of the fifteenth and sixteenth centuries raging 'in the pageant and in the street also' was thus keenly etched upon the popular imagination and still sufficiently vivid at the start of the seventeenth century to provide Prince Hamlet with a useful illustration of undisciplined bombast in his advice to the players.

Oh, it offends me to the soul to hear a robustious periwigpated fellow tear a passion to tatters, to very rags, to split the ears of the groundlings . . . it out-herods Herod. (III, ii, 10–17)

---

[1] St. Matthew, II, 1–16.

The portrait is vivid and projects across the centuries an image of an actor in a wig, gesticulating melodramatically and shouting his head off. Contemptible however as Hamlet (or even Shakespeare himself) may have found such acting in 1600, the figure of Herod that had been presented in this way was of itself dramatically striking and still capable of being remodelled into a less flamboyant but more human stage-portrait of a tyrant.

Shakespeare's Macbeth and King Herod of the religious stage share enough in common to warrant careful comparison; for once Macbeth has replaced Duncan as King of Scotland he behaves very much as Herod does and for strikingly similar reasons. In all the Cycles Herod is presented initially as a man of overweening ambition glorying in the power vested in his throne and in the fear in which he is held by his subjects. In the Chester *Magi* he is at his most lyrical on this account.

> For I am king of all mankinde,
> I byd, I beat, I loose, I bynde,
> I maister the Moone; take this in mynde
> that I am most of mighte.
>
> I am the greatest above degree,
> that is or was or ever shall be.
> the Sonne it dare not shyne on me
> if I byd hym goe downe. (lines 169–76)

In the Cycles only Lucifer is permitted such extravagance of language and sentiment: for us it brings Tamburlaine to mind and young Mortimer.[1] In the Coventry Pageant of the Shearmen and Taylors Herod is even allowed to claim supremacy over Satan.

> For all the whole Or(i)ent ys under myn obbeydeance
> And prynce am I of purgatorre and cheff capten of hell.[2]

It is to be remarked that Macbeth has come to assume a very similar image in his subjects' eyes by the time that Birnam Wood has come to Dunsinane.

[1] See Essay 10, pp. 174–5 above.
[2] Ed. Hardin Craig for E.E.T.S. (2nd ed., 1957), lines 502–3.

Young Siward: What is thy name?
Macbeth: Thou'lt be afraid to hear it.
Young Siward: No; though thou call'st thyself a hotter name
                      Than any is in hell.
Macbeth: My name's Macbeth.
Young Siward: The devil himself could not pronounce a title
                      More hateful to mine ear.
Macbeth: No, nor more fearful.
Young Siward: Thou liest, abhorred tyrant. (V, vii, 5–10)

In the Cycles Herod's initial, diabolic self-confidence is
swiftly shaken by the visit of the Magi, the three wise men with
visionary powers who can foretell the future.

Tertius Rex: By prophesies well wotten we,
                      that a Childe borne sholde bee
                      to rule the people of Iudy,
                      as was said many a yeare. (Chester, viii, 213–16)

In this version Herod and his councillors spend the next two
hundred lines in examining the writings of the Prophets.[1]
Convinced at last, he flies into a rage.

Herode: Alas! what presumption shold move that peevish page,
                  or any elvish gedling to take from me my crowne?
                  but by Mahound! that boy for all his great outrage
                  shall dye under my hand. (lines 317–320)

Some fifty lines later the three Kings set out for Bethlehem and
as soon as they are gone Herod qualifies his anger with sentiments of shame, grief and anxiety.

>   Out alas! what the Devil is this?
>   for shame almost I fare amisse,
>   for was I never so woe, I wis,
>   for wrath I am nere wood. [*wild*]
>
>   For every man may say well this
>   that I maynteyne my Realme amisse,
>   to let a boy inherit my blisse
>   that never was of my blood. (lines 374–81)

---

[1] The Towneley play also incorporates this treatment of prophecy. In the York,
Coventry and *Ludus Coventriae* plays there is this same concern with prophecy, but
it is handled differently.

Macbeth's anxieties, once he has seized the throne, take much the same form. He too has met with visionaries, three weird sisters who spoke about the future not only to him but to Banquo.

> He chid the Sisters.
> When first they put the name of King upon me,
> And bade them speak to him; then prophet-like
> They hail'd him father to a line of kings:
> Upon my head they put a fruitless crown,
> And put a barren sceptre in my gripe,
> Thence to be wrench'd with an unlineal hand,
> No son of mine succeeding. (III, i, 57–64)

Macbeth's fears are more complicated than Herod's since the price that he had to pay for his 'fruitless crown' has been a King's murder. Nevertheless his reaction to this situation follows the pattern set by Herod. The prophecy must be thwarted; the innocents must die. Macbeth, like Herod, summons hired assassins to do this work for him.

In the Cycles there is considerable variety in the treatment accorded to this decision and its consequences. The Chester and York dramatists make Herod encourage the three Kings to complete their journey, report their findings to him: as thanks, Herod plans to reward them with execution. When the Kings, warned by an angel in a dream, return to their own countries 'by another way' and thus frustrate this plan, Herod decides to eliminate the threatened rival. Summoning his soldiers he says,

> You must hy you out of this towne
> to Bedlem, as fast as you mone,
> all knaves Children, by my Crowne!
> you must slay this nighte. (Chester, x, 149–52)

Only in the Coventry play do the soldiers show any kind of imaginative awareness of the enormity of the crime they have been asked to commit.

I. Myles: My lorde, kyng Erode be name,
Thy wordis agenst my wyll schalbe;
To see soo many yong chylder dy ys schame,
Therefore consell ther-to gettis thou non of me.

II. Myles: Well seyd, fello, my trawth I plyght.
                Sir kyng, perseyve right well you may,
            Soo grett a morder to see of yong frute
            Wyll make a rysyng in thinoone cuntrey.

(lines 793–800)

The actual killing of the children is carried out on the stage with a callousness and brutality of word and deed only matched in the Cycles by the treatment accorded to Christ at his Crucifixion. Only two soldiers are used, except in the Towneley play where there are three: each speaks directly to the mother whose child he is about to kill.

Secundus Miles: Com hedyr, thou old stry!
               that lad of thyne shall dy.
Secunda Mulier: Mercy, lord, I cry!
               It is myn awne dere son.
ijus Miles: No mercy thou mefe / it mendys the not, mawd!
Secunda Mulier: ffy, fy, for reprefe! fy, full of frawde
             . . . . . . *[He kills the boy]*
             Outt! morder! man, I say / strang tratoure & thefe!
             Out! alas! and waloway! / my child that was me lefe!
             My luf, my blood, my play / that never did man grefe!

(Towneley, lines 348–364)

Despite the small number of soldiers and women used to stage this scene (or perhaps because of this very economy) the emotional impact of the horror and pathos of which it is compounded is shattering.

The deed done, the soldiers report back to Herod. In the Towneley play Herod rewards them with women and money, and concludes,

Now in pease may I stand / I thank the, mahowne! (line 460)

The York dramatist does not let Herod get away with murder so easily: for the soldiers, when questioned, admit that they do not know whether they have succeeded in killing Jesus— 'token had we none / To know that same brat by'—and Herod is left as uneasy in his mind as he was before. The Coventry play develops this idea by adding a Messenger.

> Erode, kyng, I schall the tell,
> All thy dedis ys cum to noght;
> This chyld ys gone in-to Eygipte to dwell. (lines 888–90)

The author of the Chester play advanced on these ideas and makes one of the soldiers kill Herod's own son by mistake. When the 2nd soldier has killed the child of the 2nd woman she cries out,

> This Child was taken to me,
> to looke to—Theves, wo be ye!
> he was not myne, as you shall see,
> he was the kinges sonne. (x, 381–4)

Told of this, Herod dies in an apoplexy of rage and is carried off to hell by Devils. *Ludus Coventriae* supplies a further variant, by allowing Herod to celebrate the news of the massacre with a great feast. When the feast is at its height Death enters in company with Diabolus. Herod has a stroke and, as the Devil carries him away, Death addresses the audience.

> Off kynge herowde ałł men beware
> þat hath rejoycyd in pompe and pryde
> Ffor all his boste of blysse ful bare
> he lyth now ded here on his syde
>
> . . . .
>
> now is he ded and cast in care
> In helle pytt evyr to A-byde
>
> . . . .
>
> I come sodeynly with-in a stownde
> me with-stande may no castel
> my jurnay wyl I spede. (lines 246–66)

These and many other variants of treatment of the Herod story on the religious stage are themselves highly significant; for they illustrate as nothing else could do the dramatic potential contained within it and the further developments which this admitted.

Shakespeare, as it seems to me, was fully aware of these possibilities and used them to provide at least part of the moral basis for his *Tragedy of Macbeth*. The essentials that he drew from the play are the poisoning of a tyrant's peace of mind by the prophecy of a rival destined to eclipse him, the attempt to forestall that prophecy by the hiring of assassins to murder all potential rivals and the final overthrow and damnation of the tyrant. For the three wise men Holinshed gave him the three weird sisters. It is their prophecy in respect of Banquo which disturbs Macbeth's peace of mind once he has usurped the throne, and it is to rid himself of all fears of Banquo and his heirs that he hires murderers to kill his friend and his son. Like Herod with the Magi, Macbeth adopts a twofold plan. He aims first at Banquo and Fleance; and, when this plan miscarries, he extends his net to cover all potential rivals and strikes down Lady Macduff and her children. The last twenty lines of this scene are imbued with the sharpest possible verbal, visual and emotional echoes of the horrific scene in Bethlehem. Young Siward's image of Macbeth as both tyrant and devil in Act V, scene vii, recalls the drunken devil-porter of Act II, scene iii, and thereby the two complementary images of the religious stage, Herod the tyrant and the Harrowing of Hell, are linked to one another in compressed form to provide the thematic sub-text of this Scottish tragedy.[1] Pride and ambition breed tyranny: tyranny breeds violence, a child born of fear and power: but tyrants are by their very nature Lucifer's children and not God's, and as such they are damned. As Christ harrowed Hell and released Adam from Satan's dominion, so afflicted subjects of mortal tyranny will find a champion who will release them from fear and bondage. This Macduff does for Scotland; and in due season Fleance, who escaped the murderer's knife just as Jesus did, by flight, will have heirs who become Kings. And not the least among them will be James the Sixth of Scotland and First of England,[2] patron to Shakespeare and the company of actors that gave *The Tragedy of Macbeth* its first performance in 1606.

[1] Some people might incline to regard the spectre of Death, costumed as a skeleton, at Herod's feast as the prototype of Banquo's Ghost; but I doubt this myself as this particular variant is unique to *Ludus Coventriae*.

[2] On the connection between *Macbeth* and historical events in the early years of James I's reign see The Arden Edition (ed. Kenneth Muir), Introduction, pp. xiv–xxiv. On Shakespeare and James I, see also Essay 15 below.

14

Coriolanus[1]

Shakespeare's Tragedy in Rehearsal and Performance

I

I T is tempting for historian, critic and producer alike, when approaching one of Shakespeare's plays, to suppose that a definitive version of it exists, and that this may be found in his own mind if nowhere else. The only effective counter-weight to such beguiling self-deception is familiarity with the stage-history of the play in question; for in the course of some three hundred years, the swelling list of revivals and editions demonstrates that what one generation regarded as a final answer, the next repudiated as thoroughly misguided.[2]

The producer of the play, since it is his function as an artist to approach it as a work of dramatic art, must convince himself that he *is* possessed of a definitive version: if he fails in this he cannot hope to convince his actors and technical assistants that he can help them to define it for their audiences. On the other

---

[1] Reprinted from *Later Shakespeare*, Stratford-Upon-Avon Studies No. 8, ed. J. R. Brown and B. Harris, 1966, pp. 167–81.

[2] Analytical notes on many of the play's characters are in Harley Granville Barker's *Prefaces to Shakespeare, Fifth series, Coriolanus* (1947), reprinted in paperback (1963).

hand, if he is wise, he will not overlook what the historian and the critic can tell him about the fortunes of the play when formulating this version: for it is in this way that he may best bring those parts of his production concept which are particular to his own generation, or to himself alone, into harmony with those which governed the writing of the play. Nor has the critic or historian any less to learn from those artistic truths which producer and actors illuminate in performance when it comes to tempering the wilder aspects of their personal theories with the facts of the stage-action.[1]

Coriolanus first became public property as a printed text on 8th November 1623, when it was entered in the Stationers' Register as one of the plays included in the Folio edition of Shakespeare's plays. Most modern editors assign composition and first performance to the years 1609–10.[2] To the literate section of the Jacobean public of those years the story was not new since it was readily available in print in Latin, French, and English versions of Plutarch's *Lives of the Noble Grecians and Romans*: Thomas North's English translation was published in 1579. To the illiterate it may well have been new: but, as citizens of London, they had at least had first-hand experience in their own streets of personal disaster overtaking a soldier hero turned rabble-rouser in the Essex Rebellion of 1601. To this extent the play treated of a familiar and, maybe, even a topical subject when Richard Burbage and his fellow actors of the King's Company first brought it to life on the stage.

Subsequent generations have held it in varying esteem,

---

[1] Laurence Kitchen has an account of Sir Laurence Olivier's performance in the title-role in *Mid-Century Drama* (2nd ed., 1962). The importance of the female characters in this play is stressed, from very different viewpoints, by Una Ellis Fermor, *Shakespeare the Dramatist* (1951), and by J. Middleton Murry, 'A Neglected Heroine of Shakespeare', in *The London Mercury* (1921), pp. 386–94. *Shakespeare Survey*, X (1957), contains a retrospect review of criticism in the present century on Shakespeare's Roman plays, by J. C. Maxwell; 'From Plutarch to Shakespeare—a study of *Coriolanus*,' by H. Heuer; 'Shakespeare and the Elizabethan Romans' by T. J. B. Spencer; and 'Classical Costumes in Shakespeare Productions' by W. M. Merchant. See also the latter's *Shakespeare and the Artist*, Oxford, 1959, especially Chapter II.

[2] *Modern Editions. Coriolanus* was edited by J. Dover Wilson in the New Cambridge Shakespeare (1960); by John Munro, in *The London Shakespeare* (1957), and by Alice Walker (1964).

seldom bothering to present it on the stage, often debating the political implications of the plot and frequently contradicting one another in their assessments of the hero's virtues and vices. The play was revived in the eighteenth century by James Quin and David Garrick, and in the nineteenth by John Philip Kemble and Henry Irving. Kemble alone, however, added much to his reputation thereby.

Such then, in thumbnail dimensions, is the background against which the intending actor or producer of the play in our own time must order his own thoughts about *Coriolanus*, role and play.

Any theatrical company today, however, must also take account of another factor which cannot fail to obtrude itself upon preparatory thinking—the unprecedented number of Shakespearian revivals of the past two decades. To take England only, large-scale productions of *Coriolanus* have been mounted at Stratford-on-Avon in 1952 and 1959, at the Old Vic in 1954, at the Bath Assembly in the Roman Baths in 1952, and at Nottingham to open the new Playhouse in December 1963: it was broadcast by the B.B.C. in two separate productions in 1950 and 1959 and was served up in 1963 on television in three supposedly painless instalments. No producer who respects his audiences therefore can easily ignore the images which any announcement of a new revival at once recalls; for many people the new production will offer little by way of novelty, while for others it will have to stand comparison with memories prejudiced by nostalgia. Thus he finds himself under strong pressure to adopt an approach where shock-value takes precedence over all other considerations. This pressure exists for both professional and amateur producers, but it is likely to take different forms for each. The professional, in seeking to oblige his management with a box-office attraction or to advance his own career by means of a notable controversy in the press, is inevitably attracted to theatricality or 'gimmick-treatment'. The amateur, in deference to similar pressures of scholarly origin, is just as likely to wander into the quagmire of textual emendation and historicity of representation. Either way the resulting production is certain to depart from the essence of the play and to be carried into the realms of vulgarity or pedantry. If it is easy to obliterate the tragic stature of Coriolanus in a matter of seconds by allowing him to leap to his death in the manner of a trapeze-artist for the sake of the gasp of surprise in the auditorium, it is just as easy to let the whole play evaporate into one great yawn of boredom by refusing to cut a single line of the text. What course then is the producer of today and tomorrow to set his cast if he is to bring his play fresh and revitalized to his audiences without wrecking both on either the Scilla of pedantic historicity or the Charybdis of theatrical banality? My own experience of producing the play at Bath in 1952, together with such knowledge as I possess of the theatre practice of Shakespeare's own day, suggest that the text itself offers more guidance than is often imagined. This essay endeavours to define the nature of that guidance.

II

There is first the play's title: *The Tragedy of Coriolanus*. This supplies the producer with two clear and important directives. When all else is stripped away—generals, senators, women, citizens, servants—this play is about one man, Caius Martius, surnamed Coriolanus. It is thus in essence a personal tragedy. Moreover, the word tragedy is to be interpreted as it was understood and used by Shakespeare and his fellow actors. As I have already dealt with this question at some length in Essays 3 and 5 (pp. 44–9 and 95–7 above) I will not repeat myself here. Suffice it to say that within the context of 'The Fall of Princes' Caius Martius is not himself a Prince, but in a republican society he is a prince among patricians. The play is Senecan in that it recounts in dramatic dialogue the fall of a hero from a state of prosperity to one of adversity; but it is also the product of a Christian society in so far as it examines and attaches blame for this fall within the character of the hero. Whatever else the producer may think to do, therefore, he contradicts his author's explicit instructions if he places the man Coriolanus anywhere other than at the centre of his production. It is a title-role.

The second signpost that Shakespeare provides to indicate

his own intentions resides in the *Dramatis Personæ*. Broadly speaking, the cast list of this play divides itself into three distinct groups of people: those concerned with military life, those pre-occupied with civil life, and those whose status in the society of the time denied them the right to participate directly in either —a group of women. To some extent therefore this play is concerned with war and also with politics: one of the women, Volumnia, meddles in domestic politics and, together with her two associates, Virgilia and Valeria, erupts surprisingly upon the affairs of war in the final Act. Significantly, two of these women are closer to Coriolanus himself—Volumnia as mother and Virgilia as wife—than anyone else in the play. The third, Valeria, is something of an enigma since she is given a dominant place in the third scene of the first Act and is then denied any lines of consequence in any of the three scenes in which she subsequently appears (II, i, and V, iii and vi). This division of the *Dramatis Personæ* is paralleled in the disposition of the stage-action. Roughly half the action is set on or near the battlefield and half of it in the principal arenas of civil politics—senate houses or adjacent streets. Two scenes only are strictly domestic (I, iii, and III, ii): both of these are set in Coriolanus' own home, but in neither, significantly, is he presented as the master of his own house.

All this information stems directly from the play's title, the *Dramatis Personæ*, and the ordering of the scenes as set out in the first printed edition of the play. No producer (unless, of course, he is so smug or arrogant as to suppose himself more gifted than Shakespeare) can easily afford to ignore it: rather should he follow where it leads. In sum it suffices to wipe out any temptation to regard this play as a dramatic essay on either war and generalship or tyranny and social revolution. Clearly, both of these subjects are treated fully enough to provide the play with a special flavour of its own: both, however, are elements, like the supernatural in *Macbeth*, and not the play's centre or spinal cord. The latter is to be found as the title directs in Caius Martius himself, a man born to privilege and endowed with certain gifts of leadership, who nevertheless so mismanages his own affairs within the course of the stage-action as to be

'overcast and whelmed from (Fortune's) glorie' before its close.
This was Essex's case, favourite of the Queen, flamboyant
challenger of Irish rebels, at one moment the darling of the
London mob, yet destined the next to lose all in the ignominy of
a traitor's death on Tower Hill.[1]

Where then does Caius Martius go wrong? Is his fall occasioned by some public folly or by some inner weakness? If we
seek answers to this question, Shakespeare again provides
guidance—this time within the framework of his plot.

III

The first scene of the play is set in Rome and establishes, in the
conflict of patrician and plebeian interests, the background
against which Caius Martius' bid for the highest office in the
state, the consulship, is to unfold: this is the main plot. The
last fifty lines of the scene serve to introduce the subplot as
well, the rivalry in arms of Caius Martius and the leader of
the Volsces, Tullus Aufidius. In this way Shakespeare quickly
depicts both the good fortune to which the prince of patricians,
Caius Martius, is born and the double test to which his fitness to
govern is about to be exposed. Lest there be any misunderstanding, the point is reiterated in the twelfth line of the ensuing scene where Aufidius, addressing the Volscian senate,
describes Martius as 'of Rome worse hated than of you'. His
powers of leadership are thus to be tested in both military and
political conflicts.

With that much defined, Shakespeare then proceeds to
introduce us to the third element in his play, his hero's domestic
life. After two rough, masculine scenes, one in the hurly-burly
of the Roman streets, the other in the Volscian seat of government, we are transported into the calm and privacy of a domestic setting. Moreover, it is worth noticing that this scene is
monopolized by women just as the two former scenes are

[1] Essex's fall was lamented in such popular ballads as 'Sweet England's Pride is
gone' and 'Essex's Last Goodnight'. He too could not decide whether to seek power
in the military or the civil sphere of national affairs, and by attempting both
destroyed himself.

populated exclusively by men. This contrast is so extreme and so unusual in Shakespeare's plays—it is the only scene for women which is neither introduced nor interrupted by a man—as to suggest design rather than accident. The women in question are all closely related to the protagonist: mother, wife, friend and servants. This is itself significant, and so is the fact that the scene as a whole fails to advance either the main or the secondary action. Why then should Shakespeare have chosen to lavish so much care upon domestic portraiture, and especially at this particular point in the play? To this question should be added another which I have already raised: why should Shakespeare have troubled to invent Valeria, to place her in so attractive a light in this one scene and then dismiss her from any further significant part in the dialogue? Do these problems derive from the lazy working methods complained of by Ben Jonson, or are they important directives to the play's interpreters? In producing the play myself, I accepted the latter view, and in doing so found myself confronted with several unsuspected obligations both to my author and my actors.

The first and most important was in respect of pace. Because the three opening scenes in Act I are uniformly leisured, with only distant rumblings of trouble ahead to give any semblance of movement to the stage-action, a temptation exists to rush through them making heavy cuts in order to plunge as quickly as possible into the more evidently dramatic uproar and violence of the battle before Corioli that spans scenes iv–x. Yet haste at this juncture can well wreck any chance the play may have of reaching its full stature either in Rome or Antium in the last three Acts. Exposition is always a difficult task, and when, as in *Coriolanus*, the scope of the action to be depicted is of so large an order, patience must be exercised if we are to recognize its boundaries and not be overwhelmed by its detail. My point is simply that the producer must respect the play's architecture: for, if he fails to grapple successfully with its form, his actors have little hope of communicating its meaning. In the three opening scenes, Shakespeare provides him with the code-cypher to the play's form, and this he must endeavour to transmit faithfully to any audience. Rome is the starting point, a city which, notwithstanding its republican constitution, resembles the London of Shakespeare's time in its sense of its own achievement and destiny. The foil is the foreigner, the perpetual threat to tradition, present order, and future achievement. The Volsces therefore must be sharply distinguished from the Romans in all visual aspects of the production and most especially by those contrasts of costume, setting, accessories, manners, stage-position, and general atmosphere that can be conveniently arranged within the compass of scenes i and ii. Nowhere does Shakespeare suggest that the Volsces are savages. They govern themselves like the Romans in the democratic decency of the Senate House; they entertain their guests both civilly and lavishly; and, in the day of battle, they can raise a formidable army under leaders that even Roman adversaries respect. They are not Romans in that they are foreigners and enemies; but, just as evidently, they are not cave-dwellers. Put another way, if the Roman patricians wear togas,[1] the Volscian lords at least wear robes or gowns. Shakespeare and the audiences before whom the play was first acted had no further to look for the like of Tullus Aufidius and his compatriots than Admiral Medina Sidonia and his captains of the fabled and recently defeated Armada. If objection is raised against this opinion it should be remembered that Aufidius at least is civilized enough to do something that no one in Rome is capable of doing—to put an accurate finger on the particular failings of Caius Martius.[2]

As this background of *welt-politik* is sketched in, so the image of Caius Martius begins to grow. We see him in the first scene misguidedly dispensing the scornful banter that has to be tolerated on the barrack square to the citizens of Rome in their own streets. Spectators with eyes to see and ears to hear can hardly fail to recognize for themselves the personal arrogance and political naïveté that informs this attitude. Lest they do, however, Shakespeare spells it out through the mouths of the two tribunes.

SICINIUS: Was ever man so proud as is this Martius?
BRUTUS: He has no equal.

[1] II, iii, 104.   [2] Act IV, scene vii: see p. 241 below.

His courage is a byword at home, and, as we are informed in the second scene, knowledge that he is in arms is enough to alarm the Volsces. Moreover, their General Tullus Aufidius knows that none of them may sleep in peace till Martius is struck down, and that this is a task which he has reserved for himself.

> If we and Caius Martius chance to meet
> 'Tis sworn between us, we shall ever strike
> Till one can do no more.

It is at this juncture that we are introduced to Martius' wife, a woman as pale and negative as any worshipped in the romantic imagery of Pre-Raphaelite painters and poets. We meet her in company with Volumnia, a mother-in-law as masculine in her sentiments and as domineering in her manner as any ridiculed in music-hall.[1] Both these women, as wife and mother, in their attitudes to Martius and to one another, comment on the image of the man that Shakespeare has sketched in for us in scenes i and ii. If Martius sees himself as indispensable to Rome, that is an image of his mother's making. She even endows him with an imaginary phrase—

> Come on you cowards, you were got in fear
> Though you were born in Rome.

—which echoes with sinister accuracy the attack which we have already heard him make on the citizens in the first scene.

> What would you have, you curs,
> That like not peace, nor war? The one affrights you,
> The other makes you proud.

His wife, by contrast, is feminine. War is abhorrent to her.

> His bloody brow? O Jupiter, no blood!

Yet in her very weakness and gentleness of disposition, she reveals her total incapacity to shift her husband's image of himself or loosen his mother's control over his mind. No wonder she is

---

[1] Before the producer however yields to any temptation to ridicule Volumnia, he should read Queen Elizabeth I's speech to her troops at Tilbury on 8th August 1588. See J. E. Neale, *Queen Elizabeth*, 1934, pp. 297–8.

ignored when Martius returns to Rome as conquering hero (II, i, 160–80). Had he been married to Valeria, things might indeed have been different. She, like Virgilia, is womanly; but she is a woman of spirit, a woman of the calibre of Beatrice in *Much Ado*; and a woman with enough independence of mind to say 'Kill Claudio!' and mean it, is not one whom Volumnia can permit to marry her son. Valeria can only be permitted to remain a friend. Once Shakespeare has made this point (and Act I, scene iii, suffices to do that), Valeria can be dismissed from the dialogue. It is enough to present her on the stage as the companion of Volumnia and Virgilia in Rome and Antium, a dumb reminder of what might have been and of why things are as they are.

It is by these means in the three opening scenes that Shakespeare informs us of the fatal immaturity of character that is the particular weakness of this patrician prince and is to occasion his tragic fall. In the world's eyes Caius Martius is every inch a man; married, a father, an experienced soldier and, by the end of Act II when Corioles has fallen, a national hero. Yet for all that, he is also a man who is still so much his mother's pupil as to take Virgilia for his wife instead of someone of Valeria's spirit, and no man where matters of worldly or political judgement are in question. Aufidius, by contrast, both knows his man and picks his moment when, with calculated disdain, he taunts Martius as 'Thou boy of tears' (V, vi, 101).[1] Nor is he any further from the truth when, twenty lines later, he qualifies that description with the words 'unholy braggart'. Aufidius has of course already sized up Martius (IV, viii, and V, iii, 190–203) and decided to liquidate him (V, vi, 1–60) before Martius presents himself to the Volscian Senate. All that Aufidius has left to do is to provoke Martius into an outburst of personal feeling sufficiently tactless to serve as his death-warrant. This he accomplishes with considerable finesse. Martius rises to the bait.

---

[1] Robert Hardy, in the television production, gave substance to this taunt by actually sobbing at the close of the admonition scene (III, ii). Sir Tyrone Guthrie, in his production at the Nottingham Playhouse (1963), carried the matter beyond immaturity and into homosexuality: see *The Times* notice, 12 December 1963.

> Like an eagle in a dovecote, I
> Flutter'd your Volscians in Corioles;
> Alone I did it. 'Boy'!

—a remark which is dazzling in its tragic irony. The squalid murder follows, assuming some gloss of respectability as an act of popular revenge if not of justice. At the same time, while in our horror at the baseness of this deed we acknowledge the stamp of greatness in the murdered man, we also pity the streak of immaturity that put both the consulship outside his grasp and his own person at the mercy of his smaller-minded adversary.

Remote though Coriolanus may be from us by being a Shakespearian character in the first place and a figure of Roman antiquity in the second, his like is still among us in the former captain of games who is deceived into thinking that his prowess on the sports-field endows him with some special right to hold positions of command in any walk of later life. It is excusable if proud parents and schoolmasters encourage a boy in this belief while he is still at school: but the Caius Martius that we are shown by Shakespeare has long left school behind him, and Volumnia, Virgilia, Menenius, and Cominius are all in their several ways to blame for preserving him in the fatal immaturity of this deception. Cominius admires Martius for his professional virtues and eulogizes him before the Senate (II, ii, 80–125): being a professional soldier himself, he fails to see that the qualities which he commends may require some tempering before they can be assets in civilian life. Menenius loves Martius as a favourite son, but to a point where he becomes a bad lover: he recognizes some of Martius' faults, but he prefers to try to excuse them (even to the point of admitting them) rather than to discipline and correct them in Martius himself. Swaddled then as Martius is by all his friends in self-esteem, he cannot but regard himself as indispensable first to Rome and then to Antium. Even banishment from Rome fails to bring any serious awakening; and when the moment of truth is at last spelt out before the Volsces, it is too late. Aufidius is his superior in political shrewdness if not in arms, and deals out death with truth. The key to the truth is appropriately placed well in advance of both this scene and that of Volumnia's supplication for Rome before her son. In IV, vii, Aufidius discusses Martius with a lieutenant and advances in lines 35–55 three reasons for his rival's failure to reap the harvest of his own success—pride, defective judgement, and misuse of power. The second and third of these reasons overlap each other in that it is often hard in politics to distinguish between wasted opportunity and lack of diplomatic tact: and where both faults are in evidence it is likely that they have a common origin in exaggerated self-esteem. Too much praise can swiftly translate self-confidence into tyranny: 'thus strengths by strengths do fail.'

If I am correct in my interpretation of the signposts to the play's meaning that Shakespeare bequeathed to us within the form of his text, then the producer's task in assisting his actors to release its meaning in performance is greatly simplified. A quiet and leisured pace in the playing of the first three scenes is a necessary, explanatory preface to what follows. The rest of the play moves swiftly to two climaxes, the one leading inexorably to the other. The battle scenes at Corioles in Act I, scenes iv–x, are so ordered as to present young Martius in the most favourable light possible. His conduct on the field of battle at least is exemplary, and should command the affection of the audience as it commands the loyalty of his hard-pressed soldiers. His physical courage in moments of crisis and his self-effacement afterwards are Shakespeare's means to this end. Important, therefore, though the smoke and noise of battle must be, they must neither of them obscure or drown what Martius has to do or say. His costume must arrest the eye and yet allow him to move with the freedom of an athlete within the limits of the set. And despite this activity, he must occupy positions where his voice can top all other noise. The roar of battle stilled, we may then warm to the man who can remember his debt to a prisoner when fainting himself from loss of blood (I, x, 80–94). Such a commander in the field is worthy of the hero's welcome that he is then accorded in Act II on his return to Rome, and the plotting of the non-combatant Tribunes to feather their own nests at his expense appears as mean as it is small-minded: and in this contrast lies the germ of the play's first climax, the confrontation of headstrong youth, seconded by courage, with cowardice and envy, seconded by political experience and guile. The catalyst is the consulship.

SICINIUS: On the sudden
I warrant him consul.
BRUTUS: Then our office may,
During his power, go sleep. (II, i, 203–5)

The result of this struggle is a victory for the patient and cunning exploitation of others by the Tribunes and banishment for Coriolanus.

Thus the confused clamour of battle gives room to the stately progress into Rome and the formal proceedings of the Senate until this solemn, ceremonial atmosphere itself gives way to the ever-quickening pace of a major political crisis. The storm breaks in Act III, scene iii, where Coriolanus, finding to his uncomprehending astonishment that he *is* dispensable, admits defeat in an agony of subdued rage. Unable to come to terms with the situation, the baited bull rounds on his attackers, reduces the screaming mob to silence by his posture, and launches into an alliterative execration of unparalleled ferocity.

You common cry of curs, whose breath I hate
As reek o' the rotten fens: whose loves I prize
As the dead carcasses of unburied men
That do corrupt my air: I banish you. (III, iii, 121–5)

Within this dragon's breath, however, the choice of metaphor betrays the arrogance that brought things to this pass and that will carry the dragon himself in a blind quest for vengeance directly to the second crisis.[1]

On entering Antium, Coriolanus again betrays his own naïveté. He can see that he risks execution, but only admits this possibility in terms of justice (IV, v, 23–5). His experience in Rome has taught him little: that the reward of service given to a former enemy could be murder is as far from his thoughts as that the flattering thanks of his friends and family could lead to his own banishment. To him, dishonour in Aufidius is as unimaginable as ingratitude in the citizens of Rome. This might

[1] It is as a dragon that he sees himself once banishment has become inevitable (IV, ii, 27–32).

be taken as evidence of nobility of soul; but, as a measure of political wisdom, it is small. For was it not this same Martius who called his fellow-men 'rats', 'curs', and 'abated captives' to their faces? The author of these sentiments should at least have recognized, as Sicinius does, that these commoners

> Upon their ancient malice will forget
> With the least cause these his new honours. (II, i, 209–10)

What is there so special or so sacred about Martius that will make men whom he rates as rats behave as if they were angels of virtue to him alone? Failure to ask this question is the fundamental cause both of his banishment and of his violent death.

IV

The play abounds with good acting parts, especially for the junior members of the company. Roman citizens and army messengers, Volscian servants and conspirators all have a chance to impress themselves upon the audience, thanks to their author's skill in characterization and the modulation of mood from scene to scene. Whether it be two officials attending to the seating arrangements in the Roman Senate (II, ii, 1–36) or two Intelligence Officers from the opposing armies at a chance meeting on the highway (IV, iii), young actors are given the invaluable experience of presenting a character that is both an interesting human being and an essential component in the play's design.

The large number of good parts of this kind—I reckon there are nearly twenty of them—presents the producer with three problems which are particular to this play. The first is the casting of these parts. Few professional companies can admit a salary bill that will allow each of these parts to be played by a separate actor: few amateur companies can muster talent enough to fill half of them. Doubling and cutting are the usual answers. Both are dangerous since in cutting there is a risk of damage to the fabric of the play's structure and in doubling there is an equally serious risk of blunting the edges of character delineation. The second problem is one of personal relations in rehearsal: for, if the producer gives these cameos the degree of care in rehearsal that alone will make them worth including, the players of the larger parts begin to suspect that he is neglecting their own needs. To forestall the trouble that can arise on this account, he must not only allocate time with exceptional care in the preparation of his rehearsal schedule, but bring to rehearsal an exceptional sensitivity to the emotional cross-currents flowing through the company from day to day. The third problem is one of vocal balance. Not only have enough actors to be found with a command of two regional dialects distinct enough to contrast Volscians consistently with Romans, but most of these actors are called upon to speak against a background of general tumult and still remain audible. This in my opinion is by far the most difficult technical problem with which the producer is confronted by this particular play.

No producer, professional or amateur, is likely to be so fortunate as to find all these problems solved for him; and clearly each must seek his own solution. What matters is that he should be aware that they exist and that he has found his answers to them *before* he contracts to direct this play. *The Tragedy of Coriolanus* may have affinities with *Hamlet, Macbeth,* or *King Lear* in that the title-role is the play's focal centre; but it differs greatly from them all in the style of the text. Poetic soliloquy is rare, and even then the language in which it is cast is extraordinarily condensed.

> O world, thy slippery turns! Friends now fast sworn,
> Whose double bosoms seem to wear one heart,
> Whose hours, whose bed, whose meal and exercise
> Are still together; who twin, as t'were, in love
> Unseparable, shall within this hour,
> On a dissension of a doit, break out
> To bitterest enmity. (IV, iv, 13–18)

Even the finest imagery is cast in a forbidding form. Volumnia, awaiting Martius' return to Rome, hears trumpets and declares:

These are the ushers of Martius: before him, he carries noise; and behind him, he leaves tears:

Death, that dark spirit, in's nervy arm doth lie
Which, being advanc'd, declines, and then men die. (II, i, 141–4)

Nor is comparison with the other 'Roman' plays or the histories appropriate, since in none of them do crowd scenes outnumber scenes for small groups in the heavy ratio of two to one as is the case in *Coriolanus*. Problems of vocal balance and contrast, therefore, here take on the proportions of an oratorio and even, at times, of opera. I cannot myself see, for example, how Act II, scene i, and Act III, scenes ii and iii can be put on to the stage with success unless in terms of opera: another instance is the final uproar in the Volscian Senate. In all these scenes the orchestration of noise both for crowd and soloists must be approached with the same strict attention to clarity of tempo and melodic line as a conductor brings to an operatic score, the actors' moves and positions being determined by considerations of vocal tone and audibility in the first instance and by theatrical effectiveness only in the second. (See *Plate XII*, no. 16.)

The Tragedy of Coriolanus then is perhaps the most rewarding of all Shakespeare's plays to produce because of the challenge implicit in the scale of the action compressed into play-form, but only for the company that possesses the technical skill to tackle it: for it is unquestionably the most demanding. I suspect myself that the play was written for an occasion when both halves of 'The King's Men', London and provincial touring company, were available to work together as an ensemble. If this surmise is correct, then Shakespeare was writing with a company of some thirty to forty professional actors in mind instead of the usual sixteen to twenty. In the title-role this play calls for an actor of quite exceptional physical agility and vocal virtuosity. The major supporting roles, male and female— Aufidius, Menenius, Cominius, Volumnia, and the two Tribunes—are no less varied and rewarding for the actors than those in any other play of Shakespeare's. In addition, the play offers an unequalled range of small, speaking parts, each sufficiently exacting to test the strength of the most junior members of the company to the utmost. And even after these demands have been met, there remains a need in several scenes for yet more

actors to embellish the stage-action with ceremonial detail—
Captains, Heralds, Lictors, Aediles, and the like. The demands
on the numerical strength of the company are multiplied pro-
portionately in the technical and financial demands that the
play makes upon it—costumes, accessories, properties, and so
on. Failure by the producer, particularly in an amateur company, to ensure that the back-stage organization is adequate to
cope with the strains this play places upon it, can quickly prejudice whatever success he and his actors may be in sight of
before the dress-rehearsals start. And lastly, there is the problem of the text itself, tough, muscular, seldom poetic in an
obvious way, yet supercharged by the consistent condensation
and economy of its vocabulary. In few of Shakespeare's plays
is so much reliance placed on the interior-springing of the lines
whether verse or prose. If the rhythms are lost by actors who
misplace the accents (or perhaps never find them) much of the
dialogue appears nonsensical: this, when allied to the resulting
drabness of delivery, serves to alienate an audience's attention.
Shouting only makes matters worse, reducing whole scenes or
large sections of them to 'inexplicable dumbshow and noise'.

These are some of the traps that lie in wait for the producer
whose enthusiasm for the printed version of the play outruns the
degree of competence that the play in action demands from him
and his actors as artists in the theatre. If, however, the producer
can bring himself to trust the guidance and advice that Shakespeare generously provides concerning the direction of the
play, his production, for all its particular shortcomings, will
yield up a meaning from within the play's form profounder and
more striking than any which he may himself invent or pre-
sume to impose upon it.

15

The Winter's Tale

A Comedy with Deaths

CENTRAL to *The Winter's Tale* is the personification of Time. Central to critical discussion of the play is the disparate nature of the scenes set in Sicilia and those set in Bohemia, bridged as it would seem only by this theatrical 'speaking-clock'. The contrasts between Court and country, age and youth, winter and spring and the defiance or disregard of the dramatic unities of time, place and action implicit in these contrasts have struck both readers and spectators so forcefully that critics, in attempting to defend Shakespeare, have found themselves obliged to excuse the play either as a poem in dramatic dialogue or as a carelessly constructed essay on the regenerative power of youth. The possibility that the moral meaning of the play (and thus its unity) might lie in the fusion of seemingly irreconcilable opposites seems not to have been considered. Since artistic unity of some sort is a producer's first concern, it is this possibility which I wish to consider in this essay.

The first question to be asked then is whether we have any right to regard the views of neo-classical theorists and critics about the proprieties of unity of time and unity of place as having any bearing on the writing of the play. The temptation to assume that they have and thus to use them as a datum point for criticism is very strong since one of Shakespeare's own contemporaries singled out this play on two separate occasions for stricture on this very account. Ben Jonson, first in his Prologue to *Bartholomew Fair* and later in conversation with Drummond of Hawthornden,[1] calls attention to the liberties that Shakespeare took with time and place respectively, much to the detriment of the play considered as a work of art. Given a start of this sort, subsequent critics have found it very difficult to avoid an apologetic approach: and once the assumption is made that Shakespeare has somehow to be defended for breaking the rules, the question of whether these 'rules' were those by which he worked or of whether they were of any consequence to him when he came to construct this play is quickly lost sight of. Much the same of course applies to *Troilus and Cressida* where Chapman's translation of Homer's version of the Trojan War has served to eclipse and indeed to reverse standard mediaeval and Tudor attitudes to the conduct of Greeks and Trojans in that epic conflict. In both instances, *Troilus and Cressida* and *The Winter Tale*, if precedence is given by critics to the theoretical views of Chapman, Jonson and their successors rather than to the assumptions of popular tradition, the resulting damage to our appreciation of the structure and meaning of these plays is very great.

What guidance then may we hope to obtain from popular tradition? For a start, I would suggest that we take a look at that most popular of English pastimes, civic pageantry, a pastime which in Shakespeare's lifetime attracted the attention of such notable men of the theatre as Peele, Dekker, Middleton, Webster, Heywood, Burbage and Garret-Christmas the painter. In London the most important example was the annual Lord Mayor's Show. Two of these, as it seems to me, are especially significant in this context: Anthony Munday's Show for 1605, *The Triumphs of Reunited Britania*, and Thomas Dekker's Show for 1609, *Troia-Nova Triumphans*. Both of these shows have at least one feature in common, the direct association of sixteenth-century London with ancient Troy: that London was and is

---

[1] See *Jonson*, i, p. 138.

New Troy is proclaimed publicly by actors in both Pageants to all London's citizens from the new Lord Mayor down to the humblest apprentices.

It is to the character of Virtue in the first of his four pageant-devices that Dekker entrusts this message. She addresses her welcome to the Lord Mayor:

> Haile, worthy Praetor, stay, and do me grace.[1]

She is presented emblematically to view, seated on a throne attended by 'the Liberall Arts' within a colonnade.

> And, to maintaine/This greatnesse [she continues],
> twelve strong pillars it sustaine [i.e. *the Aldermen*],
> Upon whose capital twelve societies [i.e. *the City Companies*]
> (Grave and well-ordred), bearing chiefe command
> Within this city, and, with love, thus reare
> Thy fame, in free election, for this yeare.
> All arm'd to knit their nerves in one with thine,
> To guard this new Troy.

Dekker did not need to elaborate any further on this association of London with Troy since Anthony Munday, four years earlier, had spelt out this association both verbally and visually to this same civic audience in *The Triumphs of Reunited Britania*.[2] Both in the actual Pageants and in his introduction to the printed edition of the text, Munday retraced Geoffrey of Monmouth's account of the conquest of Albion by Trojan Brutus, his slaying of the Giants, his renaming of his new kingdom Brutayne or Britain and his building of a capital city on the banks of the Thames which he called New Troy. From Geoffrey of Monmouth's 'History' these ideas had of course percolated downwards in mediaeval society until they came to be assimilated in the popular mind with other legendary material relating to folklore and the historical past: in that form it was like a well, ready to be drawn up and used by any poet, preacher or playmaker whose purposes it could profitably serve. Chaucer and

---

[1] F. W. Fairholt *Lord Mayor's Pageants*, Percy Soc. X, 1844, vol. 2, p. 19.

[2] A single copy of the 1605 edition survives in the British Museum. It has been reprinted by J. Nichols, *Progresses of James I*, i, 564 *et seq.*, and by R. T. D. Sayle, *Lord Mayor's Pageants of the Merchant Taylors Company*, 1931, pp. 84 *et seq.*

Lydgate had turned it to such use, and even the historian Camden at the close of the sixteenth century was ready to admit its continuing usefulness within that context.

> For mine owne part [he says], let Brutus be taken for the father and founder of the British nation: I will not be of contrarie minde.[1]

The ideas therefore that London was New Troy and that the British people were the lineal descendants of the Trojans were not new when expressed in the Lord Mayor's Shows of 1605 and 1609 by Munday and Dekker. Rather were they taken for granted by the populace and only questioned by the most sceptical of intellectuals. The question therefore that we should ask of Munday's and Dekker's use of these ideas is not 'where did they come from?' or 'who gave credence to them?', but 'what was their *special* usefulness at this *particular* time?' In seeking an answer to this question we need not look far, for Munday himself supplies it in the title of his Show. Brutus, so the old story went, divided his kingdom on his death between his three sons; and thus divided into three parts—Scotland, Wales and England—it was destined to remain until in the fullness of time divine providence should produce a second Brutus to reunite the kingdom. Merlin had prophesied that King Arthur was not dead, but sleeping and that he would return to accomplish this feat. Tudor historians had seen in the accession of the House of Tudor and most especially in the birth and christening of Henry VII's eldest son Prince Arthur just such a figure; these hopes, swiftly dissappointed as they were by his early death, nevertheless survived the century in other forms and were at last seen to be fulfilled in the Coronation of James VI of Scotland as James I of England and its Principality of Wales. James succeeded Elizabeth in March 1603, but because of the plague that year he did not enter London and there was no Lord Mayor's Show. His entry and Coronation took place in 1604. Both Ben Jonson and Anthony Munday submitted schemes for the Lord Mayor's Show that year and Ben Jonson's appears to have been adopted, but the text has not survived.

[1] See E. A. Greenlaw, *Studies in Spencer's Historical Allegory* (Johns Hopkins Monographs in Literary History, vol. 2), Baltimore, 1932, p. 23.

Munday, however, was successful the following year and was commissioned by the Merchant Taylor's Company to present *The Triumphs of Reunited Britania*. The Show cost the company a total of £710 2s. 5d. and the most singular feature about it is that it is designed as much as a welcome to the new sovereign as to the new Lord Mayor.[1]

James, King of Scotland, Wales and England and the second Brutus of ancient prophecy are directly equated. The principal scenic device of the show was 'a Mount triangular, as the Island of *Britayne* it selfe is described to bee'. Seated on its summit was Britannia, Brutus' wife,[2] 'a fayre and beautifull Nymph' together with Brutus himself dressed 'in the habite of an adventuruous warlike Troyan'.[3] The three kingdoms into which Brutus had divided Britain were personified in his three sons, Camber, Albanact and Locrine, who sat below their mother and father in the Pageant: below them sat personifications of the rivers which served as boundaries to the kingdoms. Each in their speeches made their own part in the story explicit to the citizens, but the character with most to say was Brutus. First he reminds his hearers of his marriage and his conquest of the Western Isles.

> Then built I my *New Troy*, in memorie
> Of whence I came, by *Thamesis* faire side,
> And nature giving me posterity,
> Three worthy sonnes, not long before I died,
> My kingdome to them three I did devide.
> And as in three parts I had set it downe,
> Each namde his seat, and each did weare a Crowne.
> (Sig. Biij)

After letting them take up their parts of the tale, he resumes his own and invites his audience to turn their minds away from

---

[1] Some of this exceptionally heavy cost is accounted for by the fact that the weather was so bad on St. Simon and St. Jude's day that the Show had to be postponed till All Saints Day, and the damage done to the pageants repaired. The bill of expenses is given in *Malone Society Collections*, III, ed. J. Robertson and D. J. Gordon.

[2] Her real name was Imogen, but this was changed to accord with her new dignity as Queen of Britain.

[3] 1605 Edition, Sigs. B and Bv. All quotations are taken from this edition.

the past and towards the present, 'to tell olde *Britaines* new borne happy day'.

> That separation of her sinewed strength,
> Weeping so many hundred yeeres of woes
> Whereto that learned Barde[1] dated long length
> Before those ulcerd wounds againe could close,
> And reach unto their former first dispose.
>> Hath run his course thorough times sandie glasse,
>> And brought the former happines that was.

> *Albania, Scotland,* where my sonne was slaine
> And where my follies wretchednes began,
> Hath bred another *Brute,* that gives againe
> to *Britaine* her first name,[2] he is the man
> On whose faire birth our elder wits did scan,
>> Which Prophet-like seventh Henry did forsee[3]
>> Of whose faire childe comes *Britaines* unitie.

> And what fierce war by no meanes could effect,
> To re-unite those sundred lands in one,
> The hand of heaven did peacefully elect
> By mildest grace, to seat on Britaines throne
> This second Brute, then whome there else was none.
>> *Wales, England, Scotland,* severd first by me:
>> To knit againe in blessed unity.

(Sig. Biij v°)

Brutus then proceeds to expound the emblematic, visual iconography of the Pageant.

> For this *Britannia* rides in triumph thus,
> For this these Sister-kingdomes now shake hands,
> *Brutes Troy,* (now London) lookes most amorous
> And stands on tiptoe, telling forraine lands,
> So long as seas beare ships, or shores have sands:

---

[1] I.e. Merlin.

[2] James had designated his conjointed kingdoms 'Great Britain' by Proclamation in 1604.

[3] I.e. by marrying his eldest daughter, Margaret Tudor, to James IV of Scotland in 1503. On this point Munday is much more explicit in his introduction to the text. '. . . a second *Brute,* by the blessed marriage of *Margaret,* eldest daughter to king *Henrie* the / seaventh, to *James,* the fourth king of *Scotland,* of whom our second *Brute* (Royall king *James*) is truely and rightfully descended' (Sigs. Bv° and Bii).

So long shall we in true devotion pray,
And praise high heaven for that most happy day.

(Sigs. Biijv° and Biv)

Then follows a choric song of welcome to King James. The rest of the Show is devoted to the more normal celebration of the Lord Mayor himself and his Livery Company.

Munday's verse is tame and the form of his Show is broken-backed, but its importance does not lie so much in its artistry (or rather, lack of artistry) as in the highly evocative nature of its appeal to popular sentiment and national pride. London, as the capital city of a country that had recently emerged as the victor in a war on two fronts, is here invited to regard its triumph as part of a divinely ordered plan, the seed of which was planted even as Troy fell, which was nurtured through the centuries by the faith of prophets and the industry and valour of the people, and which promises, in the reunion of the King-dom, a future of imperial splendour. And if the miraculous element of the fable appealed primarily to the illiterate and superstitious 'groundlings' and 'stinkards', the hard historical facts of the political situation viewed in realistic perspective must have struck hard-headed merchants and sceptical intellectuals alike as little short of a miracle. The Grand Armada of imperial Spain had been defeated against all reasonable odds; nearly a century of war and threatened invasion from a Catholic Scotland had suddenly been translated into as nearly unbreakable a Protestant alliance as the minds of men could imagine; the long nightmare of a sovereign without an heir had ended. Ahead lay prospects of stability at home and of new worlds with dreams abroad of the unparalleled trading oppor-tunities that newly won command of the northern seas brought with it. (See *Plate Twelve*.)

That Shakespeare shared this vision of New Troy triumphant in a re-united Britain seems to me to be indelibly imprinted upon both the subjects and the form of many of his later plays. In play after play written between 1603 and 1613, from *Troilus and Cressida* to *King Henry VIII*, aspects of this swelling theme reveal themselves in small or large degree.

The utterances and actions of Trojans and Greeks in *Troilus and Cressida* where love and honour are concerned bear a very different complexion for those who believe themselves to be King Priam's heirs than for those who regard Athenian democracy as the alpha and omega of civilization: no citizen of 'New Troy', when that 'deformed and scurrilous Grecian' Thersites describes himself as, 'bastard begot, bastard instructed, bastard in mind, bastard in valour, in every thing illegitimate' (V, vii, 17–18), would so far take leave of his senses as to suppose that Shakespeare was speaking his own mind through this cankered creature in the way that many latter-day critics educated in 'the classics' have done: nor would citizens of Troynovant or Troynewith have any difficulty in knowing what interpretation to place on Troilus' final lines.

> Strike a free march to Troy! with comfort go:
> Hope of revenge shall hide our inward woe. (V, x, 30–1)

The play's audience was itself the living proof of the success of this revenge. Hector is dead, but Hector's heirs have just defeated another invading fleet that sailed in mistaken confidence from Spain instead of Greece.

In *King Henry VIII* it is the prospect of Britain re-united in James I rather than the renewal of Troy which fires Shakespeare's imagination. In Act V, scene v, the infant Elizabeth is brought to her christening and there Archbishop Cranmer, like Merlin before him, is possessed of prophetic utterance. Having sung the praises of the newly baptized infant, he continues:

> but, as when
> The bird of wonder dies, the maiden phoenix,
> Her ashes new create another heir
> As great in admiration as herself,
> So shall she leave her blessedness to one—
> When heaven shall call her from this cloud of darkness—
> Who from the sacred ashes of her honour
> Shall star-like rise, as great in fame as she was,
> And so stand fix'd. Peace, plenty, love, truth, terror,
> That were servants to this chosen infant
> Shall then be his, and like a vine grow to him:

Wherever the bright sun of heaven shall shine,
His honour and the greatness of his name
Shall be and make new nations: he shall flourish,
And like a mountain cedar, reach his branches
To all the plains about him. Our children's children
Shall see this, and bless heaven.

This may well pass as simple flattery from King's Man to Royal Master; but it also echoes unequivocally the popular sentiments made explicit in *Troja-nova Triumphans* and *The Triumph of Reunited Britania* and in a manner where the imperial theme is sounded louder and more clearly than ever it was by Dekker or by Munday.

The Roman plays, *King Lear*, *Macbeth*, *The Winter's Tale*, *Cymbeline* and *The Tempest* are all touched at some point by these sentiments. *Macbeth*, with its compliment to King James in Fleance's escape and its direct comparison of this to Christ's escape from Herod's massacre of the innocents of Bethlehem which I have already discussed in Essay 13, requires no further comment here. The Roman plays, as far as I can see, bear no direct relationship either to a regenerated Troy or to King James himself; but the nascent national interest in an imperial future (so clearly manifested in *King Henry VIII*) could well have prompted the temporary switching of Shakespeare's interest away from Chronicles of English history towards an exploration of those of Roman achievement—primitive, republican and imperial in *Coriolanus*, *Julius Caesar* and *Antony and Cleopatra*. Much clearer echoes of the Troy story emerge from *King Lear* and *Cymbeline*. Both plays invite the spectator to glimpse a Britain civilized by Brutus but not as yet by Christ. In *Cymbeline*, where the imperial Roman eagle has already been planted on British soil, the pseudo-historical affairs of state provide a frame for the romantic fable of an exiled prince who returns, after many vicissitudes, to claim his ancient rights and honours: and the play's closing lines—

Never was a war did cease,
Ere bloody hands were washed, with such a peace—

invite a comparison with events of recent memory. One strand of this play, the return of the exile to his own, is taken over and reworked within *The Tempest*, where the miraculous change of fortune is achieved by the forgiveness of enemies in one generation and the marriage of their children in the next.

If it is the happy ending of the Troy–Brutus story which touches the two comedies, *Cymbeline* and *The Tempest*, it is the 'follies wretchedness' of the early part of the tale that informs *The Tragedy of King Lear*. Lear's division of England between his three daughters exactly parallels Brutus' division of Britain between his three sons and the results are as disastrous: and if, moreover, there is to be any question of important characters precipitating themselves from cliffs to rocks beneath, it might be observed that this would predictably occur at Dover, since this was the spot where Brutus himself was said to have defeated the last of the Giants, Corineus, by breaking his ribs and causing him to topple over the cliff's edge into the sea below!

Nothing could be more diverse than the plays I have mentioned, ranging as they do from *Troilus and Cressida* to *Henry VIII*, from *Macbeth* to *Cymbeline*, from the Roman plays to *King Lear* and *The Tempest*: and no one would wish to suggest that they were not drawn from sources just as diverse, ranging from Holinshed to Plutarch, from Chaucer and Boccaccio to Tudor plays. In greater or lesser degree however each of them bears some easily recognizable imprint of the Trojan Brutus legend; and if we ask why this should be, the answer is evident enough in the messianic quality which King James I's accession possessed for his subjects in the early years of his reign. And in no play, as it seems to me, is this made more explicit than in *The Winter's Tale*.

The acknowledged primary source of *The Winter's Tale* was a novel by Robert Greene first printed in 1588 and entitled *Pandosto*. Its sub-title is 'The Triumph of Time'. In Anthony Munday's Pageant of 1605 it is also the triumph of time which translates Brutus' divided kingdom into 'reunited Britania'.

> That separation of her sinewed strength,
> Weeping so many hundred yeeres of woes

. . . .

Hath run his course thorough times sandie glasse,
And brought the former happines that was. (Sig. Biijv°)

These lines, which refer directly to the political situation brought about by James I's accession, supply an equally appropriate synopsis of the action represented in *The Winter's Tale*. Leontes and Polixenes, respective Kings of Sicilia and Bohemia, from being close friends and allies are translated into enemies only to be reconciled when time has brought their children into amity. If then, as I suspect, Shakespeare spotted the correspondence between the human situation depicted in Greene's romance and the national situation implicit in the popular image of his patron's accession which Munday had so recently made explicit in his Lord Mayor's Show, the way lay open to combine the two within a drama that derived its story line from the novel and its theme from topical events. This welding of the one into the other however could not be accomplished without regarding disparateness of locality and an extended passage of time as assets rather than as hindrances in respect of dramatic technique: for if the views of Ben Jonson and his scholarly friends on the desirability of unity of time and place in tragedy and comedy, the segregation of people of high and low degree according to the genre of the play and the avoidance of deaths in comedy with the corresponding eschewing of drollery in tragedy had to be taken seriously, there was no translating either *Pandosto* or *The Triumphs of Reunited Britania* into a stage play, let alone both. To do this the playmaker must trust to his own instinct and make virtues of necessity when getting to grips with the structure of his scenario. Here Shakespeare's experience and the native English tradition of dramaturgy upon which he relied so heavily served him well. His theme, with its objective of reconcilement of division achieved through forgiveness of past follies and dissensions, dictated comedy as the form for the play; but if topical events were to be truly reflected within the mirror of the fable, then the normal limits of the formula would have to be stretched to include a double cause of initial misunderstanding and subsequent adversity instead of the usual one, since neither England nor Scotland could be held wholly to blame for the disastrous state of Anglo-Scottish relations during the sixteenth century. For despite the auspicious marriage of Margaret Tudor to James IV in 1503, the battle of Flodden was fought within a decade of it engendering a bitterness that reached its climax in the execution of Mary Queen of Scots on English soil in 1587. Within the play therefore the respective images of Scotland and England must be sharply contrasted in terms of atmosphere, yet shown to be equally susceptible to the breeding of contention notwithstanding this contrast. Even Eden had its serpent, and in this comedy there may have to be real deaths as opposed to feigned ones notwithstanding John Fletcher's views on tragi-comedy which he had claimed to be so-called apropos *The Faithful Shepherdess* of 1608/9 'in respect it wants deaths, which is enough to make it no tragedy, yet brings some near to it which is enough to make it no comedy' (*Preface to the Reader*). Disparity of locality therefore must be accepted as a deliberate premise in the formulation of this comedy. By the same token, and notwithstanding the comic framework for the play as a whole, death as a product of dissension must be allowable; and if such a fable were to succeed in embracing in its implications subjects as well as sovereigns, the *dramatis personæ* must include comic and sage illiterates as well as wise and foolish courtiers. Perhaps most importantly of all, time, as the force which allows dissension to breed from suspicion and by healing dissension to restore harmony, must not be artificially restricted to a single revolution of the sun, but be put to work and dignified by elevation to a place within the ranks of the *dramatis personæ*. Munday's 'sandie glasse' and Greene's sub-title 'The Triumph of Time' here conspired to provide Shakespeare with his cue to present 'Time as Chorus'.

It is against some background of this sort that I believe Shakespeare set to work on the construction of this remarkable comedy. I do not wish to suggest that any direct parallel was intended between particular characters in the play and particular figures at King James' Court: but I would maintain that Shakespeare did invite his audience to compare events in the Sicilia and Bohemia of his play with events in living memory in England and Scotland. In other words, it is through the structure rather than through the details of characterization and incident that the emblematic nature of the play is revealed. I only want therefore to look at the way in which certain features of the play's form help to make its moral meaning explicit.

First, then, I think we should recognize that whatever respect some of Shakespeare's contemporaries and most of his successors have had for the classical unities of time and place, Shakespeare jettisoned both in this instance as being irrelevant to his purpose. Rather did he envisage from the outset a parable set in two localities which were at least as remote from one another as London and Edinburgh yet whose peoples were linked by ties of close affection if not of blood.

Archidamus and Camillo make these points succinctly in the opening lines of the play. Archidamus insists upon the 'great difference betwixt our Bohemia and your Sicilia'. Camillo insists however that Leontes' welcome to Polixenes springs from happy childhood memories.

> They were trained together in their childhoods; and there rooted betwixt them then such an affection, which cannot choose but branch now.

Even when duties of state keep them apart,

> they have seemed to be together, though absent.

Our first impression of the two kings when they are presented to us confirms this account of their friendship; yet even in this instant the seeds of suspicion, jealousy and discord between them have inadvertently been sown. Much here depends upon the actors and the director, for Leontes' suspicion of his wife's unfaithfulness grows in his mind out of what he *sees* rather than out of what he hears. The positioning of the three actors is thus crucial, so that what they actually say to one another may be supplemented by gestures of affectionate familiarity between Polixenes and Hermione which Leontes (and the audience) can reasonably regard on the evidence of their eyes as ambiguous and even as suspicious.

261

From this point onwards the initial misinterpretation by Leontes of innocent intentions on the part of his queen and visitor rattles downhill at frightening speed, arousing a blind rage within him which aims first at Polixenes' life and then at the Queen's.[1] Both, in the event, escape; but death strikes swiftly in other quarters. The first victim is Mamillius, Leontes' son and heir, in the suddenness of whose unexpected death we are to see a punishment brought upon the king for his wanton defiance of divine providence presented here as Apollo's oracle at Delphi.

> There is no truth at all i' th' oracle!
> The sessions shall proceed: this is mere falsehood.

No sooner is this blasphemy pronounced than news comes pat of Mamillius' death. With the Queen reported to be dead, her second child (now known to be Leontes' own) banished 'quite out of my dominions', Sicilia is like Elizabeth's England, possessed of a sovereign but lacking an heir. And there ends the first of the two catastrophes on which this comedy is built.

The second catastrophe is set in another country, a country possessed of a wild and tempest-ravaged coastline much more appropriate to Scotland than to land-locked Bohemia.[2] This country is indeed as different from Sicilia as Archidamus promised Camillo he would find it; but for all its arcadian beauty (plucked in part at least from Fletcher's *The Faithful Shepherdess* of 1608/9) this country is the home of wild beasts, both animal and human. Antigonus, having deposited Leontes' daughter on the sea shore (and who must now be eliminated from the story lest he embarrass the dénouement) is pursued by a bear, struck down and eaten.[3] And, as we are later to learn, this country also harbours Autolycus, a human predator whose comic caperings cannot conceal the vicious thief and liar behind the pedlar's songs and trinkets any more successfully

---

[1] This can be treated with relative brevity here since it had already received extended treatment at the hands of the same dramatist and leading actor in *Othello*.

[2] The modern Czechoslovakia.

[3] See Nevill Coghill's essay in *Shakespeare Survey*, XI, 1958, 'Six Points of Stagecraft in *The Winter's Tale*', pp. 34-5.

than Lucifer's adder's coat and smiling face could change the reason for his presence in the Garden of Eden. This then is the setting for a tale of young love which Polixenes, having learnt nothing from earlier experience, is to treat with the same rash intolerance in regard to his son that Leontes accorded to his wife and daughter and to Polixenes himself. Prince Florizel, like his father before him, seeks safety in flight and the fourth Act ends with Bohemia as sorely discomfited as Sicilia had been at the end of Act III. Thus two sequences of circumstances, each highly propitious in point of initial environment, are separately transformed by human capacity for discord into near tragic conclusions, with the frail figures of Perdita and Time carrying the double burden of a linking device between the two sequences of events and the sole cause for hoping that a happy issue may yet come out of these afflictions. It is a singular tribute to the vitality of Shakespeare's art that he could tackle the challenge of this double catastrophe within the slender frame of a comedy and make something that was artistically so taxing appear to be so simple and so buoyant. It is in the fifth Act however that his supreme mastery of his medium is revealed: for there not only have the two disparate catastrophes to be dovetailed into one another (a task for a good craftsman) but within this dovetailing must occur the reconcilement that will transform the 'yeares of woe' into 'the former happiness that was' (a magician's assignment for a major poet). The key to both lies in the substitution of a figure akin to that of Merlin's prophecy for the dead Queen of Greene's *Pandosto*. This Shakespeare achieved in the creation of Hermione who, like King Arthur, 'is not dead but sleeping'. The discovery of Perdita's identity and its impact on Leontes and Polixenes, which might have served another dramatist well enough to conclude his play, is banished by Shakespeare to the tiring-house and recounted by three gentlemen to the audience at second hand. In this way however the ground is prepared for the far more difficult and potent magic of the statue scene with its miracle of regenerative love. Shakespeare's artistry thus leads him to dismiss an obvious but banal conclusion to his story and to rely instead upon the power of ancient ritual.

Quem quaeritis in sepulchro, O Christicolae?
Jesum Nazarenum crucifixum, O Caelicolae.
 Non est hic, surrexit sicut predixerat; ite,
nuntiate quia surrexit de sepulchro.
 Resurrexi.

With Hermione's statue behind its closed curtains in Paulina's chapel we are back in the dawn of English drama. As the curtain is withdrawn, and as the figure of the Queen that was but is no more appears standing before the group of mourners, astonishment and incredulity possess them. Perdita falls on her knees and cries impetuously,

> Give me that hand of yours to kiss

only to be prevented by Paulina:

> O, patience!
> The statue is but newly fixed, the colour's
> Not dry.

Paulina could as easily have said, '*Noli me tangere*', and been as clearly understood.

In every production of this play that I have seen, Hermione's 'statue' has been visualized and presented in a stance more appropriate to the terrace of a garden loggia or to a grotto than to a chapel. This is evidence in itself of the hold that neoclassical critical values have taken upon the imaginations of artists and audiences alike. Yet it was surely Shakespeare's intention (made explicit by the fact that the statue is in the chapel and not in a garden or in the long gallery with the other objects that Leontes so admires) that this particular statue should resemble the effigies which normally graced the tombs of the gentry in cathedrals and parish churches in Elizabethan and Jacobean England—painted effigies modelled from the death masks and actual clothes of the deceased. (See *Plate XIV*.)

If this question of the nature of the statue is related by the critic or the producer to that of the setting for this scene as a whole, I think it must be conceded that the scenic property used by the King's Men to identify this 'chapel' in 1610 was the tomb (see Essay no. 8, pp. 141–3 above) and that this particular tomb took the form of the normal sarcophagus surmounted by a

264

niche containing a standing effigy, in *pious* posture, of the supposedly dead Queen. It would then be quite clear to the audience that Hermione was not rising like Lazarus (or even Christ) from within the sarcophagus, but that the already life-like effigy was translating itself from the semblance of painted stone to life indeed. Granted these funeral furnishings by way of stage setting for this scene, it at once becomes obvious that as Paulina draws the curtain and as the *penitentes* (Leontes and Polixenes) and the *catachumens* (Perdita and Florizel) approach the tomb a second Easter dazzles their sight and ours.

Paulina: No longer shall you gaze on't, lest your fancy
May think anon it moves.

and later,

Leontes: What you can make her do
I am content to look on: what to speak
I am content to hear; for 'tis as easy
To make her speak as move.
Paulina: It is required
You do awake your faith.
(See Essay 1, pp. 11–13 above)

Thus is Hermione redeemed from death to life. Thus have Florizel and Perdita redeemed the sins of their fathers. Thus has Britannia been reunited with a second Brutus in New Troy. Time has brought this miracle to pass and Shakespeare is more than usually careful to state on no less than three occasions that the gap between the deaths of Hermione and Mamillius and the betrothal of Perdita and Florizel was sixteen years. Where Britons were concerned, Mary Queen of Scots was executed in 1587 and James I accepted the English crown in 1603.[1] The time gap is precisely sixteen years. As coincidences go, this is at least remarkable.

---

[1] If it is objected that 1610/11 is rather too late for a celebration of this Union, it should be remembered that Charles I still thought this achievement remarkable enough to merit a commission to Rubens to record it in paint and place it in the ceiling of Inigo Jones' Banqueting House, flanking the apotheosis of his father. (See *Plate XVI.*)

Index

INDEX

INDEX

groups of encounters, 205–8; reckoning, 207–8; testing, 205–6; tripartite pattern, 205

Harbage, Alfred, 154, 155

Hardison, O. B., 6, 14, 21

'Harmartia', 49, 57, 63, 175–8

Harrington, Sir John, on Masks, 114–15

'Harrowing of Hell, The' (playlet in Miracle Cycles), 215–21, 224, 225, 231: and the *Elevatio*, 216–18; connection with *Macbeth*, 215, 218–220, 224; derivation from liturgical ceremonies, 216–18

Hearne, print of Hell-castle, *111*

'Heavens', 122, 130, 147–8, 156

Hell, mediaeval stage representation of, 216, 218–19, 222–3: image of Hell-castle, 219, 223; *111*, *126*; image of prison, 222

Hemings, John, 160

Henrietta Maria, Queen, 88, 116

Henry VII, 70, 75, 76, 252

Henry VIII, 37, 70, 75–7: forbids doctrinal discussions on stage, 36

Henslowe, Philip, 122, 130, 143, 147: building of the Hope, 133, 147; Papers, 141

Herod plays and *Macbeth*, 224–31: comparison of King Herod and Macbeth, 226–8; treatment of Herod as character, 225–6; varieties of treatment, 228–30; and Mortimer, 175n

Heywood, Thomas, 47, 124, 126, 152, 250: approach to tragedy, 55

Hippolytus (Seneca), 70–1

Holinshed, 231, 258

Holland, Aaron, 147

Homer, 77, 86, 102, 250

Hope Theatre, builders' contract for, 133, 136, 147, 156, 159

Horace, 43, 47, 58, 69, 77, 87, 109: Jonson and, 90–1

House, Humphrey, 49

Hue and Cry after Cupid, 103

Hymenaei, 103

῾Ιεφθαε (Christopherson), 81

'Inner stage' theory, 137, 159, 161

Interludes, *see* Moral Interludes

Introits and Introit ceremony, 7–8, 11–12

Irving, Sir Henry, 234

Jacobean and Carolean Stage, The (Bentley), 153, 155

James I, 86, 96, 102, 149, 231, 252, 256, 258–60, 265: and Masks, 103, 107; commands plays at Court, 138; equated with Brutus, 253

Jew of Malta, The, 45, 124, 126; stage directions, 128, 129

Johnson, Dr., 86

Jones, Inigo: and the Stuart Masks, 103, 104, 106–12, 114, 139–40, 144; *78*, *174*, *175*; ascendancy over Jonson, 110–11, 145; claims precedence over Jonson, 109; Cockpit-in-Court design, 145, 148, 151–62; *63*; collaboration with Jonson, 106, 108; costume and scenic designs, 114; Master Surveyor of the King's Works, 109, 111, 154; system of changeable scenery, 111

Jonson, Ben, 30, 37, 48, 56–60, 63, 69, 77, 79 n., 87–94, 96–101, 135, 160, 238: and Fletcher, 87–8; and Lord Mayor's Show, 252; and the Stuart Mask, 103, 106, 108–14; collaboration with Inigo Jones, 106, 108; conception of dramatic art, 84–5; death, 110; 'Expostulation with Inigo Jones', 109–11, 145; influence of Aristotle and Horace, 90–1; monosyllables and polysyllables, 100; on unities of time and place, 250, 259; praise of Shakespeare, 88; scholarship of, 91, 100; strictures on Shakespeare, 84, 87–8, 90; ventures into tragedy, 46; vocabulary, 92, 101

Julius Caesar, 86

Julius Caesar, 100–1, 257

Katherens, Gilbert, 133, 147

Katherine of Sutton, Abbess of Barking, 217

Keith, William G., 152, 153, 158

Kemble, John Philip, 234

271

INDEX

104, 106–12, 139–40, 142, 145;
Jonson, 103, 106, 108–12, 145;
Mask of Augurs, 109; *Mask of
Blackness*, 106; *Mask of Queens*, 112;
Milton, 113; Nicoll, Allardyce, 103;
Sabol, Andrew, 110; *Salmacida
Spolia*, 62, 103, 116; Shirley, 113;
Simpson, P., 114; Townshend, 111;
Vision of Delight, 109; *Vision of
Twelve Goddesses*, 103, 105, 106
Mass, the, and origin of dramatic
performances, 11–12, 17
Massacre at Paris, The, stage directions,
126, 127, 129
Measure for Measure, 47
Mediaeval Drama in Chester (Salter), 5
Mediaeval Heritage of Elizabethan Tragedy
(Farnham), 48
Mediaeval Stage, The (Chambers), 5,
21 n., 22 n.
Medwall, Henry, 28, 31, 68; *15*:
dramatic skill, 32
Menaechmi (Plautus), 93
Mendelssohn, 181
Mendicant Friars, the, 17
Michelangelo, 90
Middle Ages, drama and religion in,
3–23: adjustments to current
attitudes, 3–5; campaign of the
mendicant Friars, 17; change of
attitudes towards Eucharist, 17–19;
change of emphasis in Christian
thought, 16–17; critical pre-
conceptions, 3; divine and human
qualities of Christ, 17; differences
between liturgical music-drama
and vernacular drama, 6–7;
institution of Corpus Christi Feast,
15–16; Introit Ceremony, 7–8, 11–
12; Morality Plays, 20–3; origins,
7–12; plays combining liturgical and
vernacular types, 21; Protestant
prejudice, 3, 15; traditionally
accepted pattern of development,
4–6, 8, 9
Middleton, Thomas, 50, 250
Midsummer Night's Dream, A, 156; *158*:
setting and text, 180–90:
adolescent attitudes to sex, 182–4;
fairies, lovers and mechanicals, 181,

188; four acts with recapitulation
and cadenza, 188–9; parody of
Romeo and Juliet, 185–6, 189;
relationships of setting to plot,
181–3; scenic requirements, 189–90;
significance of the wood, 182–4;
similarities with *Comus* and *The
Faithful Shepherdess*, 181–3; use of
scenic emblems, 180, 182–4; use of
the mechanicals' story, 185–7
Miles Gloriosus (Plautus), 82
Milton, 45, 113–14, 181–4, 189
Molière, 87, 98
Mons Passion Play, 220
Monteverdi, 70
Moral Interludes, 26, 35–9: criticism
of political institutions and social
injustice, 26; development of farcical
element, 38; threat from
Elizabethan censorship, 38; vitality,
30
Morality Plays: and the Revels, 25–6;
borrowing from the Tournament,
28; *chansons de geste* and jongleurs,
28; Christian ethics and personal
conduct, 22; co-existence with
Corpus Christi Cycles, 20–1;
concepts of moral order, 26;
differences from Corpus Christi
Cycles, 22; dramatic qualities, 24–41;
founded on the vernacular sermon, 22,
27; instrument of propaganda during
Reformation, 35–6; narrative and
plot material, 29–30; polemical
plays, 36–8; relations between actors
and spectators, 40; skill in plot-
construction and characterization,
37–8; structured on contention or
debate, 22; transformed into Moral
Interludes, 26; troubles with Church
and State officials, 22; vices and
virtues, 27
More, Sir Thomas, 68, 75
Morton, Cardinal, 68
Mother Bombie, 30
Motter, T. H. Vail, 78, 79 n.
Much Ado About Nothing, 241
'Mumming at Hertford', (Lydgate), 28
Munday, Anthony, and Lord Mayor's
Show for 1605, 250–5, 257, 258, 260

273